Pro and Contra Wagner

THOMAS MANN

PRO AND CONTRA WAGNER

TRANSLATED BY

ALLAN BLUNDEN

WITH AN INTRODUCTION BY

ERICH HELLER

THE UNIVERSITY OF CHICAGO PRESS

Original German edition *Thomas Mann:*
Wagner und unsere Zeit first published
by S. Fischer Verlag, Frankfurt am Main 1963
© 1963 Katja Mann. By permission of
S. Fischer Verlag GmbH, Frankfurt am Main

The University of Chicago Press 60637
Faber and Faber Limited, London WC1N 3AU

Printed in Great Britain by
Butler and Tanner Limited

94 93 92 91 90 89 88 87 86 85   5 4 3 2 1

Library of Congress Cataloging-in-Publication Data

Mann, Thomas, 1875–1955.
Pro and contra Wagner.

Translation of: Wagner und unsere Zeit; with additions.
Includes indexes.
1. Wagner, Richard, 1813–1883—Addresses, essays,
lectures.   2. Mann, Thomas, 1875–1955—Knowledge—
Music.   3. Music and literature.   I. Title.
ML410.W1M253 1985   782.1′092′4   85-20819
ISBN 0-226-50334-8
ISBN 0-226-50335-6 (pbk)

Contents

Editorial Preface

This book is substantially based on *Wagner und unsere Zeit*, a collection of Thomas Mann's writings on the composer edited by the author's daughter Erika Mann, published by the S. Fischer Verlag in 1963, and reissued in 1983.

While many of the items in this collection have been available before in English versions, these are no longer always easy to find, and it seemed that English and American readers would welcome a book that may fairly be said to assemble everything significant that Thomas Mann wrote about Wagner (outside the fiction, where his debate with the composer is continued by other means, notably in works like 'Tristan', 'Blood of the Walsungs', and *Doctor Faustus*). The book includes not only the two major essays ('The Sorrows and Grandeur of Richard Wagner', and 'Richard Wagner and *Der Ring des Nibelungen*') but also much lesser-known material, some of it now available in English for the first time. Assembling Mann's writings on Wagner in chronological sequence makes it possible to read them not just as isolated pieces but to follow the continuities and discontinuities in Mann's lifelong preoccupation with the composer.

With the exception of a short foreword by Willi Schuh, an afterword by Erika Mann, and a very few sentences in certain letters where Mann makes comments entirely incidental to the subject of this book, *Wagner und unsere Zeit* is here published complete, and in a wholly new English translation by Allan Blunden. The opportunity has been taken to augment Erika Mann's selection with five additional items which cast new light on Mann's view of Wagner. The first of these, extracts from notes for 'Mind and Art' – an essay on which Mann was working between 1909 and 1912 – show him more critical of the composer than at any other time in the fifty-year span over which he wrote about him.

While there is obviously no direct connection between Mann's views on Wagner and his scenario for a projected film of Gottfried von Strassburg's version of the Tristan legend (to which Wagner had his own debt to declare), this scenario and its author's reflections on it could not have been written without Wagner's opera in mind and ear. So this seemed as pertinent an occasion as any to bring them into English for the first time.

The two other new items will, it is hoped, amplify the context of the single most important piece in the book, 'The Sorrows and Grandeur of Richard Wagner', by showing the reaction it provoked in a Germany adjusting hastily to the Third Reich. The 'Protest' against Mann's lecture marking the fiftieth anniversary of the composer's death, a document signed by Hans Knappertsbusch, Hans Pfitzner, Richard Strauss, and a great many others who should have known better, is printed here in full, together with Mann's letter reproving Pfitzner (whose opera *Palestrina* the writer greatly admired) for compounding the fault of his signature by publishing a personal polemic against him. In July 1933 no journal in Germany was prepared to print Mann's letter; it was not published until 1974.

Also new to this book is the introduction by Erich Heller, distinguished author of *Thomas Mann: the Ironic German* and many vigorous and influential studies of other great German writers, such as Goethe, Nietzsche, Rilke, Kafka and Karl Kraus. Surprisingly, Professor Heller had never devoted an essay to the fascinating topic of Thomas Mann's enthralment to Wagner. Having shared the experience of hearing the *Ring* with him at Bayreuth, I was delighted when he agreed to contribute to this book, and to advise on its presentation.

Editorial omissions indicated by square brackets are Erika Mann's; those in round brackets are mine and are largely confined to the 'Mind and Art' extracts on pp. 37-44. Textual interpolations in square brackets and in italic type are by Erika Mann. It seemed desirable that this English edition should include some modest extra annotation – not in the no-stone-unturned academic tradition, but simply in order to identify Mann's correspondents and some of the names and allusions in the text. In supplying this I have made no attempt to gloss passing references to names or works with which the reader will certainly be familiar, or others that are mentioned *en passant* and have no direct bearing on the sense of the text. I have supplied brief introductions to the 'Mind and Art' extracts, and to

'The Sorrows and Grandeur of Richard Wagner'. Very long paragraphs have occasionally been subdivided.

The sources of the various pieces, with the exception of extracts from letters included in the three-volume *Thomas Mann: Briefe* edited by Erika Mann, Frankfurt, 1961, 1963, 1965, are given in the footnotes.

PATRICK CARNEGY

Acknowledgements

Thanks are due to Secker and Warburg Ltd, and to Alfred A. Knopf Inc., for permission to publish new translations of material to which they hold existing English copyrights: 'Leiden und Grösse Richard Wagners' (translated by H. T. Lowe-Porter as 'Sufferings and Greatness of Richard Wagner'), 'Richard Wagner und *Der Ring des Nibelungen*' (translated by H. T. Lowe-Porter as 'Richard Wagner and the *Ring*'), a brief extract from *Die Entstehung des Doktor Faustus* (translated by Richard and Clara Winston, and published under different titles in England and America, see note on p. 206), and the selection of Thomas Mann's letters made and translated by Richard and Clara Winston and published as *Letters of Thomas Mann*, 2 vols., London and New York, 1970.

We are also grateful to Thomas Mann's German publishers, the S. Fischer Verlag; to the editors of the journals where certain items were first published; to Professor Golo Mann for his support and encouragement; to Professor Hans Wysling of the Thomas-Mann-Archiv in Zurich; to Antony Beaumont, Barry Millington, Stewart Spencer, and Friedelind Wagner for help with annotation; and to Inter Nationes for the translation subsidy without which this book could not have appeared.

Introduction
by Erich Heller

This book, in bringing together most of what Thomas Mann said about Richard Wagner, is at the same time an essential fragment of the novelist's intellectual autobiography. With the first entry coming from a time when Mann was 27 and the last written almost fifty years later, it is also a singular history of how Wagner's work was received by an exceptional intelligence that in devotion and criticism was, as if by elective affinity, attracted to it from beginning to end. The same is true of his relationship to Nietzsche, of whom he once said to André Gide that, among Germans, this philosopher was the only authentic critic of Wagner; all the others, compared to Nietzsche, produced rubbish. Therefore, when he spoke of Wagner, Nietzsche always was within earshot. Although one might thus allude to a prompter, here it means close kinship.

Elective Affinities – *Wahlverwandschaften*: the scientific term has through Goethe acquired classical erotic connotations; and Thomas Mann's mind was enthralled by the art of the composer–dramatist in a manner impossible to describe without calling on Eros. Did he also 'believe' in Wagner's art as one believes in the integrity of the spirit that makes itself heard through the music of Bach, Haydn or Mozart? Far from it. 'Questionable', 'dubious': these adjectives he uses again and again not only when speaking of Wagner's personal character, but also of the character of his music and its calculated effects. Certainly, Mann's love of this music was 'a love devoid of belief', as he said in July 1911 in a short essay on Wagner. But he added that to him 'it had always seemed ... pedantic to insist that one cannot love without also believing'. Elsewhere he would even say of passion itself that it feeds on the uncertainty of its prospects and rightfulness.

July 1911: It was the time when he was preoccupied with writing *Death in Venice*, the story of Gustav von Aschenbach's passion for the exquisitely beautiful boy Tadzio; and in this Venetian tale he made Aschenbach, the celebrated author, write what is unmistakably that essay on Wagner, and write it in the sight of Tadzio on the beach. Thomas Mann himself, without using this incognito, wrote the essay on paper bearing the letterhead *Grand Hotel des Bains, Lido – Venise*. He stayed in that hotel when – well, when Aschenbach fell in love with Tadzio and wrote – Aschenbach? Thomas Mann? Thomas Mann, of course – of his doubtful love of Wagner's music, of that 'sceptical, pessimistic, clear-sighted' affair that was none the less intensely passionate and of 'indescribable charm'; and at this point Thomas Mann abandons himself to an enthusiasm that no 'sceptical' writer has ever allowed himself in describing a theatrical-musical experience: 'Wonderful hours of deep and solitary happiness amidst the theatre throng, hours filled with frissons and brief moments of bliss, with delights for the nerves and the intellect alike, and sudden glimpses into things of profound and moving significance, such as only this incomparable art can afford!' Can this simply be about the author's listening to, say, *Tristan und Isolde*? If so, it is also about the hours spent by Aschenbach, solitary amidst the bathers by the sea, lost in the sight of Tadzio's incomparable beauty and loving him with a love 'devoid of belief'.

Part of this ecstatic passage of the short essay on Wagner he wrote in July 1911, he repeats verbatim in the great essay 'Sorrows and Grandeur of Richard Wagner', written in 1933, almost twenty years later, for the fiftieth anniversary of the composer's death. This was the essay that had such formidable consequences in Thomas Mann's 'real' life. He gave the lecture, extracted from the long essay, not only in the University of Munich but also abroad, in Amsterdam and Paris – and afterwards preferred not to return to Germany where in the meantime Hitler had consolidated his tyrannical regime, and a group of well-known artists, at the instigation of a well-known conductor, responded to those lectures with an asinine and vicious manifesto. Spread by press and radio, it purported to be the 'Protest from Richard Wagner's Own City of Munich' against Thomas Mann's denigration of the German genius in foreign lands. (It was a uniquely 'German' – not only Hitlerite – event, saying as much about the 'cultural' mood of the nation at that time as it does about the historical role Wagner played in that country. For in no political circumstances whatever would it be imaginable that, say, in Italy, a distinguished writer would endanger his citizenship or even his life with a lecture given abroad, a lecture, like Thomas Mann's, hymnic in tone and critical only in its reflections, about Dante; or a Frenchman celebrating in this manner Molière; or an Englishman paying his – however reserved – respects to Shakespeare. Could a people reveal more conspicuously its cultural insecurity, heightened no doubt by alarming political circumstances, than by such a protest?)

Richard Wagner, Thomas Mann, *Death in Venice* – it is unnecessary to add that Wagner, in 1883, died in the Palazzo Vendramin by the Canal Grande; or that 'Tristan' was the name of the work that gives the title to Thomas Mann's collection of six short stories, 'Tonio Kröger' among them, published in 1903. Thomas Mann was 37 when he wrote the story of Aschenbach's *Liebestod*, his love-death, the story of the defeat inflicted upon reason and moral steadfastness by the irresistible allurements of 'decadence'. Yet he was only in his early twenties when he entered the literary scene with a much lengthier treatment and fuller orchestration of 'decadence' in *Buddenbrooks*, the novel that established the young man as a major writer. He gave the novel the subtitle 'Decline of a Family'. If it was a remarkable work of literature, the writing of it was also a flagrant act of desertion. For the highly respectable family tradition of the Manns, a tradition of merchants like the Buddenbrooks, came to its end with this emergence of literary genius, and for years to come Thomas Mann would look at his new vocation – 'Who speaks of vocation?' he once asked and exclaimed, 'Literature is a curse!' – as a betrayal of 'life' by cursed 'art'; and yet he pursued this art with single-minded dedication. Single-minded? Yes, if there can be single-mindedness in the persistent literary exploitation of such ambivalence. Thomas Mann's name for this ambivalence is Richard Wagner. He is the main source of the suspicions with which this writer encircled art, so much so that even in his last years he tried to complete the story that, conceived with outrageous humour at the time of *Death in Venice*, presents the artistic temperament through the character of Felix Krull, the virtuoso *Hochstapler*, accomplished impostor and elegant fraud who charmed and took in the whole world by the impeccable employment – in 'life', not on a stage – of his histrionic genius.

Of course, the story of Felix Krull could not possibly, like that essay on Wagner, draw upon itself the title 'Sorrows and Grandeur'.

Nevertheless, there is, even in the most serious passages of that early work, *Buddenbrooks*, a whiff of corruption and the aroma of sinister magic in the air when the spirit of Wagner appears. Thomas, the last burgher-merchant of the family who, with an utmost of effort, struggles to live by the principles of the renowned family in the medieval Hanseatic city (Lübeck was Thomas Mann's birthplace) and yet enters into a marriage that would have been rejected as eccentric by any previous Buddenbrook. Gerda, coming from a southern foreign country, a rather frail beauty, musical, playing the violin, unable to feel at home in the family circle of her North German husband, gives birth to a son, her only child Hanno, who is destined by nature to become a precursor of the next exotically named youngsters in Thomas Mann's fiction, Tonio and Tadzio, rather than a sturdy heir to the Buddenbrook tradition. The musical education he receives from his mother troubles the old church organist, a faithful family friend, who once scolds Gerda for playing Wagner in the presence of the boy who becomes deeply immersed in that 'infamous' music. 'Look how the child sits there listening! Are you determined to poison his mind?' And on the evening before the eruption of Hanno's illness that is to lead to his death and the termination of the family's male line, the boy improvises on the piano; and the improvisation gradually becomes a *Liebestod*, the love-death of an uncannily gifted adolescent:

> The cadence, resolution, fulfilment, perfect serenity came, and with rapturous exultation everything unfurled into a harmony, which in an ineluctably sad ritardando melted into another. It was the motif, the first motif, he was playing. And what now began was a feast, a triumph, a boundless orgy of this single phrase ... There was something brutal and stupid, and at the same time religious and ascetic ... in the fanatical worship of this trifle, this scrap of melody ..., something impious in the excessiveness and insatiability with which he relished and exploited it, something cynically desperate like the will to perish in an ecstasy, in the avidity with which he drew from it all the sweetness it would yield ...

Hanno's friend, the young Count Mölln, witnessing these brilliant excesses, blushingly says: 'I know what it means ...'

It is Thomas Mann's split sympathy with, on the one hand, the old organist's opposition to the 'infamous' music and, on the other hand, with the youngest Buddenbrook's intoxication that has, as early as his first novel, shaped his passionately ambiguous response to Wagner. Yet again and again, the burgher moralist in him lost out against the artist's admiration for this *ne plus ultra* of a music in which genius *and* virtuosity, depth of perception *and* exceedingly clever calculation are so bewitchingly mixed that in the outcome it is impossible to hold them apart. 'Wagner's art is ... dilettantism raised to the level of genius' – it was this observation in Thomas Mann's 'incriminating' lecture that, above all, seems to have infuriated the gentlemen of the Wagner City. They obviously no longer listened when Thomas Mann added, 'But *what* dilettantisms!' Dilettantisms that kindled in Baudelaire the desire to do with words what Wagner did with music, an intention that was decisive for the history of French – and not only French – lyrical poetry. No other composer could have had such effect. It had to be the most 'literary' of them all. Nor had Baudelaire's idea of 'absolute' poetry, offshoot of Wagner's 'total work of art', entirely happy consequences for poetry.

Still, Thomas Mann knew that Wagner's dilettantisms, in their entirety, lost that name once it is understood what a famous conductor meant when, exhausted after directing a performance of *Tristan*, said to Mann: 'This is no longer music.' Music no more, but perhaps perfect opera or, rather, music drama, in the sense of Goethe's saying, that the nightingale's sounds are no longer song. It is something perfect; and perfection is twofold. It puts a stop to the development of a certain genre and transcends it. The nightingale, with some of the sounds it produces, 'is still a bird; but then it rises above its kind and sings as if it wished to teach every other bird what singing really is'.

It is unlikely that birds have ideas. Wagner did – most of the time unfortunate ones; and Wagner's 'dilettantism' is in what he thought, yet hardly in what he took to be the musical-dramatic realization of his thinking, unless it be the crazy notion of the *Gesamtkunstwerk*, the total work of art, in which he undertook to cross the frontiers of every individual art, drama, music, painting, and integrate them all. And while he himself would supply the drama and the music, he would have loved, he said, to leave the design of the stage to distinguished painters of, for instance, the type of Hans Makart. Makart of all painters! What an imposition this would have been on the more recent stage directors of Bayreuth had they felt committed to such a model; and the mere suggestion of it reveals the utter foolishness of the notion 'total work of art'. If Baudelaire and the later symbolists were fascinated by it, it was because of the fantastic prospect of poetry becoming music, or at least a branch of it – and let the *meaning* of words go to hell, for only there, or in a similar region of the mind, could their meaning be ignored in favour of their sounds; the difference between a rose that is sick and a pose that is slick would no longer matter all that much.

It is surprising how little Thomas Mann – apart from simply taking notice of it – appears to have been worried by what must needs disquieten anyone who wishes to arrive at a true appreciation of Wagner: the abysmal contrast between the shabbiness of his character and the sublimity of his artistic effects, the mindless brutality of his 'ideology' and 'racism' and the redemptive aspirations of his music, the infantile nastiness of his verbal utterances and the undimmed radiance of so many of his proclamations in sound; the stupidity of his theories and the insuperable cleverness of his composing. In so bluntly stating the upsetting contrasts, the critic avoids, for the sake of distinctness, the moderating justice of some 'somes' and 'sometimeses'. For Wagner's 'philosophy' is not at every point so catastrophic and his music not always so successful. But the contrast exists. 'What I cannot get over is the fact that half a man can write a whole sentence,' said Karl Kraus. Applied to Wagner, this would have to run: '... that from such questionable substance so richly textured a work as *Der Ring des Nibelungen* can be wrought, or from such unholy meanness of opinions so "holy" a spectacle as *Parsifal* (even if it is, alas, spectacularly holy).' Indeed all ethical meditation abounds with problems; but one of its most puzzling is the relationship between what a man *is* and what he can *do*. Projected into an incomparably wider dimension, this is the deadly riddle of the age. We can *do* monstrously more than we *are*. We have, alas, come to know that our scientific and technological civilization may be brought to its end by this enormous moral paradox: that our sciences and engineering skills have given us the superiority *over ourselves* that threatens us with utter defeat. What has happened in art is, compared to this catastrophe, innocuous. Yet Nietzsche's 'Case of Wagner', the late diatribe 'of the only authentic German critic of Wagner', is profoundly conscious of the length to which the phenomenon Wagner takes this potentially fatal incongruity; and the diatribe is always present, if sometimes only as a whisper, when Thomas Mann thinks and speaks of Wagner.

Beware the word 'total'. There *is* a connection, much subtler than the first glance would perceive, between the total work of art and the total (or totalitarian) state. Thomas Mann sensed it. He was undoubtedly right when in 1949 (a little late in time) he wrote to a friend who had stayed in Germany throughout the war and kept furnishing the stage for Hitler's favourite operatic entertainment: 'There is much "Hitler" in Wagner.' Yet only the quotation marks around the unmentionable name betray what he really knew: much more than what he told his correspondent. 'Hitler' was the abbreviation for a murderously total rule. Thomas Mann said it all in *Doctor Faustus*: that the 'total order' of the musical score to which his composer Adrian Leverkühn aspired (there was to be not one 'free note' left in it) was the equivalent, if in a radically opposite manner, of the *Gesamtkunstwerk*. At least theoretically, Leverkühn's was the desperate response and attempted conquest of an epoch in music whose most powerful exponent was Richard Wagner. For Wagner was 'nineteenth century through and through', '*the* representative German artist of that epoch which will live on in the memory of mankind as great (perhaps) and ill-starred (for certain)'. But had Thomas Mann not just recollected, in the same piece he wrote in the summer of 1911, at the time of *Death in Venice*, the 'wonderful hours of deep and solitary happiness' spent in the theatre with Wagner? The ill-starred happiness, the bliss of a love in which, as we heard, he did not believe?

Indeed, immediately following upon those enthusiastic memories, Thomas Mann anticipated the uprising against the nineteenth century and the rebellion against its music:

> But if I try to imagine the artistic masterpiece of the twentieth century, I see something that differs radically – and favourably, it seems to me – from that of Wagner: something conspicuously logical, well formed and clear, something at once austere and

cheerful, no less imbued with strength or purpose, but more restrained, refined, more healthy even in its spirituality – something
that does not seek its greatness in the monumentally baroque, nor
its beauty in the sweep of emotion. A new classicism, I believe, is
on the way.

Although the uprising against the music of the nineteenth century
certainly occurred, *this* 'masterpiece of the twentieth century' was
probably never written, not even by Stravinsky who, unpredicted and
unpredictably, appeared to point that way after the turbulent and
'scandalous' success of his Diaghilev years. But delete in Thomas
Mann's invocation of the masterpiece he expected the serenity and
healthy spirituality and you have the music made by the great composer of his imagination, Adrian Leverkühn, hero of his novel *Doctor
Faustus* (1947) who is as un-Wagnerian as can be. Yet gone is the
hope that in 1911 Thomas Mann harboured for the musical future.
Conspicuously logical Leverkühn's work turned out to be, well
formed, excessively so, and clear; but it was far from 'serene' and
'spiritually healthy', inspired as it was by the Devil. For the Devil
had to intervene to endow it with greatness by imbuing its logical,
clear, austere form with the soul without which it would remain a
sterile structure. The soul it received was the soul of desperation.
None the less, or because of it, it is one of the most fascinating turns
in the story of Thomas Mann's relationship to Wagner that as early
as 1911 he made the spirit of a kind of happy Leverkühn rule over the
music of the twentieth century, an appointment made by the most
completely ambivalent Wagnerite of the age.

Yet young Leverkühn's determined austerity, excogitated simplicity,
undernourished leanness, was indeed the logical reaction to super-
abundance. The luxuriating richness of the artistic means had
become too rich for any order, and yet not rich enough to be inexhaustible. Yeats, the great Anglo-Irish poet, announced this double
menace in the chapter 'The Tragic Generation' of his *Autobiography*:
the exploratory ambitions of the epoch had become too diffuse to
point into any conceivable direction. After this refinement, and that,
and yet another one, he asked, 'What more is possible?' Anyone who
has an inkling of the *one* dialect pervading all the phenomena
brought about by the spirit of the age, will instantly grasp the mean-

ing of Yeats's answer: 'After us the Savage God', and with him the 'desolation of reality'. Or at the end of Yeats's poem 'Meru': 'Egypt and Greece, good-bye, and good-bye, Rome!' *Götterdämmerung*.

The young Nietzsche, Yeats's chosen philosopher, believed, and believed it ever more energetically as time went on, that from the 'desolation of reality' there was only one escape: art and its mytho-poeic power. Strange that after the running out of all spiritual resources - if that is what the desolation of reality implies - man's aesthetic creativity and perception might be reawakened in such a mighty way. For Nietzsche, in *The Birth of Tragedy*, appears to presuppose precisely this with his notorious sentence, the fundamental dictum of all aestheticism before and after him, the baptismal creed of Yeats's initiation into his Byzantium: 'Only as an aesthetic phenomenon are world and existence forever justified.' Thus Nietzsche sets up, fortified by his early experience of Wagner's art (and later, in this mythopoeic respect, utterly disillusioned by it) the only truth surviving the desolation of a reality deserted by God and gods. But if the only justification of the world is in apprehending it as an 'aesthetic phenomenon', in the manner, that is, in which a work of art is perceived, would not the next step be *to make the work of art total*, a *Gesamtkunstwerk* in which everything is created and directed by *one* great will, for instance the indeed great will of Richard Wagner?

But why stop at this point? Why content oneself with the annual ritual of the Bavarian Epidaurus, the very architecture of which was designed as an uncomfortable pilgrims' arena to make it easier for the seekers of the total aesthetic phenomenon to leave behind the mean comforts of the common world and to raise their minds to the heights of art, while the dispenser of these sacraments robed himself in velvet and silk? The next step follows with fatal logic. Why not transform the 'desolate reality' itself into a work of art, a pseudo-aesthetic phenomenon, and to treat anything 'real' that would not fit this 'artistic' vision as mere blemishes to be discarded as a painter may paint over what strikes him mistaken in the design of his canvas, or a writer cross out a phrase that displeases him? Thomas Mann arrived late at the insight that in Richard Wagner there was much 'Hitler', the failed artist who proceeded from painting inferior pictures to creating a colossally and repulsively total reality.

19

Thomas Mann's ambivalence towards the art of Richard Wagner has the deepest roots imaginable. His ever-present suspicion of art derives from his helpless adolescent exposure to the music dramas of Richard Wagner. These, in addition, had drawn upon themselves Nietzsche's forcefully ambivalent criticism; and Nietzsche's thought shone over the young Thomas Mann's world with the same luminosity as did the genius of Schopenhauer – and Richard Wagner. The ambivalence was religious in nature. For after all that can be said and has been said about Wagner's nasty egocentricity, his crude anti-Semitism, or the mindless, Germanic offence he took at the Redeemer's Jewishness, it is salvation around which most of his works revolve, redemption, the struggle of a soul for the peace that passes understanding. From *Der fliegende Holländer* to *Parsifal* it is almost always the crux of his dramas. And as his desire for salvation is usually intertwined, in tension or even alliance, with the craving for erotic fulfilment, Wagner was bound to stir up in his listeners the most intense emotions.

Schopenhauer, 'his' philosopher (as he was Thomas Mann's), saw in sex the 'focal point of the Will', that very agent of the unreflected life (the life force, the *élan vital*, as later it was called), insisting that the overcoming of the Will through the saintly life was the only way to salvation. Yet because he wrote about sex with a kind of rhapsodic negativity, he became inescapably Wagner's very own philosopher, quite apart from his declaring music the supreme art. Sometimes Wagner catastrophically perverted Schopenhauer's philosophy, if, superb musician that he was, he did not, after all, faithfully interpret the message that it delivered – no, certainly not in accordance with Schopenhauer's opinions but perhaps with the vibrations of his prose. Yet it sounds as if he wanted to make fun of Schopenhauer (perhaps by way of paying homage to Mathilde Wesendonck) when, at the end of 1858, in a letter to her from Venice, he 'corrected' 'in some details' 'friend Schopenhauer's' *magnum opus* by the discovery that there exists a way 'leading to the perfect appeasement of the Will' that is much simpler and more direct than Schopenhauer's strenuous renunciation: namely, the love that 'has its roots in sex'. This is how Schopenhauer became the patron philosopher of *Tristan und Isolde*, of the *Liebestod*, the most paradoxical and ravishing consummation of the erotic will, both in its triumph and its defeat. About a year later Wagner knew better and told the lady in Zurich: 'Longingly I often turn my eyes toward the land Nirvana. Yet Nirvana always becomes Tristan again.'

It is Wagner's music that bewitchingly expresses this ambivalence and through it outrages, in *Buddenbrooks*, the old organist and, on the other hand, makes a prisoner of young Hanno Buddenbrook's mind. And Thomas Mann's prose, having been through the schools of Schopenhauer and Nietzsche, was before long to form a work of art with an austerely ascetic 'conqueror of the abyss' as its hero: the writer Aschenbach who, with his inner eye on a kind of Nirvana, the pure contemplative life of the artist, dies a kind of *Liebestod*. *Death in Venice* is, on a miniature scale, the *Tristan und Isolde* of European Decadence, showing in an even more drastic manner the essential incompatibility of 'reality' with that magical love. The ambiguity at the centre of the imagination that produced *Death in Venice* is the same that is responsible for Thomas Mann's contradictory responses to Richard Wagner, forever repeated and varied. Was it not time to resolve the bothersome ambivalence, a friend appears to have asked him as late as 1942. Thomas Mann was 67 then and replied with unshakeable conviction: 'No, it is like that and cannot be otherwise. I can write about him today like this and tomorrow like that ...' It is not often that someone appears to be on such good terms with his contradictions. These are ingrained in his nature – as they are in the nature of Wagner's music.

Thomas Mann once said: 'Richard Wagner – a dubious character, theoretical charlatan, political blusterer but a great artist.' Although he never bravely and thoroughly examined this problem, it is obvious that he was not quite happy to leave it at that, despite his insistence on its inevitability. It is almost true to say that privately he solved or dissolved it by shedding tears over it. Yet there are tears and tears; and the tears he laughed when in Schoenberg's Californian house the composer Hanns Eisler demonstrated at the piano some of Wagner's crafty and impish tricks in his compositional demagoguery and, shaking his finger in the air, exclaimed, 'You old scoundrel!', would no doubt instantly dry the tears that came to Mann's eyes whenever he heard a mere scrap of the Prelude to *Lohengrin*.

There is a purity of art that is unattainable to a character lacking integrity. Dare we call this, after all, the morality of music? Karl

Barth, the severe Protestant theologian and relaxed lover of music, was fond of telling the anecdote of music-making angels in Heaven. When the Lord asked them to play for Him, they played Bach. But left to themselves, they played Mozart. Unimaginable that on any occasion they would perform Wagner. But then, composers don't write any more music suitable for such ensembles.

To Kurt Martens*

Dear Herr Martens,
Back behind my desk again, I feel compelled to write and thank you
and your dear wife once more for your kind hospitality. I shall not
easily forget those few tranquil summer days I was privileged to
spend with you and your family. You are very lucky, my dear friend,
and for that you must always be grateful. I wonder if *this* Flying
Dutchman will ever be granted a 'redemption' anything like yours?

[...]

* Kurt Martens (1870-1945), author and intimate friend of TM. He became features
editor of the *Münchener Neueste Nachrichten*.
† 'fänd er ein Weib' (if only he could find a wife): from Senta's ballad, *Der fliegende
Holländer*, Act II.

To Kurt Martens

[...] So: how are you? And – even more important, perhaps – how
is your work? I assume it is finished? I had hoped that you might
send me the second and third acts as well when they were ready;
now I suppose I shall have to wait for the Munich performance,

assuming that the piece* is not going to be published just yet (?). Didn't you find, by the way, that Bayreuth intimidated you and undermined your faith in your own work? That's how it would have affected me, for certain. I am totally defenceless in the face of Wagner's art, and I'm sure I wouldn't be able to do a stroke for a whole fortnight after seeing *Parsifal*. [...]

* A forgotten play by Martens.

From 'Notes'*

There's more Novalis than Schopenhauer in Wagner's *Tristan*, as somebody has probably pointed out before. But what does that matter to me?

* 'Notizen', *Der Tag* (Berlin), 24 December 1905.

From 'An Essay on the Theatre'*

My present task, speaking only for myself and without claim to scholarly credentials, is to consider the view that the drama deserves pride of place among the literary arts. Let me begin by observing that in the present day and age – the era of sub-genres, hybrids and mixed forms, where the artist has become a law unto himself, and formal distinctions have all but disappeared – that it is folly, today, even to think of ranking the arts in any kind of order. But quite apart from that, the claim for the drama's pre-eminence is downright presumptuous, to put it bluntly; and the aesthetic arguments invoked in support of that claim are so much academic claptrap.

'The drama', as the schoolmaster used to say, 'is the highest expression of literature, for it comprehends all other forms within itself.' Quite so. And to the point, in fact, where it is sometimes the *epic* element that really carries the drama. I am thinking of Wagner – and who could fail to think of him when the theatre is mentioned? I often find it difficult to see him as a dramatist. Is he not rather a practitioner of theatrical epic? An undercurrent of epic is present in all his creations, and what I have always loved most – apart from his descriptive musical preludes – are his great narrative passages, including the scene with the Norns in *Götterdämmerung* and the incomparably epic game of question and answer that is played out between Mime and the Wanderer. What is the dramatic Wotan whom we saw on stage in *Das Rheingold* compared with his epic counterpart in Sieglinde's account of the old man with the hat? Grillparzer rejected the dramatic cycle as a legitimate form. The drama (he said) exists in the here and now, and must contain within itself everything that belongs to the action. The interrelationship of the various parts gives the whole thing a certain *epic quality*, which admittedly enhances its grandeur ... But that is precisely the effect of the *Ring*! And I cannot understand how people can view the leitmotif

* 'Versuch über das Theater', *Nord und Süd* (Berlin), January and February issues, 1908.

as an essentially dramatic device. It is epic through and through, and it starts with Homer ... [...]

But the schoolmaster took a different line. He had read his Friedrich Theodor Vischer,* and was armed with the famous quotation:

> When that subjective penetration of the world which has been achieved in lyric poetry is joined with the advantages enjoyed by the epic in virtue of its objective character: when the heart that is filled with the experience of this world gives it forth again, so that it takes shape as an image at once objective and born from within: then the circle of poetry is made perfect and complete – the drama is the poetry of poetries.

Well, no doubt a man is entitled to his point of view. But it was Goethe who called the novel a 'subjective epic', in which the poet asks permission to treat the world after his own fashion; and Vischer's definition applies word for word to *Wilhelm Meister*. What it does *not* apply to, however, is one in every two dramas written. 'The dramatic poet', he writes, 'expresses his innermost thoughts and feelings through the characters into whom he transforms himself, and whom he causes to appear before us on the stage.' Now there are many instances, large and small, where that is not true. But even assuming that it were true, then the difference between the epic and the drama would consist in the fact that the narrative poet expresses his innermost thoughts and feelings not only through the characters, *but also through inanimate objects* – which suggests, at the very least, that the narrative writer has more to do than the dramatist: everything, in fact, that the latter can leave to the actor, the director, the scenery painter, the machinist and even the musician. The theatre operates on the principle of division of labour (under the direction, if you will, of a diminutive and big-headed manager and maestro from Saxony) – and the total work of art [Gesamtkunstwerk], good men of Bayreuth, cannot possibly be theatrical.

As for the drama's existence in the here and now (assuming that this is seriously claimed as an advantage), it rapidly becomes clear

* Friedrich Theodor Vischer (1807–87), author of essays on aesthetics which were influenced by Hegel and, under the pseudonym Deutobold Symbolizetti Alegoriowitsch Mystifizinsky, of a famous parody of Goethe, *Faust: Der Tragödie dritter Theil.*

that this is a ticklish point. Does the drama really show what is present, here and now? Would an art that purported to show the present actually be art at all – and not simply cheap illusionism? Does not all art lift us beyond the present moment, and say, with the fairy tale, 'Once upon a time ...'? Everybody knows *Les Contes d'Hoffmann* by Offenbach, that musical drama in three acts with intermezzo, prologue and epilogue, which brings its hero's tales to life on the stage before us. Now here is a spectacle that clearly makes no claim to represent the here and now, that aspires to be nothing more than dramatized narrative. Not a very edifying example, perhaps; but might it not be representative of a general truth? Does Wagner exist in the here and now? This work that unfolds up there in lofty childlike visions, while the music ebbs and flows at the feet of these happenings in a tide of song and narrative – is it really trying to create a sense of the here and now? But need I ask? Schiller supplied the answer when he said, 'Tragedy in its purest form always aspires to the condition of epic, while the epic poem seeks to descend into drama.' 'Aspire', he writes, and 'descend'. And what does this mean? It means that the most powerful German theatrical talent before Wagner regarded the epic mode as the supreme manifestation of art. So let us hear no more nonsense about old Vischer and his 'poetry of poetries'! [...]

There are personal issues at stake here. Do I owe the theatre a debt of gratitude? Has it contributed in any way to my broader education?

The theatre ... Far be it from me to disparage a place that evokes memories of so many strangely exciting impressions! As a boy I was allowed to go to the Tivoli. An ill-shaven man with a peculiar way of speaking, hidden away in some unventilated cavern that was lit by a naked gas flame even during the hours of daylight, sold the tickets – those greasy squares of cardboard that were a guarantee of exotic pleasures to come. The auditorium was in semi-darkness and smelled of gas. The safety curtain, slowly rising, the painted drapes of the second curtain, with its little peephole, the shell-shaped prompter's box, the warning bell rung three times – it all set the heart beating faster. And there I sat, taking it all in ... Confused images come back to me: a symmetrical stage set, with a door in the middle;

an armchair on the right, another on the left; a servant on the right, another on the left. Somebody behind the scenes tears open the central door, pokes his head through the opening, then enters the room, closing the leaves of the door behind him with both hands, as nobody in real life would ever dream of closing a door ... An animated scene, a comic catastrophe. An elegant youth with short hair raises a chair against his antagonist in a fit of rage ... Servants intervene to restrain him ... Cinderella and the doves on wires! King Cockatoo, a comic with a red face and a golden crown. A lady dressed up as Syfax, servant to the fairy, in green tights, claps her hands, thereby working the most incredible magic ... the ballet, the glitter of fairies ... pink legs, perfect legs, divine and without blemish, trip and whirr and spring to the front of the stage ... The lucky shoes ... And the trapdoor! In a moment of pique somebody says, 'I wish I were over the hills and far away!', whereupon he disappears through the floor and comes up again in the middle of a tropical landscape, surrounded by dancing savages, who nearly have him for dinner ... Outside in the foyer there was a counter laden with cakes, little mounds of froth with some sweet red stuff underneath. We buried our lips in the froth. There were coloured lampions. And the garden was filled with people ...

What thrills! What a sense of emotional abandon! But was it aesthetic in origin? A first experience of beauty? I don't know. After all, aesthetic experience begins very early and goes very deep. Who shall say then what is 'aesthetic' and what is not? School and home life formed but a drab background. I had entered a world of novelty, adventure and licence. Driven on by an exotic urge, I had longed and prayed for this strange infatuation; I loved it, of course, I drank of it, drank deep, intoxicating draughts, and found oblivion. I was enough of a moralist, already, to surrender myself to it. But was it really right, good and proper? Did I not sometimes burst into tears when I got home afterwards? What did it signify? An inability to face ordinary, everyday life again after this revelation of beauty? Or the nausea and remorse that follows on some particularly wearing entertainment, in which those legs, those perfect legs, may well have played their part even then? ... Did the theatre ever exercise that pure, serene, reassuring, invigorating, strengthening influence which was exercised by the fairy tales of the Grimm Brothers or Hans

Christian Andersen, or by the Homer translations of Reuter and Voss? Never!

But then Gerhäuser* came to the Stadttheater. He sang the part of Tannhäuser with characteristically impetuous warmth. Every other night he sang the part of Lohengrin. He glided on, a little jerkily, to the tempestuous sounds of the orchestra, and sang with subdued gestures: 'Nun sei bedankt' [Now be thou thanked]. He stepped forward, jingling softly as he walked, and sang: 'Heil, König Heinrich', and his voice rang like a silver trumpet. This was my first encounter with the art of Richard Wagner, this essentially modern art, which must be discovered and experienced by anyone who wishes to understand something of our age. And this vast and questionable *oeuvre*, that I never tire of discovering and experiencing, this clever and ingenious wizardry, full of yearning and cunning, this fixed theatrical improvisation, which has no existence outside the theatre – it is this and this alone that binds me for life to the theatre. As for the dramatic poets – Schiller, Goethe, Kleist, Grillparzer, Ibsen and our own contemporaries like Hauptmann, Wedekind and Hofmannsthal – nobody will ever convince me that they do not work just as well when read as when performed – if indeed they do not work rather *better*, on the whole, when read. But Wagner is to be found only within the theatre: without the theatre he is unthinkable. There is no point in bemoaning the fact. It is idle to wish that instinct and ambition had not drawn him to grand opera, impossible to isolate his impact from the theatre. With greater practical energy than Schiller he enhanced the pathos of the theatre, and won for it a new dignity and solemnity, to the greater glory of his own work. But this reformer was no radical. He did not actually renew or rejuvenate the theatre. He made no attempt to turn stagecraft into an art form, or to transform set design into a serious undertaking. He wanted to commission Makart to paint some sets for him – in itself a rather disquieting fact, which points to an underlying affinity in important matters of instinct. He left the whole childish apparatus just as he found it, and his theatre is theatre just like anybody else's. It is the triumphant celebration of our own selves, the epoch as art, yearning

*Emil Gerhäuser (1868–1917) sang in Lübeck (1892–6) and such parts as Lohengrin, Siegmund, and Parsifal at Bayreuth (1892–9).

as mastery – and it is theatre. We must reconcile ourselves to that as best we can.

And so we make our way to the temple booth, that state institution dedicated to the arts. We don our evening dress, excited by the sense of social occasion. Possibly it comes at a bad time, when we feel tired, out of sorts, in need of a rest; but a week ago we purchased our tickets from some official, at the cost of much time and effort, and now we are committed. By horse and cab we wend our way to the mercy seat. We fight the good fight of the cloakroom, justify our claim to art by showing our ticket at various points, and are shown to our velvet-covered seat amidst the assembled throng. The smell of perfume, the sound of chatter, satin corsages that creak at the seams, disagreeable faces – the faces of people who are manifestly incapable of either a good sentence or a good deed. And then, up there, the ideal world to which one gazes up, swiftly intoxicated by the music, with shame and questioning in one's heart: can it be good, can it be sublime, if it also appeals to all those other people as well? The ideal is not without its comic side. Hunding is pot-bellied and bow-legged, like a cow. Sieglinde's powdered bosom heaves up and down in the *décolletage* of her animal-skin costume – a sort of prehistoric ball gown. Siegmund, squat and tense on the edge of his chair, betrays a certain anxiety lest something dreadful happen to his tights. Nor is it remotely credible, by the way, that this plump, pink man has just stepped in from the wilderness, the tempest and the depths of despair. The fire in the hearth sends showers of sparks against the backcloth – and for a moment your thoughts stray to all those horrifying stories of fires breaking out in theatres. Later on Fricka's rams – an outsize clockwork toy, one of the star turns of the house – actually run across the stage, their hinged legs clattering at the joints. But why no bleating? Surely, in this day and age, one can expect rams that bleat! ... And in between, frissons and brief moments of bliss, delights for the nerves and the intellect alike, with sudden glimpses into the most wonderful relationships, into things of profound and moving significance, such as only this incomparable art can afford ... [...]

The essentially makeshift character of all theatre is manifest wherever theatre is still performed, spontaneously and unabashed, as a self-justifying end in itself. It is manifest in the game of charades, where, after conferring briefly on the action, the participants speak each according to inclination and ability; it is manifest in the ballet divertissement, whose dramatic design exists only in the head of the ballet mistress who arranges it; and it is most clearly manifest in that archetypal popular theatre, the puppet theatre, where Goethe's discussion between the Theatre Director, the Dramatic Poet and the Wag* becomes superfluous, because all three are effectively combined in the puppeteer. And let us not forget the 'breathless' delight that Richard Wagner felt one day when he witnessed such a popular entertainment, as he tells us in his essay 'On Actors and Singers'! Such delight is scarcely to be wondered at in the Director of the Bayreuth Festival Theatre, the man who staged *Der Ring des Nibelungen*, that supreme piece of puppet theatre, with its uncomplicated hero! For has it not occurred to anybody that this Siegfried bears a striking resemblance to the little fellow who wields the slapstick in the fairground booth? [...]

The word 'drama' is universally translated as 'action': our entire dramatic aesthetic is founded on this translation. Yet it may all be a mistake. I am reliably informed (by a certain professor of philology)† that the word 'drama' is of Doric origin, and means, in standard Doric usage, 'occurrence', 'story', in the sense of 'sacred story', the local legend around which the religious cult then grew up. 'Drama', therefore, does not connote a 'doing' but a 'happening', an event; and the word acquires this meaning once again in the neo-classical German drama. *Die Braut von Messina* [The Bride of Messina], after all, is not the only work of Schiller's to be conceived in the Sophoclean manner. Georg Brandes,‡ writing in his *Hauptströmungen* [Main Currents], says: 'Not even *Wilhelm Tell* is written from a modern point of view. On the contrary, it is Hellenic in every respect. The subject matter', he continues, 'is conceived in terms not of drama but of epic.' And the action he terms 'more of an event'. Here we see how a style of treatment that an ancient poet would have considered dramatic, and that the writer of neo-classical drama considers dramatic, is openly described as 'epic' from a modern standpoint –

* In the 'Prelude on the Stage', *Faust* Part I.
† Nietzsche, in *Der Fall Wagner*.
‡ Georg Brandes (1842–1927), Danish literary critic who was among the first outside Germany to appreciate the importance of Nietzsche.

an indication of how careful we need to be, at least in our use of 'undramatic' as a term of disapproval. If we wanted to translate the word 'drama' as action or 'doing', then we would first have to reinterpret the idea of 'action' in the sense of 'sacred act' or act of consecration; and just as the first dramatic action was *ritual* action, so it appears that the drama at the summit of its ambition always aspires to take on that original meaning once again. The scene on the Rütli meadow* is after all 'action' only in the sense of a ritual ceremonial; while in *Parsifal* we witness the return to the stage of religious cult, in the form of baptism, foot washing, the Eucharist and the exposure of the reliquary. It is well known that what we understand by 'action' today was precisely the element that was excluded from ancient drama; either it had occurred before the drama began or it took place offstage, and what the audience actually saw was an emotional scene, a lyrical outpouring, action at one remove – in a word, speech. [...]

We Germans are born with a reverence for the theatre such as no other nation knows. What all other European peoples regard as a social entertainment is to us a part of our education at the very least. Recently the Kaiser remarked to a French actress that just as the university is a continuation of the grammar school, so the theatre, to us, is a continuation of the university. And that, as I say, is the very least respect we feel is due. Only a German could have produced a work like 'The Stage Considered as a Moral Institution'†. Only a German could have planned and realized a concept like 'Bayreuth'. The belief in the possibility of the theatre as temple is an unshakeably German belief, and this deeply serious theatrical ideal may well explain why the German stage has produced only a handful of comedies. But even someone who opposes the cultural hegemony of the theatre for good reasons will find that this possibility always remains a problem of enduring fascination.

When the chorus of Greek tragedy processed in measured dance around the altar or *thymelé*, then the theatre was truly a temple. And in Bayreuth, a few thousand years later, the theatre has once again assumed the appearance, at least, of a solemn national act, a divine

* In *Wilhelm Tell.*
† 'Die Schaubühne als eine moralische Anstalt betrachtet', an essay by Friedrich Schiller.

service in the name of Art – although it is difficult to rid oneself entirely of the suspicion that what Bayreuth ultimately embodies is not the spirit of the nation, but merely the supreme ambition of one artist. At all events, the hieratic genius of Richard Wagner has succeeded in turning a specific theatre, *his* theatre, into a shrine, a house of mysteries elevated far above the ordinary business of the theatre – an enterprise in which even Goethe had failed signally. Goethe resigned his post as Director of the Weimar Theatre because the Duke had insisted that a 'special turn', as we would say today – in this case, a trained poodle – should be paraded before the theatre audience as the hero of a popular melodrama. This he saw as 'demeaning to the dignity' of the theatre. Perhaps the great wise man was less than wise on this occasion. Perhaps it is unwise to set too much store by the dignity of one particular stage, since the stage in itself, properly considered, is nothing; all the stage can ever do is to *present* something. What is the theatre, after all? A platform of wooden boards. You can walk across it on your hands or you can stand on it to recite immortal poetry. Where yesterday the legs of ballerinas flitted, today Medea paces. The theatre demands so much forgetfulness anyway that we might just as well forget its 'yesterday' too. The theatre exists in the here and now; it has no yesterday. Often enough it is only a place of low amusement. But its ambition to be a temple will always be reviving, for that is a legitimate part of its very nature. [...]

Symbolism and ceremonial: just one step further, or scarcely even one step, and we have reached the point where the dramatic action becomes ritual, an act of consecration, where the theatre attains its summit – on top of the hill at Bayreuth, to be precise; we have reached the point where the name of the spectacle is *Parsifal*. [...] The 'reality' of the theatre, its immediate impact on an assembled group of people, together with that extraordinary passion for effect that sets it apart from all the other arts – this is the reason why it has always been only too willing to make the most unscrupulous use of *non*-artistic effects, to trespass on to territory that is not its own, and to pull out all the available stops. It has harnessed forces social, political, national and moralistic, and has not been slow to make use of the most estimable force of all, the religious; in future, it may be, it will be even less slow to make use thereof. In his essay on the stage Schiller has some brilliantly illuminating observations on the affinity between religious and theatrical effects. If his thoughts are taken to their logical conclusion, then it does not appear impossible that at some point in the future, if the Church should ever cease to exist, it might fall to the theatre alone to satisfy man's need for symbolism – that it might then enter upon the Church's inheritance, and be a temple in the literal sense of the term.

To that end, of course, the theatre would need above all to rediscover its natural and original vocation as popular art, as an institution for the entertainment and edification of the people; and whether or not it really contains within itself the seeds of that venerable future we have outlined, it is virtually certain that the future as such belongs to the popular theatre. So let me conclude with a word or two on that.

That Richard Wagner, the Romantic who was befriended by a king, should be the first man in Germany – or for that matter the world – to redemocratize the auditorium, to bring it back to the level of the amphitheatre (if I may put it thus), is one of those startling circumstances that confound all our established categories and antithetical distinctions, and that so delight the liberal mind. But then, how could a dramatist and man of the theatre in the grand manner ever be anything other than a romantic democrat of the kind that Wagner is in *Die Meistersinger* – given that the ideal theatre audience cannot be other than representative of the *people*, united by common popular feeling, sharing a deep-seated popular appreciation for the sublime, yet unsophisticated and desirous of being entertained – in a word, that popular audience that Hebbel had in mind when he said that our modern theatre had never been more than an entertainment and pastime, but that as long as it remained the pastime of the *people*, the 'real, genuine' people, then it was not a lost cause.

Indeed, the theatre seems to have become a lost cause only since it became the pastime of the vulgar bourgeoisie, who are the true representatives of an anti-romantic and un-popular democracy, and who are to the genuine middle class as the modern masses to the 'real, genuine' people. The fact that Wagner's theatre, that 'Bayreuth' has been taken over by the vulgar bourgeois rabble – i.e. by international tourism – would be a supreme irony, were it not that Wagner's art, as well as speaking to the nation in a way which gives it the style and stature of myth, also contains within itself elements that account only too well for the fate suffered by Bayreuth: highly artistic and diseased elements of a cosmopolitan European spirit, without which – let us be honest – it would never have meant as much as it did to people like us either, but which, by the same token, fitted it to act as a stimulus and opiate to the fashionable bourgeoisie. And yet Bayreuth still remains a popular theatre in ideal and conception; the fact that a seat costs twenty marks is merely part of the 'image', like the audience and much else besides. But while Wagner reformed the auditorium in a popularizing spirit, he abstained (what am I saying – it was the very opposite of 'abstention'!) from a corresponding reform of the stage – although it must be said in all fairness that he did devote himself with intense interest to this problem, albeit on a theoretical level and in relation to the theatre stage (as opposed to his own stage, that of grand opera), and said practically everything on the subject that our newest innovators have so far managed to say.

The use of the word 'suggestion', for example, which figures so prominently in present-day discussions on the reform of the stage, originated with him. It was likely (he said) that the reformed German dramatic stage of the future would be concerned not with 'exposition and elaboration', but with 'meaningful suggestion'; and indeed it was Schinkel* who observed that the theatre of the ancients had deliberately avoided all vulgar illusionism, choosing instead to allow the 'symbolic suggestion' of locale to create that 'true and ideal illusion' which 'an entire modern theatre, with all its backdrops and borders' cannot convey. [...]

Let us remember that it was Wagner again who first dismissed the modern, indoor amphitheatre, where the action is presented face on through a two-dimensional proscenium arch, as unsuitable for the drama of the future, pointing the way back instead to the old style of arena that was open to the audience on all sides. Recently, in an attempt to move beyond a spatial naturalism that is both unartistic

* Karl Friedrich Schinkel (1781–1841), theatre designer and architect of neo-classical orientation.

and practically outmoded, some have proposed the adoption of that low-relief style of set design which still survives in Japan, and which was used on occasion in Germany by Goethe. In any event, the stage of the future will be dominated by symbol and artistic suggestion, to the point where it will become possible to perform the 'Prologue in Heaven' (for example) in front of an adult audience in a reasonably dignified manner, and without all the paraphernalia of gauze clouds and *trompe-l'oeil* perspective that we have to put up with today. It has to be said that a theatre that hardly knows how to cope with *Faust*, the most sublime and archetypal dramatic poem in the German language, is indeed 'condemned'.

From 'Mind and Art'

The following extracts are taken from TM's notes for an uncompleted essay that he began in the early months of 1909 and intended to call 'Geist und Kunst' (Mind and Art). These notes, running to some sixty sheets of notes bearing the title 'Zum Literatur-Essay', are now in the Thomas-Mann-Archiv in Zurich.

They are of special interest here in that in them TM develops Nietzsche's famous critique of Wagner, upbraiding him as an enemy of literature. He venomously derides the composer's immense self-esteem as a 'poet' and authority on literature: '*Überliterarisch*'. Wagners *Gedichte*. (Unter oder über? Zweifelhafter Fall!)' [*Overliterary*. Wagner's *poetry* (Under- or over-? Difficult to say!)]. TM sees Wagner as representative of an all-too-German tendency to judge literature by musical criteria, to assert or imply that the art of the prose writer is an inferior art to that of the poet and that of the musician. And TM senses in Wagnerism not just a threat to 'literature' but also to his own craft as a writer. The 'Mind and Art' fragments show him striving to clarify and assert his own commitment to Apollonian literary values and to resist the Dionysian pressure of Wagner and the subversive effects of his influence. TM's work on the essay was an act of personal exorcism.

Unable to draw the strands of 'Mind and Art' satisfactorily together, TM eventually handed over its completion to Gustav von Aschenbach, hero of *Death in Venice*, whose attributed writings include not only 'Coming to Terms with Richard Wagner' (the text of which is on pp. 45–8) but also, we are given to understand, an impassioned treatise on 'Mind and Art', 'whose analytical force and antithetical eloquence prompted serious critics to rank it alongside Schiller's 'Über naive und sentimentalische Dichtung' [Discourse on Spontaneous and Reflective Poetry]. *Death in Venice* was published in 1912 and by the end of that year TM had abandoned any hope of completing the essay that he had already allowed to be completed for him in fiction by Aschenbach.

The extracts translated here are not numbered, though the reader might like to know that they come from sections 12, 13, 16, 17, 19, 48, 52, 53, 60, 84, 97 and 114 in TM's numbering. Sections are given complete in most cases; the few editorial omissions are shown (. . .). While no attempt has been made to disguise the fact that the original German text consists of uncorrected notes, replete with alternative words and phrases, the punctuation has been slightly revised and TM's asterisked afterthoughts printed as bracketed inserts indicated thus: *(. . .). The original German text may be consulted in

37

Quellenkritische Studien zum Werk Thomas Manns (Thomas-Mann-Studien I), eds. Paul Scherrer and Hans Wysling, Bern, 1967. A valuable essay about it by T. J. Reed, ' "Geist und Kunst". TM's Abandoned Essay on Literature', is in *Oxford German Studies* I, ed. T. J. Reed, Oxford, 1966.

The snobbish disdain for 'literary' values and the 'man of letters' that is currently fashionable in Germany is also the source of the exaggerated and exaggerating desire for 'high art', 'sacred art', etc., that is causing many a talent that might have worked happily enough within its own limits to be eaten up with inappropriate and impossible ambitions. *Greatness.* Face-pulling and agonizing. The ludicrous discrepancy in Schaukal* between actual output and all the fuss he makes. (...) An impotent craving for the great, the poetic, the *more-than-literary*, the sublime, which is not to be found in any other country. Correction: d'Annunzio. A buffoon. And yet precisely this desire to write *the* comedy, *the* modern epic, *the* new tragedy, is typical of the 'literary man' in the bad sense. (One eye on literary history.) They forget that greatness can never be willed into being, that it has simply to grow out of the work. Genesis of Wagner's works (*Meistersinger*). Nowadays nobody wants to be a good novelist; they call themselves 'narrative writers' instead – it sounds less literary. The ability to write counts for nothing; but any shapeless babble that wells up from Orphic depths – or claims to do so – is highly esteemed.

Intellectuality of the typical modern artist. Ibsen, Wagner, *Klinger*,† Strauss, Mahler, Dehmel, Reger, George. Towards a critique of modernism. (...) George *not* more-than-literary. Discursive, critical, not poetic in the sense claimed. Artistic *understanding*. (I *adore* this age of ours. Nothing could be more interesting!)

Query: Did Wagner bring poetry (literature) and music closer together? He treated music in a literary manner. But is it because of this that today's composers want to be more literary, and compose 'literary lyrics'? And what about 'literary dramas'? These are prob-

* Richard von Schaukal (1874-1942), German poet and writer, personally known to TM.
† Max Klinger (1857-1920), painter and sculptor known for his representations of Beethoven and Nietzsche.

ably the less talented composers, of course – or the fashionable speculators. The absolute (genuine) musical composer = unliterary. But how did Wagner come to despise all things literary? Was it demagogy? Romanticism?

Wagner is never subtle, but always clever. His (unsubtle) obviousness, schoolmasterly insistence – dictated by the theatre, and even more by his *popular* ambition.

Modern striving for popular appeal. (...) A romantic whim. Unless one is sufficiently poetic to apply the term 'people' to the corrupt bourgeoisie. Did Wagner remain a true child of 1848 inasmuch as he confused the middle classes with 'the people'? A court-theatre audience is not 'the people'. The people's knowledge of W. extends to *Tannhäuser* and *Lohengrin* (bits of them). (...) No comparison with Verdi, Puccini, Weber.

(...) Nothing of more burning interest than the critique of modernism: that I discovered at the age of 19, when I first read Nietzsche's Wagner criticism – those impassioned polemics! And one of my favourite books is Tolstoy on modern art. In Germany there is a lack of psychology, of perception, of excitability and the maliciousness that comes with perception. There is a lack of critical vehemence ... What do people *know* of the modern artist, of his secrets, his little tricks for making virtues out of weaknesses, etc. – of Strauss, Mahler, George, Hofmannsthal, Wedekind, etc.? There isn't even such a thing as Wagner criticism, apart from Nietzsche – assuming that one would hesitate to invoke Thode, Golther or Glasenapp* as Wagner experts ... The struggle against the present age, and against the things that it holds up in triumph, does not have to be based on personal rancour. There are distinguished examples that show that it can also spring from a desire for self-knowledge, and can foster a spirit of self-knowledge and self-transcendence in the age at large. There is no doubt that we can learn more about Wagner from Nietzsche's critique than from Glasenapp, Wolzogen,† etc. Polemic

---

*Henry Thode (1857–1920), Wolfgang Golther (1863–1945), and Carl F. Glasenapp (1847–1915) were members of the Bayreuth circle; their writings on Wagner, which include a voluminous biography by Glasenapp, were invariably reverential.
†Hans von Wolzogen (1848–1938), another prolific member of the Bayreuth circle.

as a source of instruction. Good polemic is incomparably more fascinating to the psychologist than hero worship. Brandes on German Romanticism.

Coriolanus as antithesis of *Meistersinger*. The artist as *aristocrat* versus the artist as *demagogue*. *Pride* versus *ambition*. Wagner, pliant like Rousseau, had no pride – in fact he was always begging (for love, for money). But he was ambitious like him. (Hauptmann. 'The more aristocratic'?) Wagner has the nerve to keep on invoking Shakespeare! The scene where Coriolanus has to win the support of the plebs. How much better, purer, more dependable that is than *Die Meistersinger*! What fecklessness, perversity, *betrayal*, lies in an artist's craving for popularity, his demagoguery, his flattery of the people!

Wagner as 'natural genius', unliterary, divorced from tradition and his contemporaries? There was Weber and the romantic opera. There was Beethoven. Berlioz had developed orchestration. The Nibelungen theme was in the air. Hebbel. W. *Jordan.* *(Jordan (born 1819), banished from Saxony in 1846 for proposing an atheistic toast, went to Paris. His first major poetic work: *Demiurgos: a Mystery*. Extensive epic-dramatic-metaphysical composition full of deep thoughts. He translated Sophocles, Shakespeare, Homer, *the Edda* *(A penchant for the gigantic). Principal work the *double epic Die Nibelunge*, in alliterative verse, which he used to recite with great success as an itinerant rhapsodist. He wrote a work on the 'epic verse-form of the Teutons and its alliterative technique'. 'Fulfilment of *Christianity*'.) Schumann (another Romantic) had Nibelungen plans in his drawer. It was precisely W's ambition to have tradition behind him, *not* to stand alone. Look at the list of his 'precursors'. His texts, which in themselves are certainly outside any literary tradition, are curious enough. (The candid young man.) By way of explanation he emphasized often enough that he was 'no man of letters'. As a poet he was a musician (musicians write dreadfully for the most part – have no taste in matters of language), and as a musician he was a poet. His texts are not tenable as poetic works, as linguistic compositions (they would not have brought him any great fame), nor will his music stand on its own as music. The former are not possible without

40

music, the latter is essentially literary. The elemental motifs of the *Ring*, the primitive chromaticism of *Tristan*: these are conceived in a poetic manner. In explaining his music he emphasized often enough that he was no musician, or 'not just' a musician. Very true. He was certainly a poet long before he was a musician. The Dutchman, as portrayed by Van Roy,* is an extraordinarily moving poetic figure. But how vulgar is the melodic texture of this opera, compared with that of Mozart or Beethoven!

A blend, then, of Teutonic culture and Christianity. Jordan possibly more claim on both than the dubious actor's offspring.† The latter's Germanness theatrically overdone. Hebbel a German *too*.

Wagner criticism! Wagner as a classic, an authority! Musical directors conduct him; 60,000-mark tenors declaim him; officers, middle-class wives, well-bred young ladies, students (in a word, the 'people' of *Die Meistersinger*) listen with unquestioning faith. (No wonder; he was very German in his unfailingly brilliant grasp of the role of authority. The leitmotif.) He is sacrosanct, taboo – nobody thinks of criticizing him. For musicians he is a 'classic', great, remote, a titan of yesteryear. These gentlemen have strangely engineer-like notions of progress. For me, for us, who do not attach much importance to one bass tuba, one set of drums and ten cacophonies *more*, Wagner is still a burningly topical issue, a problem, the problem of modernism itself – and everything that has followed, including *Elektra*, seems uninteresting by comparison.

Wagner criticism. Let us not be deceived by the loud applause of the young people standing in the theatre stalls. The truth is that among the better-educated youth of the generation born after 1870 there is much criticism of Wagner, much instinctive, albeit unvoiced mistrust of Wagner. Hofmiller‡ says quite rightly that the younger generation regards him with *questioning* admiration. Wagner is dubious/suspect. Their devotion to Beethoven or Mozart is altogether more trusting and unequivocal. (The candid young man.)

---

* Anton van Rooy (1870-1932), who sang Wotan, Sachs, and the Dutchman at Bayreuth (1897-1902).
† An allusion to the suggestion (unproven) that Wagner's father was the Jewish actor, Ludwig Geyer.
‡ Josef Hofmiller (1872-1933), conservative Munich intellectual, critic and journalist.

Schiller too says of *culture* that 'if it had to be reduced to one basic tendency, its ultimate goal would be the creation of a state of harmony and peace, both within itself and with the world at large'. It seems that he shares this lucid ideal with the men of the Renaissance and the neo-humanists. We slower brethren hesitate and entertain misgivings. Harmony as the goal of culture? All right, but there are goals that it would be better not to attain. I suspect this goal of not being a desirable one. Is it not identical with the old concept of Nirvana? And are culture and art therefore hostile forces? For so intensely dualistic an artist as. Wagner would be unthinkable under such an ideal. Art means struggle, error and conflict (Schopenhauer's definition of melody): not peace and concord. Imagine Hauptmann suddenly a Greek! The compassionate bard of suffering humanity, the tender guardian of the pathological, the most Christian of all modern writers and the one most closely akin to Wagner!

Wagner to Uhlig*: 'The *Ring* is the greatest thing that has ever been written.' The candid young man, quite without literary bias, did not agree. If he had said: the greatest work of poetry that has ever been set to music. Less a question of intellect than of character. Is it really true, as Pfitzner† claims, that if only the 'literary barrier' were removed we would not only understand this foolery but also applaud it? It seems to me that understanding is enough. If Wagner's poetic works were not written in the language of opera texts, but were worthy of serious consideration as linguistic compositions, they would still be by no means 'the greatest thing that has ever been written'. 'The grand style' does not make the greater poet. For alongside that alfresco theatrical greatness that knows how to stylize in the ideal-romantic manner (well suited to the musical drama), and in which Wagner's real gifts lay, there is also such a thing as poetic greatness (and who is to say that this, measured against an illusory greatness, is not the more genuine article?) In terms of the personal, the characteristic, the psychological, the intimately human, and as a contemporary of Dostoevsky, in the face of the colossal *oeuvre* of

---

* Theodor Uhlig (1822–1853), violinist in the Dresden Court Orchestra and close friend of Wagner's.
† Hans Pfitzner (1869–1949), the composer. See also note on p. 79.

Shakespeare, Goethe, Balzac (already written: the *Odyssey*, the *Divine Comedy*, *Don Quixote*, *Gil Blas*, *Dead Souls*, *Hamlet*, the *Comédie Humaine*, *Faust* [...] – all purely literary works, of course, pretty dry old stuff ...), such a remark could only have come from an artist whose intellect/character was depressingly incommensurate with his talent. It was different with Schiller, whose name, ever since Nietzsche, has often been linked with Wagner's by the more sophisticated critics. He was far from allowing himself to be led astray into arrogance by his (noble) style. With the most wonderful fairness, insight and dignity he defined his own nature in relation to that of his realist neighbour, but without passing judgement, and his marvellous 'Discourse on Spontaneous and Reflective Poetry' is, despite Nietzsche, an artistic achievement compared with which Wagner's writings are nothing but vainglorious self-advertisement. 'I cannot, *cannot* forget the man!' How would Goethe have judged Wagner? Very charitably, as was his wont ... No, it is impossible to revere Wagner! Neither his character nor his intellect make it possible. His talent is admirable in its dubious modernity. But it is only in the *very* young that admiration and reverence are one and the same; and talent alone does not make a great man ... Nor does the 'grand style' ... And what is it that he lacks? What deficiency in his personality, his mental attitude, discourages reverence and makes him appear undignified, unjust, mistrustful, arrogant, self-seeking, envious, mean? It is the lack on which he prided himself all his life as a virtue, and which the Germans have likewise always regarded as a virtue in him: the lack of literature.

Goethe looked up to Shakespeare's poetic greatness, subordinated his own genius to it with the instinctive sense of rank of the noble-minded. One really should make the effort, when one is feeling strong enough, to appreciate the full extent of Goethe's nobility and virtue, the hallowed growth and kindly overshadowing splendour of his humanity, in order to be sensible to the beauty of that subordination. *(What a figure he cuts alongside him, the ambitious fool who regarded everybody who ever had any talent in this world as *his* forerunner and lackey! The German virtue of proud subordination was utterly alien to this histrionic exponent of Germanism.) Wagner never looked up to anybody and he revered nobody except as an indirect means of self-adulation.

'But Nietzsche said: "I have given the Germans the most profound book* that they possess."' An expression of irritated pride that is far more considered, for all its vehemence, than Wagner's. 'The Germans' are not 'the world', and 'profound' is far more restricted in scope than 'great'. Strident though Nietzsche's remark may sound, it is carefully gauged and probably accurate.

(...) I do not mean to say that I believe more readily in Schiller and Wagner than in Hebbel. But I *love* them, and to insist that one cannot love without also believing strikes me as pedantic. One must not take art too seriously. We Germans are inclined to do so, led astray by the *gravitas* of our national character and the ambition of some of our more forceful artists. But how much happier and richer man would be if he did not demand to believe and take seriously before he consented to love! (...)

* He meant *Also sprach Zarathustra*.

To Walter Opitz*

From the country residence of Thomas Mann
Bad Tölz
26 August 1909

[...] I am tired out by all the excitement and agitation I have been through recently. I have been in Munich a lot, at the Reinhardt Theatre – which has been an important experience for me, and given me much food for thought. Getting to know Reinhardt himself has excited me in the way that personal contact with a man of mission always does – child that I am. And then I was in Bayreuth, for the *Parsifal* – too late really, because although I've never really *believed* in Wagner, my basic passion for him has also cooled a lot in recent years. But quite apart from the sheer physical exhaustion of it all (it

* Walter Opitz (1879 – died in the 1950s in the DDR), writer and close friend of TM.

was dreadfully hot), I also found it a very demanding emotional experience. There are certain things – the 'Good Friday magic', the baptism, the majestic transformation music of Act III, and the unforgettable final scene, the supreme triumph of Romanticism – that are simply irresistible. The music is the ultimate in modernism. Nobody has ever gone beyond it. Strauss's so-called 'progress' is all twaddle. Every one of them continues to feed and draw on *Parsifal*. What a terrifyingly *expressive* art! The accents of contrition and torment that he practised all his life achieve their ultimate intensity only here. Tristan's longing pales beside this Miserere. Piercing details, gripping moments, the most refined and ardent cruelties. But does it still have a future? Does it not already belong to history in terms of ambience, tendency, taste? I do believe Walt Whitman has more influence on the younger generation than he does ... but there it is.

Do come and stay with us in September.

Yours,
THOMAS MANN

Coming to Terms with Richard Wagner*

I can never forget what I owe to Richard Wagner in terms of artistic pleasure and artistic understanding – no matter how far I move away from him in spirit. As a prose writer, story-teller and psychologist I had nothing immediate or practical to learn from that practitioner of symphonic theatre, whose poetic impact, like that of Klopstock, goes beyond the realm of the particular, and whose prose style was

---

* 'Auseinandersetzung mit Richard Wagner', *Der Merker* (Vienna), July–September issue, 1911. TM originally titled the piece 'Über die Kunst Richard Wagners'. Part of the MS was written on notepaper headed *Grand Hotel des Bains, Lido-Venise* and dated 'Lido-Venedig Mai 1911'. There can be little doubt that this is the 'little tract, a page and a half of choice prose' whose composition, in the fourth chapter of *Death in Venice*, is assigned to Gustav von Aschenbach, seated beneath the canopy of his beach-table and drawing inspiration from the sight of Tadzio playing nearby. See also TM's account of the piece in his letter of 11 August 1911 to Ernst Bertram (pp. 48–9).

always a source of embarrassment to my love. But of course the arts are only different manifestations of art itself, which is the same in all its forms; and Wagner need not have been the great blender of the arts that he was in order to have exercised an instructive and nourishing influence on every form of artistic endeavour. What also gave my relationship to Wagner a certain immediacy and intimacy was the fact that secretly I always saw and loved in him – notwithstanding the claims of the theatre – a great *narrative* artist. The recurrent motif, the self-quotation, the symbolic phrase, the verbal and thematic reminiscence across long stretches of text – these were narrative devices after my own heart, and for that very reason full of enchantment for me; and I acknowledged at an early age that Wagner's works had a more stimulating influence on my youthful artistic aspirations than anything else in the world, filling me constantly with a longing, envious and infatuated, to produce something similar, if only on a small and modest scale. And indeed, it is not difficult to catch a whiff of the spirit that informs the *Ring* in my own *Buddenbrooks*, that epic pageant of the generations, linked together and interwoven by leitmotifs.

For a long time all my artistic thinking and practice was overshadowed by the name of Wagner. For a long time it seemed to me that all artistic desires and ambitions must conduce inevitably to that mighty name. At no time, however – not even in the days when I never missed a single performance of *Tristan* at the Munich Hoftheater – could my professions *about* Wagner ever have been seen as a profession of faith *in* Wagner. As a thinker and personality he seemed to me suspect, as an artist irresistible, if also deeply questionable in terms of the nobility, purity and wholesomeness of his influence; and never did I surrender my youthful heart to him with the same trusting abandon with which I yielded to the spell of the great poets and writers – those of whom Wagner felt entitled to speak, almost pityingly, as 'literary writers'. My love for him was a love devoid of belief, for it has always seemed to me pedantic to insist that one cannot love without also believing. It was a liaison, an affair – sceptical, pessimistic, clear-sighted, spiteful almost, yet full of passion and indescribable charm. Wonderful hours of deep and solitary happiness amidst the theatre throng, hours filled with frissons and brief moments of bliss, with delights for the nerves and the intellect alike, and sudden glimpses into things of profound and moving significance, such as only this incomparable art can afford!*

But today I no longer believe – if indeed I ever did believe – that the stature of a work of art is to be measured in terms of the unsurpassability of its artistic resources. And I have the impression that Wagner's star is in the descendant in the skies of the German mind.

I am not talking about his theory. If it were not something so completely secondary, not so wholly a retrospective and superfluous glorification of his own talent, then his creative work would undoubtedly have become just as untenable as the theory: and nobody would have taken it seriously for a moment without the work, which appears to validate it as long as one is sitting in the theatre, but which in fact validates nothing but itself. Has *anybody* ever seriously believed in this theory, I wonder? In this amalgam of painting, music, words and gesture that Wagner had the nerve to proclaim as the fulfilment of all artistic ambition? In a hierarchy of genres in which *Tasso* would rank below *Siegfried*? Are Wagner's writings on art actually read, in fact? And whence this lack of interest in Wagner the writer? Is it because his writings are propaganda rather than honest revelation? Because their comments on his work – wherein he truly lives in all his suffering greatness – are singularly inadequate and misleading? This must suffice by way of excuse. But it is true enough: there is not much to be learned about Wagner from Wagner's critical writings.

No, I am talking about his mighty *oeuvre* proper, which has currently attained the peak of its popularity with the bourgeois public – about his art as a taste, a style, a particular mode of sensibility. Let us not be deceived by the loud applause of the young people standing in the theatre stalls. The truth is that among the better-educated youth of today there is much criticism of Wagner, much instinctive, albeit unvoiced mistrust, and indeed – let us be frank – much indifference towards Wagner. How could it be otherwise? Wagner is nineteenth century through and through, he is *the* representative German artist of that epoch, which will live on in the memory of mankind as great (perhaps) and ill-starred (for certain).

* This sentence is a virtually literal self-quotation from 'An Essay on the Theatre' written three years previously, see p. 30.

But if I try to imagine the artistic masterpiece of the twentieth century, I see something that differs radically – and favourably, it seems to me – from that of Wagner: something conspicuously logical, well formed and clear, something at once austere and cheerful, no less imbued with strength of purpose, but more restrained, refined, more healthy even in its spirituality – something that does not seek its greatness in the monumentally baroque, nor its beauty in the sweep of emotion. A new classicism, I believe, is on the way.

Even so, whenever some chord, some evocative phrase from Wagner's work impinges all unexpected on my ear, I still start with joy; a kind of homesickness, of nostalgia for my youth, comes upon me; and once again, as of old, my spirit succumbs to that clever and ingenious wizardry, full of yearning and cunning.

To Ernst Bertram*

From the country residence of Thomas Mann
Bad Tölz
11 August 1911

Dear Doctor,

Many thanks for your most valued and interesting letter.

My decision to write about Wagner† was taken only with the greatest reluctance and under the pressure of an old promise I had given to the editor of the *Merker*. This journal (published in Vienna) organized a kind of 'Wagner survey' for its Bayreuth number. Some six months ago I was invited to take part in this; and since I had agreed, when the journal was first launched, to contribute the occasional piece, I thought this a convenient opportunity to redeem my promise. But as the deadline approached and the editor started to press me, I found the whole thing not at all to my liking; and what

---

*Ernst Bertram (1884-1957), professor of literary history whose books include *Nietzsche* (1918). TM played chamber music with him until he (TM) gave up the violin in 1913 or 1914.

† TM is referring to the previous essay, 'Coming to Terms with Richard Wagner', pp. 45-8.

the *Merker* calls my 'Coming to Terms with Wagner' is really just a sketchy piece of journalism dealing in a rather irresponsibly perfunctory way with a subject that is really ripe for thorough and definitive treatment. ('If only I had the time ...!') So take it for what it is. The piece gives no idea of the crisis in which I find myself *vis-à-vis* this art. Last Monday I tried listening to *Götterdämmerung*. My inward resistance to this wild play-acting with human passions and human tragedy almost brought words of outrage to my lips. In my bitterness I said to myself that only a barbaric and spiritually purblind nation could raise temples to a work like this. Just as well that I didn't write such thoughts down. No doubt time will teach me to view things more calmly and justly. (...)

Yours truly,
THOMAS MANN

To Julius Bab*

From the country residence of Thomas Mann
Bad Tölz
14 September 1911

Dear Herr Bab,
Very many thanks. You are absolutely right: Goethe would have been bound to regard Wagner as a thoroughly repugnant phenomenon. He was very tolerant, of course, in his moral attitude to anything of great moment or impact, and I sometimes wonder if he wouldn't have answered us by saying: 'The man is simply too big for you.' But that would be his affair. As for the Germans, they ought to be made to choose: Goethe or Wagner. It has to be one or the other – not both. But I'm very much afraid they would go for Wagner. Or perhaps not? Could it not be, perhaps, that every German *knows* in his heart that Goethe is incomparably more deserving

---

* Julius Bab (1880-1955), editor of a five-volume history of German drama and of several biographies of writers and actors.

of veneration and trust as a leader and national hero than that snuffling gnome from Saxony, with his colossal talent and his shabby personality? Quaeritur.

With kindest regards,

THOMAS MANN

From *Reflections of a Non-political Man**

In art and literature my love of things German begins at the point
where they become possible and valid in European terms, capable of
making a European impact, and accessible to every European. The
three names that come to mind when I think about the roots of my
own intellectual and artistic development, names that form a bright
constellation of eternally united minds, shedding its glorious light
across the German heavens – these names designate phenomena, not
of a parochially German, but of European import: Schopenhauer,
Nietzsche and Wagner.

I can picture the small room high above the suburban streets
where, sixteen years ago, I lay for days on end on an oddly shaped
chaise-longue or sofa, reading *The World as Will and Idea.*
Solitary-unordered youth, filled with desire for the world and for
death – how eagerly it quaffed the magic potion of this metaphysic,
whose deepest essence is eroticism, and in which I recognized the
spiritual source of Wagner's *Tristan* music! [...]

This was also the time when my passion for Richard Wagner's art
reached its zenith – or was fast approaching that point. I say 'passion'
because more sober words like 'love' or 'enthusiasm' would not truly
express my meaning. The years when one is most capable of self-
surrender are often the years of the greatest psychological sensitivity,
which in my case was powerfully stimulated by a certain amount of
critical reading; and surrender allied to knowledge is the very definition of passion. The most personally difficult and fruitful discovery
of my youth was this: that passion is *clear-sighted* – or not deserving
of the name. Love that is blind, love that merely lauds and glorifies
– a foolish fond fancy! There is a certain type of official Wagner
literature that I could never bring myself to read. But that critical
reading which I found so stimulating came from the pen of Friedrich
Nietzsche, and more especially those writings that constitute a critique

* *Betrachtungen eines Unpolitischen* (1915–18), Berlin, 1918. See also note on p. 161.

of the artist, or – which amounts to the same thing in Nietzsche's case – a critique of *Wagner*. For wherever the artist and the business of art are discussed in these writings – and they are certainly not discussed in any indulgent way – the name 'Wagner' may safely be substituted for 'the artist', even if he is not specifically mentioned. Nietzsche had experienced and studied the phenomenon of 'the artist', if not art itself (though a case could be made out for that too) entirely through the medium of Wagner, just as his much lowlier descendant thrilled to discover Wagner's art – and almost, in that, the experience of art itself – through the medium of Nietzsche's critical writings. And this in the formative years of my youth, with the result that all my notions of art and the artist were decisively shaped by this experience – or if not decisively shaped, then at least coloured and influenced: influenced, moreover, not in any spirit of wide-eyed enthusiasm, but rather of all-too-wary and sceptical appraisal.

Discerning surrender, clear-sighted love – such is passion. I can truthfully claim that the intensity of my passion for Wagner was not in the least diminished by the fact that it was refracted through psychological and critical analysis – an analysis which, as we all know, is every bit the equal of its enchanting object in shrewdness and subtlety. On the contrary, it was this that gave it its real edge and piquancy, and transformed it into a passion in the true sense – with all the demands that only a true passion imposes on one's nervous resilience. However poetic and 'German' it may like to appear, Wagner's art as such is an extremely modern and by no means innocent art. It is clever and ingenious, full of yearning and cunning; in its resources and characteristics it knows how to combine the narcotic with the intellectually stimulating in a way that is intrinsically exhausting for the spectator. But the preoccupation with that art almost becomes a vice, a *moral* issue, a recklessly ethical surrender to all that is harmful and devouring, if it is merely naive enthusiasm – and not combined with an analysis whose most venomous insights are ultimately a form of glorification and a further expression, simply, of passionate devotion. Even in *Ecce homo* there is a page on *Tristan* that is proof enough that Nietzsche's relationship to Wagner remained one of impassioned love even after the onset of his paralysis.

The intellectual name for 'love' is 'interest', and anyone with any psychological insight knows that 'interest' connotes an emotion that is anything but insipid – which indeed is far more potent than (for example) 'admiration'. It is the writer's emotion *par excellence*, and critical analysis, far from destroying it, actually supplies it with constant nourishment, very much contrary to Spinozist doctrine. Impassioned interest seeks satisfaction not in panegyric, therefore, but in criticism, hostile, even malicious criticism – even in the downright polemical, provided it is witty and the product of passionate feeling. Mere praise tastes flat and stale by comparison; there are no lessons, it seems, to be learned from it. And should that interest get to the point of celebrating its object – be it a thing, a personality or a particular problem – in a productive form, then the resulting work will be a strange beast, one that prides itself, almost, on being misunderstood, the product of a crafty and impishly deceptive enthusiasm, which at first sight looks exactly like a lampoon. Not long ago I produced a little something along these lines myself, when I contributed to the war debate with a kind of historical essay sketching the life of Frederick the Great* – a piece inspired, indeed wrung from me, by contemporary events, which anxious friends urged me not to publish at first (the war was still in its early days then): not because it was 'patriotic' in a manner insulting to literature, but for precisely the opposite reason ...

I know full well where the argument is taking me when I say this. Nietzsche and Wagner are both leading *critics of German culture and civilization*, the latter indirectly, through his art, the former directly, through his critical writings – although (such is modernism) the artistic method is fully the equal of the critical in terms of intellectual assurance and sophistication. Leaving aside Nietzsche, Germany – as I said – has never had a tradition of Wagner criticism; for an 'unliterary' populace is by the same token unpsychological, antipsychological. Baudelaire and Barrès have said more valuable things about Wagner than can be found anywhere in the works of Wagner's German biographers or apologists; and at the present time it falls to a Swede, W. Peterson-Berger, in his book *Richard Wagner als Kulturerscheinung* [Richard Wagner as Cultural Phenomenon], to give us Germans some hints as to the attitude of mind with which one might do well to approach such an interesting phenomenon (in the most momentous sense of that term) – namely, a democratically

* 'Friedrich und die grosse Koalition' (Frederick and the Great Coalition), 1915.

honest and open attitude, which is essential if we are to understand the first thing about it. The Swede writes of Wagner's nationalism, of his art as a national German art, and observes that the only genre *not* absorbed into his great synthesis is German folk music. Although he is capable of sounding a folksy German note from time to time for purposes of characterization, as in *Die Meistersinger* and *Siegfried*, this never constitutes the basis and starting point of his musical writing – is never the *source* from which it wells up spontaneously, as in the work of Schumann, Schubert and Brahms. There is a necessary distinction to be made, he argues, between folk art and national art; the former is aimed at a domestic audience, the latter at an international one. Wagner's music is more national than popular; to the foreigner as such it may appear typically German in many respects, but at the same time it has an unmistakably cosmopolitan cachet. Well, it is easy enough to make a point by overstating one's case. In fact Wagner is so intensely German as a spiritual phenomenon that a powerful emotional experience of his work has always seemed to me an indispensable prerequisite for any kind of understanding – or if not an understanding, then at least an inkling – of the profound splendours and agonizing travails that make up the German character. But *as well as* being an eruptive revelation of the German character, this *oeuvre* is also a theatrical representation of it, [...] which appears destined to elicit from an Allied audience tremoring with horrified curiosity a cry of: 'Ah, ça c'est bien allemand par exemple!'

True and potent though it is, then, Wagner's Germanness is refracted and fragmented in the modern mode, is decorative, analytical and intellectual – hence its powerful fascination, its innate capacity for cosmopolitan, not to say planetary influence. His art is the most sensational self-portrayal and self-critique of the German character that could possibly be imagined; as such it is calculated to make German culture *interesting* even to the most doltish foreigner, and a passionate preoccupation with Wagner's art is necessarily and always a passionate preoccupation with that selfsame Germanness which it glorifies in a manner both critical and decorative. This it would be anyway; but how much more so if it is guided by a critique that appears to be directed at Wagner's art, but which in fact is directed at German culture and civilization in general, albeit not always in

54

such a directly explicit way as in the splendid analysis of the *Meistersinger* Overture that opens the eighth section of *Jenseits von Gut und Böse* [Beyond Good and Evil]. For the fact is that while Nietzsche may have his foreign rivals as a critic of Wagner, as a critic of German culture he has absolutely none, either abroad or at home: his remarks on that subject are by far the most malicious and by far the best ever written, and the soaring brilliance of his eloquence when he addresses himself to things German and the problem of German culture testifies to his profound and fierce affection for these matters. To speak of Nietzsche as 'anti-German', as people in Germany sometimes do (in other countries, with the benefit of distance, they see these things more clearly), is as crass as it would be to call him an anti-Wagnerian. [...] What I meant was that a young man compelled by taste and historical circumstance to use the art of Wagner and the critical writings of Nietzsche as the basis for his own culture, and to form his mind principally on these, was by the same token bound to perceive his own national heritage, the culture and civilization of Germany, as a wholly remarkable European element, exciting vehement criticism; and it was inevitable that a kind of psychologically orientated patriotism should develop in him at a very early stage, a feeling that naturally had nothing at all to do with political nationalism, but which none the less engendered a certain sensitivity where national pride was concerned, a certain impatience with the *cruder* forms of anti-German propaganda based on ignorance: rather as a lover of art who was once deeply immersed in the experience of Wagner, but who has now repudiated this art for higher spiritual reasons of his own, will be moved to impatience by the abuse of ignorant and reactionary philistines. To reverse the emphasis of my earlier definition: 'interest' is the intellectual name for an emotion whose sentimental name is – 'love'. [...]

Rarely, I imagine, will the influence of Wagner on a non-musician – and an even more confirmed non-dramatist – have been so powerful and decisive as I confess it was in my case. He influenced me not as a musician, not as a dramatist, nor yet as a 'musical dramatist', but simply as an artist, as the modern artist *par excellence*, as Nietzsche's writings had taught me to see him – and above all as the great master of musical-epic prose and symbolism that he is. All that I know about the handling of artistic resources, about artistic effect as such (as opposed to mere showiness, striving after effect for its own sake), about the epic mode, beginnings and endings, the role of style as a mysterious assimilation of the personal to the objective, about the creation of symbols, the organic coherence of the individual work and the biographical unity of the complete *oeuvre*: all that I know about these things, and have attempted to practise and develop within my own limits – I owe it to my passion for this art. Even now, when some evocative phrase, some disjointed chord from Wagner's musical cosmos impinges all unexpected on my ear, I still start with joy. But to the young man for whom there was no place at home, and who was living in a kind of voluntary exile in an unloved foreign country,* this artistic world became quite literally his spiritual homeland. A sightseeing tour followed by a concert on the Pincio ... and lost amidst the throng of the international smart set, taking their banal pleasures, the shabby and rather down-at-heel young man stood at the foot of the podium, beneath a dense blue sky that never ceased to oppress him, beneath palm trees that he despised; and weak-kneed with rapture, he received the romantic gospel proclaimed in the *Lohengrin* Prelude. Did he think back to these times twenty years later, when the spirit that informed the *Lohengrin* Prelude found itself at war with the international smart set? Are memories such as these partly to blame, perhaps, for his unselectively non-literary stance in this war?

An anti-Wagner demonstration in the Piazza Colonna! Maestro Vessella, the then conductor of the municipal orchestra (with kettle drums: whenever kettle drums appeared in the Piazza, people knew that the municipal orchestra – and not the stupid military band – would be playing, and that Wagner would be on the programme) – Vessella, the champion of German music in Rome, is playing the lament for the fallen Siegfried. Everyone knows there will be an uproar. The piazza is crammed with people, every balcony is packed. The piece is heard out in silence. Then all around the square the battle begins between defiant applause and national protest. One faction cries 'Bis!' and claps furiously. The other shouts 'Basta!' and whistles. It looks as though the opposition will win the day; but Vessella goes for the encore. This time the protesters carry on with-

* Italy. In 1896–8 TM lived in Rome, and it was there that he began *Buddenbrooks*.

out regard for the performance. The *piano* passages are shattered by whistles and loud calls for Italian music, while shouts of approbation from the Wagnerian camp dominate during the *forte* passages. But I shall never forget how the Nothung motif welled up for the second time, amidst the cries of 'Evviva!' and 'Abbasso!', unfolding its mighty rhythms above the brawling factions, and how, when it reached its climax in that shattering dissonance that precedes the twice-repeated C major chord, a great howl of triumph broke forth, engulfing the helpless, broken opposition, and cowing them into discomfited silence for some considerable time ... The 20-year-old foreigner – foreign to this place like this music, *with* this music – stood hemmed in by the crowd in the square. He did not join in the shouting, for he was too choked with emotion. His countenance, turned towards the podium, which furious *Italianissimi* were trying to storm while the musicians defended it with their instruments – his uplifted countenance smiled in the consciousness of its own pallor, and his heart beat with a fierce pride, with the morbid feeling of youth ... A pride in what? A love for what? Merely for a controversial taste in art?

It is very possible that twenty years later,* in August 1914, his mind went back to the Piazza Colonna and to the tears of emotion that once welled up in his eyes at the triumph of the Nothung motif and coursed down over his cold visage, tears that he could not dry because the press of that foreign crowd pinned his arms to his side. None the less I am not deluded. Even if the intense experience of that art did become a source of patriotic feelings to that young man, it was a spiritual experience of supra-German significance, an experience that I shared in common with the European intelligentsia, like that of Thomas Buddenbrook. For this German musician was no longer a 'German music-maker' in the old, cosy, traditional sense. Very German he undoubtedly was (and indeed, can one be a maker of music *without* being German?). But what fascinated me was not the German-nationalist element in his art, nor its specifically German poeticism or romanticism – or at least, only in so far as all this appeared intellectualized therein, as decorative self-portrayal: but rather the all-powerful European appeal that emanates from it, and

---

* TM's first trip to Italy, when this incident probably took place, was in fact in the summer of 1895.

to which Wagner's current, almost extra-German status bears witness. No, I was not so German that I failed to see the profound psychological and artistic affinity between his artistic devices and those of Zola and Ibsen, both of whom, like him, were pre-eminently masters of the symbol, the tyrannical formula, and of whom the French novelist in particular, a Naturalist and a Romantic like himself, appears as his true confrère in his desire and capacity for intoxicating and overwhelming a mass audience ... The Rougon-Macquart cycle and *Der Ring des Nibelungen*: the average 'Wagnerian' does not lump them together in his mind. Yet they *do* belong together – a fact acknowledged by the understanding, if not by the affections. For there *are* cases where the intellect insists on a parallel that the emotions would prefer to reject out of hand. The Rougon-Macquart cycle and *Der Ring des Nibelungen*! I hope I am not asked to choose between them. I fear that I would make the 'patriotic' choice. [...]

Aestheticism in the literal sense is the most un-German thing in the world, and the most unbourgeois. One is not schooled to be an aesthete in the academy of Schopenhauer and Wagner; here one breathes the air of moral pessimism, the air of the German bourgeoisie. For they are one and the same, the German and the bourgeois; if 'mind' as such is an inherently bourgeois concept, then the *German* mind is bourgeois in a very special degree, German *culture* is essentially bourgeois, and the German bourgeois tradition is essentially *humanistic* – which means that it is not *political*, like Western culture (or at least, has not been so hitherto), and can only *become* political by turning aside from its own humanistic tradition ...

To say that Schopenhauer and Wagner inhabit a bourgeois domain, that what one receives at their hands is a bourgeois education, seems an absurd claim; for it is difficult to reconcile the idea of bourgeois tradition with that of genius. And indeed, what could be less bourgeois than their careers, highly strung and tragic as they were, full of turmoil and torment, and ending, finally, in the brilliance of world renown! Nevertheless, they are both true children of their bourgeois age, and the bourgeois element is everywhere discernible in their human and intellectual being. Consider the life that Schopenhauer led: his origins in the Hanseatic mercantile tradition; his long years of unbroken residence in Frankfurt; the pedantic, Kantian

uniformity and regularity of his daily regime; the sensible care
he took of his health, based on a sound knowledge of physiology
('The wise man seeks not pleasure, but the absence of pain'); his
meticulous habits as a capitalist (he kept an account of every penny,
and by careful management succeeded in doubling his small fortune
during his lifetime); the unhurried calm, persistence, economy and
regularity of his working habits (he wrote for publication only during
the first two hours of the morning, and in a letter to Goethe he said
that *loyalty and honesty* were the two virtues chiefly responsible for
his achievements and successes – virtues that he had translated from
the practical sphere to the realm of theory and intellect): all this
testifies to the bourgeois character of his private life, just as his
bourgeois *intellectual and spiritual values* are revealed in his utter
abhorrence of Romantic medievalism, with its scheming priests and
valorous knights, and in his unquestioning allegiance to classical
humanism. [...]

As far as Wagner is concerned, however, both his private and his
artistic persona exhibit elements that smack not just of the solidly
middle class, but of the vulgar and the downright *parvenu*: that taste
for the opulent, for satins, luxury, riches and bourgeois ostentation
– a private, personal trait in the first instance, but one that reaches
deep down into his intellectual and artistic being. I am not sure if I
was the original author of the observation that Wagner's art and
those elaborate dried-flower arrangements by Makart (complete with
peacock feathers) share a common historical and aesthetic origin.
But if Wagner was a trifle inclined to bourgeois vulgarity, he was
also a good 'burgher' in the best German sense; and his self-
dramatization as 'German master craftsman' (even in his wardrobe)
had its own innate and natural justification. It would be wrong
to see only the white-hot eruptive fire in his work, the daemonic
and the brilliant, and to ignore the element of traditional Old
German craftsmanship – that honest perseverance, pride in workmanship, and ingenious diligence ... 'By their fruits ye shall
know them.' Wagner's European intellectualism reappears in Richard
Strauss, while his German-bourgeois portion is seen again in the
folksy craftsmanship and honest industry of the endearing Engelbert
Humperdinck.

The bourgeois as artist: a paradox become reality, but a paradox none the less, ambivalent and problematic by any reckoning, despite the special legitimacy that this intellectual life form enjoys in Germany. When I spoke of the decisive influence that Wagner's art had on me, I omitted to mention one rather disquieting aspect, which I have been putting off until now: and that is not so much Wagner's own bourgeois identity as his relationship to bourgeois culture, and the *effect* he has on the average middle-class person. It is at *this* point that Wagner's influence can become a kind of corruption – as perhaps it did in my case: I am referring to what Nietzsche calls the 'double focus',* the artistic view combined simultaneously with the bourgeois, the instinct (and it *is* an instinct, of course, not a calculated intention, something wholly objective, not at all subjective) for satisfying sophisticated needs *and* more cheerfully commonplace ones, for winning over the select few *and* capturing the masses – an instinct that relates, in my own view, to Wagner's appetite for conquest, his thirst for this world, his 'sinfulness' in an ascetic sense: to what the Buddha calls 'attachment' or 'craving', his desire, his sensual-metaphysical longing for love. For there is a kind of art, of course, that knows nothing of all this, or of this one particular thing: an art that is chaste, austere, cold, proud, even forbidding, that nourishes for 'the world' nothing but contempt and scorn in its heart and mind, and remains utterly untouched by any form of demagogy, any consideration or condescension (be it ever so unconscious), any profane desire for influence, community or love. Wagner was far removed from this. There is one passage in his work that sums him up in every respect, including this one: I refer to the moment in Act II of *Tristan* when he invokes the so-called 'longing' motif on the word 'Welt' [world] ('Selbst dann bin ich die Welt!' [Then I, I am the world!]). Nothing will convince me that Wagner's appetites, his world-eroticism, are not the source and origin of what Nietzsche called his 'double focus': a capacity, born of imperative need, to captivate and charm not only the most refined spirits – *that* we take for granted – but also the broad mass of the common people. I say 'born of imperative need' because I believe that every artist, without exception, creates precisely what he himself *is*, what accords with his own aesthetic judgement and needs. A dishonest artistry, calculating and creating effects that it scorns, effects that are beneath it, that are not

* See note on p. 128.

first and foremost effects on the *artist*, their author – such an artistry does not exist. It follows from this that the objective effects achieved by an artist – including the broad bourgeois appeal of Wagner – are always a direct reflection of his own being and nature. As an artist Wagner was filled with longing – or ambition, to put it more bluntly. But what one desires as a young man, *really* desires by the laws of nature – not what one has mistakenly and spuriously talked oneself into desiring – that one has in abundance in old age; and the end result of that aristocratic/democratic, artistic/bourgeois view is *success*, which in this case necessarily means a twofold success: success with the artistic community *and* with the bourgeoisie, for neither the applause of fellow artists nor the applause of the public at large is sufficient, on its own, to constitute 'success'. And let nobody think I am being in the least smug when I add that I too, in my small way, can tell a tale or two about 'success'. I see it as just one of life's experiences like any other, and I know that it says something highly equivocal about those to whom it comes. Put plainly, it signifies that they needed to appeal to the fools as well.... But I also know that any 'success' that is the end result of that double focus learned in sin and iniquity from Wagner offers but a precarious and uneasy refuge; that it bears within itself a mortal peril and a Furies' vengeance; that a man who has achieved this success must expect, in the long run, to fall out with both parties, the bourgeoisie *and* the radicals. [...]

As far as Wagner is concerned, it is clear that he was a revolutionary all his life, both as artist and as thinker. But it is equally certain that this champion of national cultural revolution did not intend political revolution, and never felt at all at home in the climate of 1848–9. In his memoirs he speaks of the 'appalling superficiality of the spokesmen of that age', of their 'stale, hackneyed rhetoric both at public gatherings and in all their personal dealings with others'. He was astonished (he tells us) to hear and read 'at what an incredibly banal level of argument the debate was conducted, and how they all ended up saying nothing more than that the republic was the best form of government, but that a monarchy might be just about acceptable in the meantime, provided the monarch behaved himself'. And how repugnant and offensive it must be to liberal critics, those who see a necessary antithesis between worldly power and things of the mind, to hear Wagner say, of the Frankfurt Parliament, that it was hard to see what could possibly come of all this inflated talk on the part of men who were *totally powerless*. Powerless indeed! This brutal fanatic had a weakness for 'power', it seems, and in 1870 he did not hesitate to place himself on the side of 'power' – indeed, to acclaim it, to acclaim it with rapturous delight, and to show himself far more enthusiastic in its behalf than ever he was back in the heady days of the National Assembly.

And yet the liberal critics would have us believe that he was 'no militant'? Good heavens! He extolled Bismarck's 'tremendous courage', hailed the German army before the gates of Paris; the victory over France, the re-establishment of the Reich, the crowning of a German Emperor – it was all too much for his artistic soul, which burst forth into a kind of hymn along the lines of: 'Full bright is mankind's morn; now break, thou day of the gods!' In short, he was more fanatical than any of those who welcomed war in 1914; for none of us was big enough or unbridled enough by nature to compete with him in philistine impropriety.

For an insight into Wagner's relationship to politics in general (and to 1848 in particular) which makes the situation almost laughably clear, one need only recall that he had just completed *Lohengrin* at the time, crowning his achievement with the Prelude, that most romantically joyous piece in the entire musical repertoire. *Lohengrin* and 1848 – two worlds apart, with at most only one thing in common: their national pathos. And the liberal critic is guided by a sure instinct when he makes fun of *Lohengrin* in satirical social novels by translating it into the political sphere. Wagner could probably hear the fine bass of his own King Henry in his mind when he made that thoroughly bizarre speech before the Dresden Fatherland Association, in which he proclaimed himself an ardent royalist and a despiser of constitutionalism in all its forms, and called upon Germany to cast out 'alien, un-German notions' – by which he meant Western democracy – and to re-establish the one true saving and Old-Germanic relationship between the absolute monarch and the free people: for in the absolute monarch (he said) the very concept of freedom is raised to the highest level of divinely inspired consciousness, and the people can be truly free only under the rule of *one* –

not under the rule of *many*. Even Friedrich Wilhelm Foerster* is not more eccentric in his political beliefs than this. But such things he said, this most implausible of revolutionaries! Like his claim that art had been *conservative* in its heyday, and *was destined to become so again*. Or the terse and indelible proposition: '*Germans are inherently conservative.*' Or a proposition that only a Frenchman or a radical utopian would question: 'The future is conceivable only in so far as it is conditioned by the past.' Or that immortal and definitive proposition, which is not open to question at all: 'Democracy in Germany has been transposed into another language. *It exists only in the press.*' Naturally Wagner loved the idea of the brotherhood of man, but he was far removed from any internationalist leanings: otherwise words like 'alien', 'transposed', 'un-German' would not have connoted judgement, condemnation, even hatred – as from his lips they clearly do. But why did he hate democracy? Because he *hated politics per se*, and because he recognized that *politics and democratism are one and the same thing*. Why is it that nations endowed with a special relish and talent for political life believe in democracy, desire democracy, and indeed have democracy? Precisely because they are the nations that enjoy political life! Nothing could be plainer. A nation's taste for democracy is in inverse proportion to its distaste for politics. If Wagner was in any sense an expression of his nation, if in any thing he was German, German-humanistic, German-bourgeois in the highest and purest sense, it was in his hatred of politics. It is tempting to see the intellectual disillusionment that resulted from his participation in the Dresden uprising of May 1848 as the reason why he vowed immediately afterwards never to get involved in that sort of thing again, and declared politics to be 'thoroughly futile'. But statements such as 'A politically minded man is repugnant' (from a letter to Liszt) spring from deeper, impersonal sources. What Englishman, Frenchman, Italian, or even Russian would ever have made such a remark? In this case it sprang from an artist's nebulous and earnest speculations about the supposed corruption, the anarchic-doctrinaire politicization of mankind, dating from the dissolution of the Greek *polis* and the destruction of tragedy; about a

---

*Friedrich Wilhelm Foerster (1869–1966), political and educational theorist who in 1920 resigned his professorship in Munich in order to be free to pursue ethical. pacifism.

'fundamentally social movement' which had nothing at all to do with political revolution, but which would, on the contrary, usher in a human condition that would mean the 'end of politics', where there would be no more politics of any kind, and where, *for that very reason*, 'art in all its truth' would become possible; about a depoliticized, humane and artistic form of life and mind, therefore, that would be a thoroughly German form of life and mind, favourable to all things German. For: 'We Germans, it seems, will never be great politicians; but perhaps we shall be something far greater, if we gauge our talents aright ...' It was of a world depoliticized and made humane, a world made 'German' in the most civilized and anti-political sense of the word, that he dreamed, this amalgam of German cultural tradition and artistry, when he spoke of the desire that seeks 'after the only truth – man himself': very much in contrast to the liberal critic, whose dream, rather, is of a Germany 'made humane' by a process of democratic politicization ...

But I did say earlier that the liberal critic knows what he is doing when he satirizes Wagner. He knows by instinct, for he has certainly not read him, and does not understand a single note of his music. What probably would be news to him, however, and at the same time further grist to his mill, is the fact that Wagner was an imperialist, on top of everything else – *and* there is proof! As early as 1848, in that same thoroughly bizarre speech that he made before Dresden's democratic Fatherland Association, he called for the establishment of German colonies. 'We shall do a better job than the Spaniards,' he said, 'who turned the New World into a priest-ridden slaughterhouse, and better than the English, who made of it a shopkeeper's till. We shall do it in splendidly German fashion!' The colonial ideal never ceased to exercise his mind, and in this he may have been influenced by reminiscences of Frederick and Faust. But how could the liberal critic be other than satirically disposed towards an intellectual stance that is both anti-political *and* nationalist, anti-political *and* imperialist, when he himself contends, with practised vehemence, that one *must* be politically minded, but may on no account entertain nationalist sentiments, and when he invariably speaks of 'imperialism' as if it were the vilest work of the Devil and a crime against humanity?

The present war teaches us once again that all manner of interests are served by times of great turmoil and tumult. There is no philosophy, no ideology, no doctrine, no fad or fancy that does not find its confirmation and justification in war, that is not joyously convinced that its time has come, that its future is now dawning. Wagner discovered something of himself in the so-called German Revolution; he was young enough and idealistic enough to believe that it would make his cultural dreams come true – his dreams of the 'end of politics' and the dawning of a new humanity. It brought him profound disappointment, and he disavowed his involvement in it as an 'act of folly'; its mortal foe, the wily and brutal founder of the Second Reich, he hailed with delight, even though Bismarck's solution to the German question, far from signalling the 'end of politics', in fact heralded their real beginning for Germany; and although that 'act of folly' had very serious and weighty practical consequences for Wagner's outward life, it would be quite absurd to claim that the political upheaval of 1848 was an inward experience of the first importance for him, *the* decisive experience of spiritual self-discovery. That came to him much later, and in the most unpolitical form imaginable – a thoroughly German experience, moralistic and metaphysical. It came to him in the solitude of his Swiss exile, and it was only a book: it was the philosophy of Arthur Schopenhauer, in which he discerned the spiritual redemption of his own being, the true dwelling-place of his soul. [...]

Art will never be moral or virtuous in any political sense: and progress will never be able to put its trust in art. It has a fundamental tendency to unreliability and treachery; its delight in the outrageously irrational, its predilection for the 'barbarism' that begets beauty, are indestructible; and although some may call this predilection hysterical, philistine, immoral to the point of endangering the world, yet it is an imperishable fact of life, and if one wanted to eradicate this aspect of art – if indeed one could eradicate it – then one might well have freed the world from a serious danger: but in the process one would almost certainly have freed it from art itself – and there are few who would wish that. An irrational force, but a powerful one; and mankind's attachment to it proves that mankind is neither able nor willing to survive on rationalism alone, as summed up in the celebrated three-part equation of democratic wisdom: 'reason = virtue = happiness'. In this connection it is worth rereading Baudelaire's wickedly enthusiastic description of the *Tannhäuser* March: 'Who among us,' he exclaims,

> who upon hearing these chords so sumptuous and proud, this glorious rhythm so elegantly measured, these regal fanfares, could picture to himself anything but a scene of fantastic splendour, a procession of heroic men in shining raiment, all of lofty stature, all imbued with strength of will and childlike faith, no less magnificent in their joys than terrible in their feuds?

And who among us (we would add) could fail to see that the ideas and images evoked by this art are *extremely questionable* in terms of any political virtue?

To Ernst Bertram

Poschingerstrasse 1, Munich
4 June 1920

[...] I was better prepared for a reading of your piece than you can imagine. On the eve of the evening before, from 5 until 10 yesterday, I had listened to *Die Walküre* with my two eldest, who are more and more a delight to my eyes and a joy to my heart.* In my mind's eye I had never lost sight of the four-evening cycle, which to me will always be the very archetype of 'the work' as such; but it was quite a few years since I had seen any of its parts in the theatre. Antaeus! He felt himself not a little 'electrified', while the children marvelled, moist-eyed from time to time. To be more precise: the work that I surveyed as a whole from this vantage point appeared at first in a rather cold light. I missed that element of the mysterious, the nebulous and half-discernible, which had enhanced its grandeur and rendered its depths the more profound to my youthful mind. But I also realized that its effect on me at that time had really been only artistic, whereas now I felt much more able to respond to it on a human

* Erika, b. 1905, and Klaus, b. 1906.

66

level. It is beyond all question the most powerful of the four pieces in human emotional terms. Siegmund being told of his impending death while his beloved slumbers in his lap; Wotan laying his greatest and dearest child to rest for her epic sleep – these are things on whose sublime humanity the grown man gazes not with the nervous awe of youth, but with the emotion born of experience. In any event Wagner is still the artist I understand best, and in whose shadow I continue to live. The relationship of this proto-democratic European to German culture was a romantic one, like his relationship to 'the people' and popular culture – and indeed to music itself. For romanticism is intellectualism allied to longing. One can readily see that the democratic character of his artistic devices and effects was bound to appear vulgar and destructive to cultural conservatives, and as long as such people exist, so it must always appear. Ultimately this is music for the unmusical – or rather, for the unmusical *as well*. Anyway, it is one form of democracy that commended itself to me early on – the characteristically German form, evidently. I can't see it working out in any *other* shape in this country ... [...]

To Paul Steegemann*

Fürstenhof, Garmisch
18 August 1920

[...] Most of the great moralists were also great sinners. They say that Dostoevsky was a child-molester. He was also an epileptic, and today we are on the point of declaring this mystic illness to be a form of sexual malpractice. At all events, the yawning chasms of lust open up at every turn in the works of this religious believer – as they do in many a great, sublime and sacrosanct work, in whose presence stupid minds (even if they noticed anything) would not dare to giggle or voice their outrage. Wagner's *Tristan* is a thoroughly obscene work. In *Ecce homo* Nietzsche uses the phrase 'the lust of hell' to

* Paul Steegemann (1894-1956), publisher.

67

describe it, and adds that the use of an expression borrowed from mysticism is not only permissible here, but positively enjoined. It is interesting to note that certain turns of phrase in the text of *Tristan* are taken from Schlegel's *Lucinde* – that *notorious* book. Other things are taken from the *Hymnen an die Nacht* [Hymns to the Night] of Novalis, or at least from the same general area of Romanticism, which (not that the philistine would notice) is likewise an extremely lascivious area. [...]

Tristan and Isolde*

One Tristan, at the court of King Mark of Cornwall, nephew to the King and the son of his deceased sister Blancheflor, and Isolde, princess of Ireland, daughter to the Irish King Gurmun and his Queen Isolde, are personages of great renown in the courtly circles of their day, and each has heard much about the other by way of rumour.

Although they have never seen each other, Tristan represents for Isolde the ideal of manhood, while she embodies for him all his dreams of womanly beauty and nobility. Tristan's renown rests on his bravery, cleverness and noble breeding, which is a legacy of his Breton blood. (His father, Rivalin of Parmenie, came thence to the court of King Mark at Tintagel; the story of his love for Blancheflor ended in tragedy.) Not only is he the most handsome and graceful youth in all the land, a shrewd general who has performed many great warlike services for his uncle, a dazzling knight whose heroism has won the day in many a passage at arms and many a knightly exploit: but he is also the most cultivated man of his age, accomplished in languages and song and all the arts of peace, and endowed with political acumen – not just a blunt man of action. Likewise, travellers acquainted with Ireland and its capital city of Develin† cannot praise too highly the charms of the fair-haired Isolde, which are likewise conjoined with extraordinary qualities of mind and intellect. (From her mother she has learned many secrets of the healing art.) Thus do they each carry in their heart the image of the other, and their thoughts meet across the distance that separates them. (Opening shots!)

But that their ways should ever meet is highly improbable, for there exists an ancient feud between Ireland and Cornwall. Repeated wars have been fought between them, with varying issue; rivers of

---

* A film scenario, based on Gottfried von Strassburg's *Tristan* poem of the early thirteenth century, which TM wrote in 1923 in collaboration with his brother Viktor. It was first published in Viktor Mann's *Wir waren fünf*, Konstanz, 1949. See TM's remarks on pp. 76–7 about the genesis of the scenario.
† Dublin.

blood have flowed; and the hatred on both sides, but particularly the Irish, is so fierce that under Irish law any Cornishman attempting to land there must be put to death.

At Tintagel, King Mark's castle, the situation is that Mark loves his nephew dearly and has designated him to be his heir, for which reason he is resolved not to marry. But Tristan has many enemies at court among the great men of the land, the barons – men who are jealous of him, conspire against him, and are forever urging Mark to bestow a queen upon the land and a direct heir to the crown. Tristan for his part, quite without thought for his own advantage, is devoted to Mark in absolute fealty, and this loyalty combines with his interest in the much-renowned Princess Isolde to suggest the idea of winning her to be his lord's bride. The true greatness of the plan lies in its political significance: Tristan hopes to bring about peace between the two countries, which have inflicted so much damage on each other through hatred and war. The plan is bold, and seemingly impracticable – as the King himself thinks when Tristan proposes it in the Council. But in the end Mark accedes to the plan, solely in order to put a stop to the importuning of his barons. He announces that he will marry Isolde and none other. If she is not to be won, then he will not marry at all, and Tristan will be heir to the crown.

The barons want Tristan to be charged with this perilous enterprise, and they try to persuade the King to send him to Ireland alone (in the hope that he will perish in the attempt). The King refuses angrily, and wants them to go without his nephew. But Tristan claims the commission for himself as a supreme personal honour, and asks only that a number of barons be sent to accompany him. With reluctance and misgivings they consent to this arrangement. They set out. As they are approaching the Irish coast, Tristan, clad now in the most wretched clothes he can find, takes his harp and transfers from the barque into a small skiff. He commands the others to return home with the message that he will return either with Isolde or not at all. Then he casts himself adrift in his skiff, to be carried ashore by the tide.

A lookout in Develin spies the helpless craft, and a party is sent out to investigate. As the servants despatched from the mainland approach, they hear the sound of singing and harp-playing, so sweet and bewitching that they listen absolutely motionless, relinquishing oars and helm. Then they lay hold of the alien craft and find Tristan inside, who spins them a yarn about how he is a court minstrel from Spain who launched out into commerce; how he was making for England with a wealthy associate and a valuable cargo when he was attacked on the high seas by pirates; and how, while his fellow merchant and the entire crew were slaughtered, he alone was spared by the pirates because of his beautiful singing, and was cast adrift in this tiny boat with a little food to sustain him.

The Irishmen bring him ashore, just as Isolde is passing by with Brangane and her other ladies on her return from bathing. A great crowd gathers, the Princess is informed, and Tristan – who calls himself Tantris and pretends to be weak with exhaustion – is brought before her at her request. She commands him to sing and play; he obeys, and makes the most profound impression, not least by his words and general demeanour. She gives orders that the shipwrecked minstrel shall be taken to the royal castle and bestowed in a small chamber where he can rest and recover.

And so Tristan enters the court circle, where he soon wins all hearts by his talents and his personality. He is superior to them all in intellect, breeding and learning. He tutors Isolde in music and languages, and gives her instruction in 'morality' – the art of seemly conduct. They fall in love. But for Tristan this emotion is entirely subordinate to his sense of mission and purpose and his duty to King Mark; and when he observes that Isolde loves him he is pleased for the reason that she will follow him the more willingly to Cornwall, although the discovery also makes him only too happy in himself. She for her part lives in the belief that her feelings can never lead to anything, since their object is a poor, nameless minstrel and merchant, albeit a man of quite remarkably commanding presence.

Finally Tristan declares himself to her. There follows a scene filled with the most confused and conflicting emotions. She learns that the one she loves is Tristan, the dream of her girlhood, and that he has come by stealth and subterfuge to woo her, not for himself, but for King Mark. She is to go with him – but only to be delivered into the arms of his uncle. With the passionate intensity of his own feelings he woos her in the name of Mark and in the name of his political ideal, and in the end she assents. All is revealed to the royal parents, surprise, anger, rejoicing, reflection and consent follow, and Tristan conducts Isolde back to Cornwall.

During the sea voyage their strange relationship continues. Isolde is torn between her love and her hatred for the deceit practised upon her, Tristan between his passion and his fealty to the King. The issue is determined in the following manner.

Queen Isolde, accomplished in the arts of healing and magic, has brewed a love potion which she has placed in a glass flask and entrusted to Brangane. Isolde is to give it to Mark to drink on their wedding night, so that he will be inflamed with undying love for her. But on the homeward voyage the ladies feel seasick, and the vessel puts in to a harbour. Most of the travellers go ashore, including Brangane. The two lovers remain on board with a few junior servants. Feeling thirsty, they call for wine, and a little maid, finding nothing but the love potion, which looks like wine, brings them this: they drink, Brangane returns, realizes with horror what has happened, and tells them all. Now she is their guilty accomplice, who has forfeited the right to stand guard over Isolde's purity – and anyway regards the attempt as useless. Henceforth she is the servant of their love, which has been set free by the potion (and against which honour can avail nothing) and now abandons all restraint. The couple consummate their union and live together as lovers for the remainder of the voyage, whose end is to them an unthinkable and terrible prospect.

Mark receives them in Cornwall with great pomp and splendour, the marriage is celebrated, and on the wedding night the guilty Brangane is prevailed upon by the lovers to sacrifice her virginity to the King in place of Isolde. Then, when Tristan brings the customary drink of wine, Isolde changes places with Brangane, and Mark spends the rest of the night with her.

From now on, since Tristan has free access to Isolde, Mark is continually deceived by the couple. By himself he would never have suspected anything. But their ill-fated happiness is observed by a man who likewise adores Isolde passionately, the King's Lord High Steward, Marjodoc. He sleeps in the same room with Tristan, whence the latter steals forth at night to visit Isolde's bower. One night, when he has the dream about the boar, Marjodoc follows Tristan, guided by his footprints in the snow, and spies Tristan and the Queen in bed, despite Brangane's attempt to mask the light with a chess-board. Great are his pain and rage. But he does not tell the King he has spied on them: instead he merely warns him about certain rumours, destroys his peace of mind, and keeps a sharp watch on the lovers himself.

Mark is racked with doubt and torment because the rumours concern his so seeming-pure 'wife' and the friend who is dearest to his heart. The Aquitanian dwarf Melot is induced by him and Mar-jodoc (whose suspicions allow him no rest) to play the spy in return for promises of reward. Tristan is forbidden to enter the Queen's bower.

Now parted, the lovers fall to grieving, as Mark does not fail to observe. He announces a great hunting party to last for twenty days. Tristan excuses himself on the grounds of illness. Brangane now gives the lovers the advice about the olive-tree shavings. They follow her advice and meet in the garden beneath the tree, where the dwarf eavesdrops on them, but without recognizing the Queen for certain. He puts Tristan to the test by bringing him a fictitious message from Isolde, but is roundly rebuffed.

Thereupon Melot rides to the King and takes him to the olive tree by the spring. The scene where they sit in the tree, Tristan and Isolde notice their shadows cast on the ground, and proceed to play the innocents. Mark's faith in them is restored, and he throws Melot in the brook. The couple are now allowed to meet freely again.

But Marjodoc and Melot continue to watch them, reviving Mark's suspicions anew. The rumours persist. Mark torments himself with doubt and eventually resorts to the method of trial by ordeal (which Isolde herself proposes at a special council, trusting in the favour of God). She arranges for Tristan to come to Carleon, the scene of the trial, in the guise of a pilgrim, and plans in advance the scene (stumbling with her in his arms) to which her disingenuous oath refers. She carries the red-hot iron without hurt or injury.

Triumph! The lovers can again carry on undisturbed. But Mark observes their looks, which frequently reveal their true feelings. Despite God's judgement, which he begins to doubt, he is soon racked once more with suspicion and jealousy, and finally he can stand it no longer. Unwilling to go on sharing in their pleasures with dishonour, he banishes them both from the court.

They withdraw to the wilderness and make their abode in a rocky grotto built by the giants in ancient times. Meanwhile Mark is tortured with longing for Isolde, and he curses that strict sense of honour that would not allow him to share his pleasure with Tristan. Forewarned, the couple are discovered; Mark observes them through a window high in the cavern wall, sees the sword lying between them, and deceives himself that all is well again. After consulting with his nobles, Mark recalls them to the court, implores them on bended knee to avoid anything that could give rise to scandal, and is free to enjoy Isolde once more. He knows and yet refuses to know, living in dishonour with Isolde, who can no longer be accused of deceiving him. There now follows the summer scene in the garden, where Tristan and Isolde fall asleep on the couch after taking their pleasure, and are discovered by Mark. The flight of Tristan, after Isolde has given him the ring. When Mark returns with his councillors he finds the Queen alone, and the barons chide him for tormenting himself with vain fancies. He takes no action against Isolde.

Tristan roams far and wide, eventually fetching up after various adventures in the duchy of Arundel, which lies between Brittany and England. The land is ruled by Duke Jovelin and his Duchess Karsie, together with their children Kaedin and Isot as blanche mans (Isolde of the White Hands). The castle in which they live is called Karke, and here Tristan is received with great honour. They delight in their renowned guest, who soon becomes their friend. Kaedin worships him with boyish admiration, while his relations with Isolde of the White Hands, whose name made a profound impression on him from the first and whose gentle charms win his heart, soon become close and tender, encouraged and abetted by Kaedin. Tristan's inward struggle over his loyalty to the Irish Isolde. His feelings play tricks with him because of the name. Breaking faith in the act of fidelity. He excuses his feelings by imagining that Isolde is lying in Mark's arms (fantasy image). Isolde of the White Hands loves him; if nothing else, courtesy requires him to return her favour. He tells her stories, sings, writes and reads with her. Composes canzonas in which the name Isolde recurs constantly, so that everybody thinks he is referring to her of the White Hands. Finally he kisses and embraces her, and goes to her parents to ask for her hand in marriage. They give their joyful consent.

The wedding takes place with feasting and tournaments. In the bridal chamber Isolde of the White Hands is brought to bed. Then Tristan is disrobed, and as the silken gown is removed the ring given to him by the Irish Isolde falls from his hand. He gazes long upon it, wrestling inwardly with himself. He cannot deceive the fair-haired Isolde, but neither may he fail in his duties as a husband. Confusion of the heart alone has brought him to this pass, and he deceives himself more than the two ladies whom he deceives one with the other. Finally he goes to Isolde, but asks his tender bride to be patient with him, as his heart is beset by a magic spell from which he hopes to be released in time. She submits lovingly to his request. And so they live together as brother and sister only.

Later on Duke Jovelin's lands are invaded by powerful neighbours, and his troops find themselves hard-pressed. Deeply unhappy as he is, Tristan seizes eagerly on the opportunity to throw himself into the fray, hoping to find a merciful death. Together with Kaedin he rides forth to battle, where his skill and bravery carry the day: the enemy is routed, but Tristan is wounded by a poisoned arrow and brought back to Karke, where he languishes beyond recovery. All remedies fail. So he entrusts Isolde's ring to his faithful young friend Kaedin, and asks him to journey to Cornwall and persuade Isolde to come to Arundel. She alone can help him (he says), and she is sure to come for the love she bears Tristan. Kaedin is to travel in the guise of a silk merchant, show Isolde the ring in secret, swear to her that Tristan has never loved or touched another, and remind her of all the joys and sorrows they once shared together. Kaedin's sister has remained a virgin for the sake of that love. Tristan asks him to reveal nothing of all this to his sister, except to say that he is going to fetch a foreign lady physician. He is to take Tristan's own ship, in which he will find two sails, one white and one black. If he returns with Isolde he is to run up the white sail; if he comes without her, the black. Kaedin willingly promises to do all that Tristan asks.

But Isolde of the White Hands has overheard their conversation, listening through the wall behind Tristan's bed after she and the others have been sent out of the room. Now she knows why her life has been empty of joy, and the gentle young maid becomes a spitting wildcat, vowing revenge. To Tristan, however, she continues to put on the face of love and devotion.

Kaedin sets course for Cornwall, lands near the royal palace, and hawks his wares – cloth, falcons, gold trinkets. He takes a selection of fine things to the castle, sells something to the King, and while displaying his wares to the Queen contrives to show her the ring. Isolde grows pale, takes him aside, and he tells her all. She is profoundly affected, and confers with Brangane, who arranges for one of the gates to remain unguarded that night; Isolde slips out and boards the ship with Kaedin. A fair wind speeds them on their way, and he hoists the white sail.

Meanwhile Tristan is pining away, despatching messengers by the hour to see if the ship is yet in sight. He even has his attendants carry him down to the sea himself; but for fear of seeing the black sail he returns to his chamber, preferring to receive the news from the lips of another. Then Isolde of the White Hands enters, bearing the false and treacherous news that a black sail is approaching. He despairs and dies.

Great is the general lamentation. The body is laid out in state by nobles and servants. Meanwhile Isolde has landed, and hears the sound of weeping and wailing in every street and the tolling of funeral bells from every church and chapel. She makes enquiry – and an old man tells her Tristan is dead. Numb and dry-eyed she strides ahead to the palace, leaving her retinue behind, while all who see her marvel at her grief and beauty. Tristan's body lies in candlelight. She embraces him, kisses him, and sinks to the ground by the bier. She has died of a broken heart.

On the Film Scenario for *Tristan and Isolde**

The news that I am engaged in the preparation of a film scenario entitled *Tristan and Isolde* is not entirely true inasmuch as I delivered the completed manuscript several months ago, having found the writing both easy and pleasurable. But it was necessary to wait

* 'Über das Filmmanuskript *Tristan und Isolde*', a letter in the *Frankfurter Zeitung*, 14 May 1924.

for the 'good' season before the location shooting could begin, since it proved difficult to find suitable landscapes and settings.

However, I hear that the film is now well into production, and it will certainly not be the fault of the Rolf Randolf Company if the end result is not well worth seeing. If it is a flop I shall feel responsible – and that would effectively deter me from dabbling a second time in this curious field.

The first point about my text is that it is not connected in any way with Richard Wagner's musical drama of the same name. It is a dramatic version of the wonderful epic poem by Gottfried von Strassburg, which of course has had to be shortened and condensed at many points, but whose rich psychological meaning I have endeavoured to translate as faithfully as possible into theatrical terms.

On a purely visual level the completed feature film will not even attempt to compete with the great monster spectaculars like the *Iliad* or the *Nibelungen*; and although it offers plenty of scope for gorgeous visual imagery, particularly in terms of splendid landscapes (and seascapes), its main emphasis will be on the human and the dramatic element.

As for the connecting text – or the 'titles', as they are called – I have tried to bring them to life by addressing myself as far as possible directly to the audience, rather like a man using a pointer. For I see film as a truly popular medium, an institution with enormous educational potential – a technically and thematically more sophisticated version of the old fairground ballads with picture-and-music accompaniment.

My intimate and creative involvement with Gottfried's masterly poem, which I had never really studied closely before, has given me much pleasure and enjoyment; and if my labours can help to bring him closer to the many thousands who today regard the cinema as second only in importance to their daily bread, then I shall be well satisfied.*

* The film was never made.

To Josef Ponten*

Poschingerstrasse 1, Munich I
21 January 1925

[...] It was a Frenchman, Maurice Barrès, who called *Iphigenie* a
'civilizing work'. The term is possibly even more aptly applicable to
that other work of self-discipline and self-chastisement (not to say
castigation), much derided for its atmosphere of culture, courtliness
and prim delicacy: *Tasso*. Both are works of 'renunciation', characterized by a Teutonic-improving eschewal of the allurements of barbarism, which that unabashed sensualist Richard Wagner appro-
priated to such devastating effect – with the inevitable price to pay
that his ethnic-voluptuous *oeuvre* is now the object of a popular cult
that grows more vulgar by the day. And there really *is* an inevitability
in all this. For is not that improving duty to renounce, which Goethe
took upon himself, something more than personal? Is it not the
decree of destiny, the inborn and absolute imperative of all German
culture, to be ignored at our great spiritual peril, that was ever meant
to grow in some way – and in whatever measure – towards formative
responsibility? [...]

* Josef Ponten (1883–1940), author of a six-volume novel that remained uncompleted
at his death.

To Hans Pfitzner*

Poschingerstrasse 1, Munich
23 June 1925

[...] I realized, of course, that my recent intellectual resolves were bound to be distasteful to you. But believe me at least when I say that they spring from good intentions – and from a feeling of responsibility that may well be more exacting than that which rests upon the musician. You followed blithely the power of love ... Such is not given so readily to every man, and there are instances of a deliberate self-disciplining, not without its pain, that earn for the individual concerned the name of Judas. Our play, dear maestro, is long since done; in its great and representative manifestations it belongs to the intellectual history of a bygone age. We of today are merely a modern journalistic rerun of the case of Nietzsche contra Wagner. In his intellectual origins Nietzsche was, like Wagner – whom he repudiated with the judgement of his conscience, but whom he loved until his dying day – a late son of Romanticism. But Wagner was the puissant-fortunate self-glorifier and self-consummator, while Nietzsche was the revolutionary self-conqueror who 'turned Judas': and that is why the former was never more than the last glorifier and infinitely enchanting consummator of an epoch, whereas the latter has become a seer who leads mankind forward into a new age. [...]

*Hans Pfitzner (1869-1949), composer of late Romantic operas, one of which, *Palestrina* (1917), left a profound impression on TM and which he discussed at length in *Reflections of a Non-political Man* (1918). Pfitzner later signed the infamous indictment of TM for his address 'The Sorrows and Grandeur of Richard Wagner', see pp. 149-51. See also pp. 154-67 for TM's remarks apropos Pfitzner's part in the indictment.

A Facsimile Score of *Tristan und Isolde**

[...] In closing, I should like to speak briefly of a publication, as curious as it is impressive, which might have some interest for Americans. For some time I have been guarding a treasure: it is a veritable copy of the score of Wagner's *Tristan und Isolde*! It was given to me on my birthday; daily I do it reverence. I will not say it is the one genuine original score of this highly developed opera – for that is in Bayreuth. But, in a magnificent binding, contrived with the aid of the most refined technique, it is so perfect a facsimile of Wagner's minute-colossal manuscript that one needs no imagination to accept, without effort, its authenticity and originality and to feel himself bewilderingly in the possession of something holy. These scattered groups of precise Gothic notes signify something ultimate, supreme, profoundly precious – something to which Nietzsche bade for us a final farewell, a farewell until death: they signify a world which, for reasons of conscience, we Germans of the present are forbidden to love over much. This is the pinnacle, the consummation, of romanticism, its furthest artistic expansion, the imperialism of a world-conquering oblivion – of an intoxicating self-annihilation. And all of this is uncongenial to the soul of Europe which, if it is to be saved to life and reason, requires some hard work and some of that self-conquest which Nietzsche upheld with heroism and exemplariness. Never, to those at least who were born to love that world which the younger men hardly know – has the contrast between aesthetic charm and ethical responsibility been greater than today. Let us acknowledge it as the source of irony! A love of life defends itself ironically against the fascination of death; but in art it is uncertain whether an irony which turns against life and virtue and knows how to treasure the allurements of forbidden love is not indeed a more religious thing. And so it happens, that we in our work-room, have formally made of the facsimile of the original score of *Tristan*, a melancholy and ironic cult.

The Drei-Masken-Verlag in Munich is the publisher of these remarkable editions. A reproduction of the *Meistersinger* manuscript preceded *Tristan*, and a *Parsifal* is soon to follow.

* From 'German Letter (VI)' in *The Dial* (New York), October 1925.

From 'What Do You Owe to the Notion of Cosmopolitanism?'*

The 'mediocre' element in Wagner, i.e. his whole 'German master craftsman' affectation, was quite overpowering. In this context the idea of 'seduction' almost takes on the sense of 'deceit' or 'trickery'. For whole nations can be taken for a ride by the heroes who have been summoned to transform them: all they need to do is dress up as 'master craftsmen'. To think that Wagner can still be misrepresented today, while attempts are being made to restore Bayreuth, as the patron saint of an antediluvian Germanism and the epitome of a rough-and-ready worthiness – when artists and decadents of European rank, such as Baudelaire, were the first to acclaim his genius! Nietzsche's measureless scorn for the misunderstanding that Wagner has engendered among us Germans remains the single most powerful critical experience of my life.

* 'Was verdanken Sie der kosmopolitischen Idee?', *Die Literarische Welt* (Berlin), 16 and 23 October 1925.

To an Opera Producer*

Munich
15 November 1927

Dear Sir,
I was very interested to hear about your theatre's new production of *Lohengrin*, which you wish to commemorate with appropriate literary contributions. You put me in mind of the many things I have said about Wagner – and against Wagner – in various books and

* Letter in *Die Lesestunde* (Zeitschrift der Deutschen Buchgemeinschaft, Berlin), 16 November 1927. The producer and the theatre have not been identified.

essays; but I think this is definitely *not* the occasion for a progress report on the continuing decline of the Wagnerian star in the firmament of the German mind (- indeed, it could even be said to have disappeared below the horizon altogether). The summary dismissal of genius by some wretched critic who fancies himself an authority on the subject has always been thoroughly repugnant to me, and I should despise myself if I felt even remotely inclined to cut a figure by passing judgement and denying the most profound, instructive and formative experiences of my youth. I am well aware that the Bayreuth of today is concerned more with the visiting gentleman from San Francisco than with the German mind and its future. But that does not alter the fact that Wagner, considered as an artistic force, was something almost without parallel, probably the most formidable talent in the entire history of art. Where else has there ever been such a conjunction of greatness and guile, of ingenuity and sublime depravity, of popularity and devilish finesse? He remains the paradigm of world-conquering artistry, and Europe succumbed to his talents, just as it succumbed to the statecraft of Bismarck. Neither was much acquainted with the other, yet together they constitute the high point of a romantic hegemony of the German spirit.

When we are talking about Goethe, that is the time to speak of the human, the moral and the poetic dimensions. The *Ring* remains for me the epitome of the work *per se*. In contrast to Goethe, Wagner was a man wholly concerned with the work in hand, a man devoted absolutely to power, the world and success, and in that sense a political man; and despite the roundness, unity and completeness of his life's work I sometimes think that people like him live their lives less than fully. In order to have lived fully, it seems to me, he would have had to keep a diary, say - a secret and totally truthful diary side by side with his public, political *oeuvre*. I don't know if I am making myself clear. He was a man of action, without any profounder intimacies. His autobiography is null and void. Immortality, it could be said, belongs not to the man but to his work - that *efficacious* work, in which his entire life has been subsumed.

Nobody is better fitted than he to stimulate our productive instincts. Our human-poetic portion turns instead to Goethe. In the former respect I owe him an immeasurable debt, and I have no doubt that the traces of my early and continuing experience of Wagner's work are manifest in everything I have written. *Lohengrin* was my first discovery. I have heard it countless times, and today I still know the words and music almost by heart. The first act is a marvel of dramatic economy and theatrical effect, the Prelude something utterly magical, the very peak of Romanticism. There was a time when I never missed a performance of *Tristan* at the Munich Hoftheater – that most sublime and dangerous of Wagner's works, which in its sensuous-suprasensuous passion, its lascivious desire for bed, is really something for young people, at the age when the erotic is all-important. The most brilliant psychological insight into *Die Meistersinger* comes from Nietzsche. Here I am thinking not of his admirable analysis of the Prelude, but of a note on the work as a whole and its intellectual significance: '*Meistersinger*', he writes, ' – a lance against civilization: the German against the French.' What is meant here by 'civilization' and 'the German' is something I dealt with at some length during the war in my *Reflections of a Non-political Man*. But to Nietzsche's observation in cultural psychology we might add that *Die Meistersinger* was a great and universally acknowledged German victory, a total triumph of the German spirit in its opposition to civilization – and will always remain so historically, *whatever the circumstances*.

Today, oddly enough, my interest is focused primarily on the work of Wagner's old age, on *Parsifal* – perhaps because it was the work I got to know last, and therefore the one I still know least. Despite *Tristan und Isolde*, and despite a certain feeling of the now-routine about all its artistic devices, it stands as the most extreme of all his works, with a capacity for matching style to psychological nuance that surpasses at the last even what we have come to expect from Wagner, filled with sounds in which I immerse myself each time with renewed disquiet, curiosity and enchantment.

Yours very truly,
THOMAS MANN

Ibsen and Wagner*

The dramatic *oeuvres* of Ibsen and Wagner are the two outstanding manifestations of the Nordic-Germanic artistic spirit in the nineteenth century worthy to be ranked alongside the great creative achievements of other races: the novel in France, Russia and England, French Impressionist painting. In their greatness and their sophistication, their titanic morbidity, they will stand as perfect exemplars of the age that brought them forth – that same nineteenth century which it is now fashionable to dismiss with contempt, but which in sheer terms of scale, at the very least, was so far superior to the thoroughly meagre showing made by the Europe of today. Grandeur was the essence and hallmark of the age, a gloomy and afflicted grandeur that is at once sceptical and passionate – fanatical even – in its pursuit of truth, and that can find a fleeting happiness, without creed or religion, in surrender to the transient moment of consuming beauty: and when one reflects on the bonds that unite Wagner and Ibsen, its true sons, one finds it very difficult to distinguish between their broad historical affinity and some more intimate rapport. Our experience, the experience of a whole generation, links them together as it links them with Tolstoy and Zola; but it also sees in them a very special togetherness that sets them apart from these two. When a famous Bayreuth conductor saw a play by Ibsen for the first time in Munich, his final judgement was: 'It's either ridiculous – or it's as great as Wagner.' He was sufficiently confused to posit the first as a hypothetical possibility, but it is quite clear that such a choice automatically rules out its negative option, and is therefore no choice at all. Ridiculous or great can mean only great, great like Wagner, great (that is to say) in the same 'modern', bold and enormously interesting way as Wagner. Although the man in question, Hermann Levi, was a musician and probably not much at home in literary matters, he was enough of an artist to recognize, in the dialogue of the 'domestic drama', techniques, effects, charms, profound attractions that were already familiar to him from that world of sounds, and to sense not only the fellowship *of* greatness, but a fellowship *within* that greatness which will always be sensed, always noted.

* *Vossische Zeitung* (Berlin), 18 March 1928.

One does not love Ibsen and Wagner as one loves Goethe – not with the same kind of love. With them the focus of our love and esteem is not (as it is with him) on the life: it is on the *work*, and they are much better fitted to stimulate our productive instincts than Goethe, who certainly inherited his father's work ethic, his insistence on 'finishing the job', but whose autobiographical writing, for all its richness, its canonical fullness of humanity, has a certain carelessly fragmentary and occasional quality about it. That splendid, civilized and refined world of experience, of self-representation and confession, for which objective reality exists only in the guise of poetic irony – shall we declare a special and exclusive preference for that world? Is productivity to be understood as a mere sign of life, a pleasing incidental – or as the very form, the primal expression of the will itself? It is more important to make the distinction than to make up our minds. In contrast to Goethe, Ibsen and Wagner were wholly concerned with the work in hand, men devoted absolutely to power, the world and success, and in that sense political men; and this is the key to the amazing unity, the perfect roundness and completeness of their mighty theatrical *oeuvres*, full of social revolution in their youth, and paling with old age into the realms of magic and ceremonial. *When We Dead Awaken*, that eerie, whispered confession of the obsessively productive artist who now *repents*, a declaration of love for life that comes late – too late: and *Parsifal*, the oratorio of 'redemption' – how accustomed I have grown to seeing them as one, feeling them as one, these two valedictory dramas of consecration, the 'last words' of the artist before he is silenced for ever – the celestial works of two aged men of great ambition, filled with a majestic sclerotic weariness, having that sense of the now-routine about all their artistic devices, and all the marks of lateness: recapitulation, retrospective, self-quotation and dissolution. As for what was termed *fin de siècle*, what was it but the paltry satyr play of a minor age to the century's true and awesome finale, enacted in the last works of these two great sorcerers? For Nordic sorcerers they were, the pair of them, crafty old magicians both, thoroughly versed in all the insinuating and captivating wiles of a devilish artistry as shrewd as it was slick, accomplished in the management of effects, in the meticulous cultivation of detail, in every kind of ambiguity and symbolic allusion, in the celebration of ideas and the poeticization of the intellect – and at the same time musicians both, as Nordic dwellers naturally are: not only Wagner, who consciously set out to learn music because he needed it as an instrument of conquest, despite the fact that it was not inborn in him, not part of his inheritance, but Ibsen too, albeit his is a veiled and abstract musicality, underlying the spoken word.

But I know what it is that unites them most closely. It is that process of sublimation, hitherto not even envisaged as a possibility, which an old-established and by now intellectually undistinguished art form underwent at their hands. In Wagner's case that art form was the opera, and in Ibsen's the social drama. Goethe said: 'Everything that has been perfected in its kind must go beyond its kind to become something else, something unique. In many of its notes the nightingale is a bird like any other; but then it transcends its own class, as if to show the whole feathered species what singing really means.' Wagner and Ibsen 'perfected' the opera and the domestic drama in exactly this way – by transforming them into something else, something unique. Even that element of reversion-to-type in Goethe's example of the nightingale is to be found in them: in Wagner, even the late Wagner of *Parsifal*, the traditional opera still recurs from time to time, while Ibsen's plays still creak from time to time with dramatic contrivances à la Dumas *fils*. But both men are 'creators' in the sense that they perfect and transcend the material they are given, making from it – and herein lies their true affinity – something that is wholly new and unexpected.

From 'Recollections of the Stadttheater'*

Later on it was to the theatre in my native city† that I owed one of the cardinal artistic experiences of my life, my first encounter with the art of Richard Wagner – an encounter whose decisive and forma-

* 'Erinnerungen an das Stadt-Theater', *Jahrbuch des Lübecker Stadttheaters 1930/31*, Lübeck, 1930.
† Lübeck.

tive influence on my own artistic thinking I have always spoken of whenever I have had occasion to comment on the intellectual antecedents of my books. At that time the young Emil Gerhäuser was the resident heroic tenor. When his voice was in its prime he used to sing the parts of Tannhäuser, Walther Stolzing and (more often than not) Lohengrin. I do not want to appear over-presumptuous, but I fancy the Stadttheater never housed a more receptive, more enraptured listener than me on those magical evenings. I was there as often as I could possibly manage it, with or without permission. I had my own personal seat, so to speak, in the stalls, which was the next cheapest category after the standing room – a seat that was not numbered, like the rest, but identified by the letter A. This seat was my favourite, my regular, for which I paid my money to old Weingarten (or Weingartner – I'm not exactly sure of his name any more), the box-office clerk, a pensioned-off actor who could not bear to leave the theatre behind, and who sat in a kind of unventilated cavern, lit by a gas flame, issuing the greasy cardboard tickets that were subsequently collected on the door to be resold over and over again. One day a 'benefit' was given in honour of Weingarten or Weingartner. I think they did the *Hüttenbesitzer** or some such old-fashioned thing – which was just right for him – and at the end the old man was applauded on to the stage, where he blew kisses in the daintiest way imaginable to the notabilities in their boxes in the dress circle ...

Today I should no doubt find all kinds of fault with the sort of *Lohengrin* production that used to enthral me in those days and vouchsafe me all the thrills of romanticism. The tone of the violins in the small orchestra may not have been the purest, even though my violin teacher, Winkelmann, was one of their number; the swan may have come on stage a little jerkily at times; and some of the characters in the chorus, especially, may have been rather peculiar. I particularly recall one member of the Brabant gentry, an aged tenor, who always used to stand downstage beating time with his index finger, and whose voice came out as a ghastly strangled falsetto on the line 'Gar viel verheisset uns der Tag' [Great the promise of the day] in Act II. But what of it? Youth is blessed with wonderful

---

* *Der Hüttenbesitzer*, a play (and also novel) by the French writer Georges Ohnet (1848–1918), original title *Le maître de forges* [The Ironmaster].

powers of abstraction. I was happy, I was, as the French say, *transporté*; and today, all these years later, I still know my *Lohengrin* almost by heart.

Wagner and the Present Age*

Considered as an artistic force, Wagner is something almost without parallel, probably the most formidable talent in the entire history of art. Where else has there ever been such a conjunction of greatness and guile, of ingenuity and sublime depravity, of popularity and devilish finesse? He remains the paradigm of world-conquering artistry, and Europe succumbed to his talents, just as it succumbed to the statecraft of Bismarck. Neither was much acquainted with the other, yet together they constitute the high point of a romantic hegemony of the German spirit.

When we are talking about Goethe, that is the time to speak of the human, the moral and the poetic dimensions. The *Ring* remains for me the epitome of the work *per se*. In contrast to Goethe, Wagner was a man wholly concerned with the work in hand, a man devoted absolutely to power, the world and success, and in that sense a political man ... Nobody is better fitted than he to stimulate our *productive* instincts. Our human-poetic portion turns instead to Goethe. In the former respect I owe Wagner an immeasurable debt, and I have no doubt that the traces of my early and continuing experience of Wagner's work are manifest in everything I have written. *Lohengrin* was my first discovery. I have heard it countless times, and today I still know the words and music almost by heart. The first act is a marvel of dramatic economy and theatrical effect, the Prelude something utterly magical, the very peak of Romanticism. There was a time when I never missed a performance of *Tristan* at the Munich Hoftheater – that most sublime and dangerous of

* 'Wagner und unsere Zeit' (originally called 'Skizzen'), August 1931, *Die Musik* (Berlin), February 1933. Many sentences in this piece draw almost word for word on the letter 'To an Opera Producer', pp. 81–3.

Wagner's works. The most brilliant psychological insight into *Die Meistersinger* comes from Nietzsche. Here I am thinking not of his admirable analysis of the Prelude, but of a note on the work as a whole and its intellectual significance: '*Meistersinger*', he writes, ' – a lance against civilization: the German against the French.' But to Nietzsche's observation in cultural psychology we might add that *Die Meistersinger* was a great and universally acknowledged German victory, a total triumph of the German spirit in its opposition to civilization – and will always remain so historically, *whatever the circumstances.*

To Walter Opitz

Poschingerstrasse 1, Munich 27
20 January 1933

[. . .] I have had to decline an invitation to speak at the meeting of the Socialist Cultural League, because my health really leaves a lot to be desired at the moment – and because, notwithstanding that, my time is greatly taken up with a piece of work relating to the forthcoming fiftieth anniversary of Wagner's death. Some time ago I agreed to give the commemorative address* at the Wagner celebrations in Amsterdam on 13 February, and then to give repeat performances in French in Brussels and Paris. You'll understand that it was risky from the outset for me to embark on the subject of Wagner, seeing that I of all people have not a little to say on the matter: and the trick will be *not* to write a book. [. . .]

* 'The Sorrows and Grandeur of Richard Wagner', see pp. 91–148.

To Ernst Bertram

Neues Waldhotel, Arosa

26 February 1933

Dear Bertram,

We've just returned from Amsterdam, Brussels and Paris, where we've been commemorating Wagner – and now we are resting up in this somewhat overcrowded haven. The piece on W[agner] turned out to be a small book – inevitably. It's coming out soon. But what is that, compared with everything else that's coming!

Warmest regards,

Yours,

T.M.

The Sorrows and Grandeur of Richard Wagner

This essay, TM's most important study of Wagner, was commissioned by the Goethe Society of Munich for the fiftieth anniversary (on 13 February 1933) of the composer's death, and first given as a lecture in the Great Hall of the University of Munich on 10 February. It was published as 'Leiden und Grösse Richard Wagners' in *Die Neue Rundschau* (Berlin), April 1933. While unstinting in its admiration of Wagner's artistic achievement, the lecture was an all-too-overt warning of the danger latent in uncritical attitudes to Wagnerian ideology; its sentiments were directly opposed to the Nazis' appropriation of Wagner for an unholy alliance of *Macht* and *Kultur*. As it was already imprudent for TM to have aired uncomfortable home truths about Hitler's great hero in Munich within two weeks of the Führer having become Chancellor of the Reich, it was perhaps not altogether unexpected that this lecture, which TM proceeded to repeat abroad in Amsterdam (13 February), Brussels (14 February), and Paris (18 February), should have been the immediate (though of course not the only) cause of his long exile from German soil.

On 27 February the Reichstag was burned and shortly after, while holidaying at Arosa in the Swiss Alps, TM was warned that his personal safety in Germany could not be guaranteed. 'I am on the list of those guilty of "intellectual high treason" for "pacifistic excesses",' he wrote in a letter of 13 March. His children and other friends rescued his manuscripts, including the uncompleted Joseph novel, forwarding them, together with much of his library, to addresses in France and Switzerland. In the autumn he settled at Küsnacht near Zurich, emigrating to America five years later in 1938.

'The Sorrows and Grandeur of Richard Wagner' provoked an extraordinary written protest from a group of self-appointed guardians of Munich's cultural hygiene, which included the 'Senior Public Health Officer' himself. The text of this is on pp. 149-51; TM's riposte is on pp. 151-3.

> Il y a là mes blâmes, mes éloges et tout ce que j'ai dit.
>
> Maurice Barrès

Steeped in sorrows and grandeur, like the nineteenth century that he so perfectly epitomizes – thus does the intellectual figure of Richard Wagner appear before me. I see a face deeply lined by all his traits of character, overlaid by all his drives and compulsions: and I am scarcely able to distinguish between my particular love for his work – one of the most splendidly questionable, ambivalent and fascinating phenomena in all artistic creation – and my general love for the century that his life effectively spans, that restlessly impelled, tormented and obsessive life, unrecognized and misunderstood, and ending finally in the brilliance of world renown. We of today, preoccupied as we are with tasks that are uniquely new and challenging, have no time and little inclination to deal justly with the epoch that is fading into history behind us (the so-called 'bourgeois' epoch); we look upon the nineteenth century as sons look upon their fathers – full of criticism: and this is as it should be. We shrug our shoulders both at its belief – which was a belief in ideas – and at its unbelief, which is to say its melancholy brand of relativism. Its liberal faith in reason and progress strikes us as faintly amusing, its materialism all too neat and clear-cut, while its confidently monistic view of the world now seems extraordinarily shallow. And yet its pride in science and knowledge was counterbalanced, indeed outweighed, by its deep pessimism, its musical attachment to night and death, which will probably come to be seen as the dominant characteristics of the age. At the same time this is associated with a strong predilection for the large format, for the standard work, the monumental, the grand production on a massive scale – which in turn, curiously enough, goes hand in hand with a love of the very small and painstaking, the psychologically detailed. Yes indeed: grandeur is the essence and hallmark of the age, a gloomy and afflicted grandeur that is at once sceptical and passionate – fanatical even – in its pursuit of truth, and that can find a fleeting happiness, without creed or religion, in surrender to the transient moment of consuming beauty; and a statue to the moral exertions of the age would need the physique of an Atlas, tense and straining in every muscle, like a figure by Michelangelo. What enormous burdens they bore in those days, *epic* burdens in the ultimate sense of that momentous word – which is why one should think not only of Balzac and Tolstoy, but of Wagner too. When the latter wrote to his friend Liszt in 1851, solemnly outlining his plans for the *Ring*, Liszt replied from Weimar in these terms:

Go to work and apply yourself with utter singleness of mind to your task. If you need a brief, let it be the one that the cathedral chapter of Seville gave to the architect commissioned to build their new cathedral: 'Build us a temple such that future generations will say the canons were mad ever to undertake such an extraordinary work.' Yet there the cathedral stands!

Now *that* is the nineteenth century!

The enchanted garden of French Impressionist painting, the novel in England, France and Russia, the natural sciences in Germany, German music – no indeed, it was no mean age, and in retrospect it appears as a dense forest of great men. And with the distance that retrospect brings we are able for the first time to discern a family likeness between them all, that common stamp which the epoch sets upon them for all their individual differences of character and ability. *Zola* and Wagner, for example, the Rougon-Macquart cycle and *Der Ring des Nibelungen*: fifty years ago hardly anybody would have thought of linking together the names of these two artists, these two works. Yet they do belong together. The affinity of their minds, intentions and artistic resources seems perfectly obvious to us today. It is not only the ambition to create on a vast scale, the artistic penchant for the grandiose and the massive that unites them, nor yet the technical device of the Homeric leitmotif; more than anything else they share a naturalism that is raised to the level of symbolic significance, a naturalism that enters the realm of myth. For what reader of Zola's epics could fail to see in them that symbolism, that tendency to myth which lifts his characters into some preternatural dimension? That Astarte of the French Second Empire, known to us as Nana – is she not both symbol and myth? And whence does she derive her name? It is an elemental sound, a first, instinctive utterance of mankind in its infancy: Nana was one of the epithets of the Babylonian goddess Ishtar. Did Zola know this? If he did not, so much the more remarkable and telling.

Tolstoy too has the same vast naturalistic range, the same democratic immensity. He too uses the leitmotif, the self-quotation, the stock phrase that identifies his characters. He has often been criticized for his unrelenting thoroughness of exposition, his endless repetitions and underlinings, his determination not to let the reader off for a moment, his monumental will to tedium; while of Wagner Nietzsche writes that he is at all events the most *impolite* of geniuses, treating his listeners like fools and repeating a thing so many times until it drives you mad – and you believe it. That is one kind of affinity, but a deeper one is to be found in the social-ethical ambience that they both share. It signifies little that Wagner saw art as a kind of sacred mystery, a panacea for all the ills of society, while Tolstoy dismissed it towards the end of his life as a frivolous luxury. For in so far as it *was* a luxury Wagner dismissed it too. He thought to apply its cleansing and sanctifying powers to the cleansing and sanctification of a corrupt society; cathartic and purgative by nature, seeking by means of aesthetic consecration to free society from luxury, plutocracy and lovelessness, he was closely akin to the Russian novelist in his social ethos.

Both men, moreover, have suffered the same fate inasmuch as people have claimed to see a sudden break in their lives that split them in mind and character, signifying something like a moral collapse – whereas in point of fact their two careers display the utmost consistency and unity. Those to whom it seemed that Tolstoy had fallen prey to some kind of religious mania in his old age failed to see that the final phase of his life was fully prefigured in what had gone before; they forgot – or had never noticed – that the spirit of the old Tolstoy already lives in such characters as Pierre Bezuchov in *War and Peace* and Levin in *Anna Karenina*. And when Nietzsche represents the ageing Wagner as suddenly breaking down in surrender before the Cross of Christ, he fails to see – or would have us fail to see – that the emotional world of *Tannhäuser* already anticipates that of *Parsifal*, and that the latter work is simply the summation and supremely logical conclusion of a profoundly romantic-Christian *oeuvre*. Wagner's final work is also his most theatrical, and it is hard to imagine an artistic progression more logical than his. An art based on sensuous experience and recurrent, symbolic formulas (for the leitmotif is such a formula – more than that, it is a monstrance, laying claim to an authority that verges on the religious) necessarily takes us back to Church ceremonial; indeed, it seems to me that the secret desire and ultimate ambition of all theatre is to revert to that religious rite from which it originally evolved among heathens and Christians alike. The Baroque, Catholicism and the Church are already implicit in the art of the theatre; and an artist as practised as Wagner in the manipulation of symbols and the elevation of monstrances was bound, in the end, to see himself as the fellow of the priest – or even as a priest in his own right.

I have often reflected on the bonds that unite Wagner with *Ibsen*,* and found it difficult to distinguish between straightforward historical affinity and a rapport more intimate than that wrought by mere contemporaneity. I could not fail to recognize, in the dialogue of Ibsen's domestic drama, techniques, effects, charms, profound attractions that were already familiar to me from the world of Wagner's music, nor to note a fellowship that resided in part, no doubt, in the simple fact of their greatness, but in many ways also in the *manner* of their greatness. How alike they are in the amazing unity, the perfect roundness and completeness of their mighty *oeuvres*, full of social revolution in their youth, and paling with old age into the realms of mysticism and ceremonial! *When We Dead Awaken*, that eerie, whispered confession of the obsessively productive artist who now repents, a declaration of love for life that comes late – too late: and *Parsifal*, the oratorio of redemption – how accustomed I have grown to seeing them as one, feeling them as one, these two valedictory dramas of consecration, the last words of the artist before he is silenced for ever – the celestial works of two aged men, filled with a majestic sclerotic weariness, having that sense of the now-routine about all their artistic devices, and all the marks of lateness: recapitulation, retrospective, self-quotation and dissolution.

As for what was termed *fin de siècle*, what was it but the paltry satyr play of a minor age to the century's true and awesome finale, enacted in the last works of these two sorcerers? For Nordic sorcerers they were, the pair of them, crafty old magicians both, thoroughly versed in all the insinuating wiles of a devilish artistry as shrewd as it was slick, accomplished in the management of effects, in the meticulous cultivation of detail, in every kind of ambiguity and symbolic allusion, in that celebration of ideas, that poeticization of the intellect – and at the same time musicians both, as Nordic dwellers naturally are: not only Wagner, who consciously set out to learn music because he needed it as an instrument of conquest, but Ibsen too, albeit his is a veiled and abstract musicality, underlying the spoken word.

But the one thing above all else which makes them totally alike is that process of sublimation, not previously envisaged as a possibility,

* Notably in 'Ibsen and Wagner', pp. 84–6.

95

which an old-established and by now intellectually undistinguished art form underwent at their hands. In Wagner's case that art form was the opera, and in Ibsen's the social drama. Goethe said: 'Everything that has been perfected in its kind must go beyond its kind to become something else, something unique. In many of its notes the nightingale is a bird like any other; but then it transcends its own class, as if to show the whole feathered species what singing really means.' Wagner and Ibsen perfected the opera and the domestic drama in exactly this way – by transforming them into something else, something unique. Even that element of reversion-to-type in Goethe's example of the nightingale is to be found in them: in Wagner, even the late Wagner of *Parsifal*, the traditional opera still recurs from time to time, while Ibsen's plays still creak from time to time with dramatic contrivances à la Dumas *fils*. But both men are 'creators' in the sense that they perfect and transcend the material they are given, making from it something that is wholly new and unexpected.

But what is it that elevates Wagner's work so far above the intellectual level of all previous forms of musical drama? Two forces have combined to elevate it to these heights, two forces and brilliant accomplishments that one might suppose to be mutually hostile, and whose inherently contradictory nature it has now become popular once again to insist upon: I refer to the forces of *psychology* and *myth*. Many deny their compatibility on the grounds that psychology is too rational not to be seen as some kind of insuperable obstacle *en route* to the land of myth. It is regarded as the antithesis of myth, in the same way that it is regarded as the antithesis of music – despite the fact that in Nietzsche and Wagner we have two classic instances where this very combination of psychology, myth and music confronts us as a living reality.

On the subject of Wagner the psychologist a whole book could be written, dealing with the psychological art of the musician *and* the poet (inasmuch as one can distinguish between the two in his case). The device of the musical reminiscence, already used on occasion in the old operatic tradition, was gradually developed by him into a subtle and masterly system that made music, to a degree never before realized, into an instrument of psychological allusion, elaboration and cross-reference. The poetic idea of reinterpreting the 'love potion', that magic motif of naive epic, as a mere device for liberating a passion that already exists (in fact the lovers might just as well be drinking plain water, as long as their belief that they have drunk the cup of *death* frees them in their minds from the moral law of the day): this is the thought of a great psychologist. How extraordinarily Wagner's poetic powers go beyond those of a mere librettist, right from the beginning – and not so much in terms of linguistic accomplishment as of psychological insight! 'Die düstre Glut' [This sombre fire], sings the Dutchman in his lovely duet with Senta in the second act,

> Die düstre Glut, die hier ich fühle brennen,
> Sollt' ich Unseliger sie Liebe nennen?
> Ach nein! Die Sehnsucht ist es nach dem Heil:
> Würd' es durch solchen Engel mir zuteil!

> This sombre fire that burns within my heart,
> Shall I, wretch, to it the name of love impart?
> But no! Redemption is·the thing I crave:
> If only *this* be the angel sent to save!

Those are lines written to be sung, yet never before had such complex thoughts, such convoluted emotions been sung or put into singable form. The accursed man falls in love with this girl at first sight, but he tells himself that the love he feels is not for her, but for redemption, salvation. On the other hand she stands before him as the physical embodiment of that salvation he seeks, so that he is not able – or indeed willing – to distinguish between his longing for spiritual deliverance and his longing for her. For his hope has assumed her form, and he can no longer wish it otherwise; in other words, in loving redemption he loves this girl. What an interweaving of double meanings – what a penetrating insight into the complex depths of an emotion! This is analysis – and the word suggests itself in a more modern and daring sense when we observe the first springtime stirrings of the youthful Siegfried's love life, so vividly evoked by Wagner's text and by the music he uses to underscore the meaning. What we have here, rising up from the dark depths of the unconscious, is a presentient complex of mother fixation, sexual desire and *Angst* (by which I mean that fairy-tale fear that Siegfried seeks to know) – a complex, therefore, that bears witness to the most extraordinary intuitive affinity between Wagner the psychologist and that other characteristic son of the nineteenth century, the psychoanalyst Sigmund Freud. The way that Siegfried's thoughts of his mother slide into eroticism in his reverie beneath the linden tree, or the way in which, in the scene where Mime tries to instruct his ward in the meaning of fear, the motif of Brünnhilde slumbering in the fire moves through the orchestra like a dark, distorted presence – this is pure Freud, pure psychoanalysis. And let us not forget that as in Wagner so in Freud – whose radical investigations into the human psyche and study of the subconscious are magnificently anticipated in Nietzsche – the psychological interest goes hand in hand with an interest in myth, in primitive humanity and precivilization.

'Love in the fullest and truest sense', said Wagner,

is possible only within a sexual context: only as man and woman can human beings fully and truly love, while all other forms of love are merely variants, derivatives, adjuncts or counterfeit copies of that original. It is mistaken to regard this love [i.e. sexual love] as simply *one* manifestation of love in its totality, as though there existed other, and indeed higher, manifestations besides this one.

This attribution of a sexual origin to all forms of love is plainly akin to psychoanalytic method. It is an expression of the same psychological naturalism that is embodied in Schopenhauer's metaphysical formula 'the focus of the will' and in Freud's theories about culture and sublimation. In short, archetypally nineteenth century.

The erotic mother complex also recurs in *Parsifal*, in the seduction scene in the second act – which brings us to the figure of Kundry, the most powerful and poetically extreme of all Wagner's creations. He himself seems to have realized that she was something quite extraordinary. His thinking was stimulated originally not by her, but by general feelings about Good Friday: but it was not long before his conceptual and creative interest became increasingly focused on her, and the sudden realization that the wild messenger of the Grail should be one and the same person as the Temptress, the idea (in other words) of a split personality, was the decisive inspiration and allurement, the source of his most secret delight in this whole wondrous undertaking. 'Once this dawned on me,' he writes, 'practically every other aspect of the material became clear to me.' And on another occasion: 'In particular a most unusual creation, a woman of astonishing daemonic power (the messenger of the Grail), is taking shape ever more clearly and vividly in my mind. If I ever finish this work, it ought to result in something very original.' 'Original': a touchingly unassuming and modest word to describe the thing that finally emerged. There is about all Wagner's heroines a touch of grand hysteria, something somnambulistic, enraptured and visionary, which lends a curious and disquieting modernity to their romantic posturings. But the figure of Kundry, 'the rose of hell', is nothing less than an exercise in mythical pathology; in her agonizingly schizoid condition, as instrument of the Devil and penitent hungering after redemption, she is portrayed with an unsparing clinical accuracy, an audacious naturalism in the exploration and representation of a hideously diseased emotional existence, that has always seemed to me a supreme triumph of insight and artistry. Nor is she the only character in *Parsifal* whom Wagner has pushed to the psychological limit. When it says, in the preliminary draft of this last and most extreme work, that Klingsor is the daemon of secret sin, the wild ragings of impotence in the face of sin, we feel ourselves transported into a world of Christian insight into remote and hellish psychological states – the world of Dostoevsky.

And secondly: Wagner as maker of myth, as the man who discovered myth for the opera, who redeemed opera through myth. Truly he is without peer in his mental affinity with this other world of images and ideas, without peer in his ability to evoke myth and infuse it with new life. When he discovered myth after the historical opera he discovered himself; and when one listens to him now it seems as though the music had been created to no other end, and could never be applied to any other purpose, except to be the servant of myth. Whether the latter appears as an emissary from on high, despatched to the aid of suffering innocence, but compelled to return from whence it came because faith would not stand the test; or as the story in song and narrative of the world's beginning and end, a whole cosmogony in fairy-tale form – everywhere Wagner has captured its spirit, its essence, its very *sound* with an assurance and intuitive affinity, has spoken its language with a native facility, that are quite without parallel in the whole of art. It is a language without tense, the language of times past and times to come; and the sheer density of mythological ambience – in the Norns' scene at the beginning of *Götterdämmerung*, for example, in which the three daughters of Erda indulge in a kind of solemn cosmic gossip, or in the appearances of Erda herself in *Das Rheingold* and *Siegfried* – is quite matchless. The overpowering accents of the music that accompanies Siegfried's funeral cortège no longer tell of the woodland boy who set out to learn the meaning of fear; they speak to our emotions of what is *really* passing away behind the lowering veils of mist: it is the sunhero himself who lies upon the bier, slain by the pallid forces of darkness – and there are hints in the text to support what we *feel* in the music: 'A wild boar's fury', it says, and: 'Behold the cursed boar', says Gunther, pointing to Hagen, 'who slew this noble flesh.' The words take us back at a stroke to the very earliest picture-dreams of mankind. Tammuz and Adonis, slain by the boar, Osiris and Dionysus, torn asunder to come again as the Crucified One, whose flank must be ripped open by a Roman spear in order that the world might know Him – all things that ever were and ever shall be, the whole world of beauty sacrificed and murdered by wintry wrath, all is contained within this single glimpse of myth. So let it not be said that the creator of *Siegfried* broke faith with himself when he gave us *Parsifal*.

A passion for Wagner's enchanted *oeuvre* has been a part of my life ever since I first became aware of it and set out to make it my own, to invest it with understanding. What it has given me in terms of enjoyment and instruction I can never forget, nor the hours of deep and solitary happiness amidst the theatre throng, hours filled with frissons and delights for the nerves and the intellect alike, with sudden glimpses into things of profound and moving significance, such as only this art can afford. My curiosity about it has never flagged, and I never tire of listening to it, admiring it, following it – not without certain misgivings, I confess; but all the doubts, reservations and objections have in no way detracted from its appeal, any more than Nietzsche's immortal critique of Wagner, which I have always taken to be a panegyric in reverse, another form of eulogy. It was an expression of love-hate, an act of self-mortification. Wagner's art was the great love and passion of Nietzsche's life. He loved it as Baudelaire loved it, the poet of *Les Fleurs du Mal*, of whom it is said that in the agony, the paralysis and the semi-dementia of his last days he smiled with joy – 'il a souri d'allégresse' – when the name of Wagner was mentioned. So too Nietzsche, in the dark night of his paralysis, would prick up his ears at the sound of that name and remark: 'I loved him dearly.' He also hated him dearly, for intellectual reasons to do with his own views on the morality of culture – views that are not at issue here. But it would be strange indeed if I were alone in finding that Nietzsche's polemic against Wagner serves to stimulate my enthusiasm rather than deaden it.

What I did object to, right from the beginning – or rather, what left me totally indifferent – was Wagner's theory. In fact I have hardly ever been able to convince myself that anyone could ever have taken it seriously. What possible use could I have for this amalgam of music, words, painting and gesture that claimed to be the one and only truth and the fulfilment of all artistic ambition? For an artistic doctrine that would have ranked Goethe's *Tasso* below *Siegfried*? It was a bit much, I thought, to claim that the individual arts arose out of the disintegration of some original theatrical unity into whose service, to their own great good fortune, they were now to return. Art is entire and perfect in each of its manifestations; it is not necessary to add together all its different forms and genres in order to make it perfect. Such a rigidly mechanistic line of thinking represents the nineteenth century at its worst, and what Wagner's triumphant *oeuvre* validates is not his theory, but simply itself. It lives and will long continue to live; but art will live longer yet in all the individual arts, moving mankind through them as it has always done before. It would be infantile philistinism to think that the pitch and intensity of an artistic effect was equal to the cumulative product of its assault on our senses.

As a passionate practitioner of theatre – indeed, a man utterly obsessed with theatre – Wagner did incline to such a view in so far as he felt it to be the first duty of art to communicate everything to the senses in the most direct and exhaustive way possible. And it is fascinating to see, in the case of his principal work, *Der Ring des Nibelungen*, what the fulfilment of this unrelenting demand did to the *drama*, which was after all the object of all his endeavours, and whose fundamental law, it seemed to him, was this exhaustively sensuous representation. The story of this work's genesis is well known. While working on his dramatic sketch *Siegfrieds Tod*, Wagner could not accept (as he tells us himself) that so much had to be taken for granted, that so much action preceding the beginning of the piece would have to be explained in the course of the drama. The need he felt to bring these earlier events to life on the stage was overwhelming. And so he began to write the work backwards: he composed* *Der junge Siegfried*, then *Die Walküre*, then *Das Rheingold*, and would not rest until he had put everything on to the stage as it actually happened – the whole story in four evenings, starting with the primeval cell, the ultimate beginning, the first E flat of the double bassoon that opens the *Rheingold* Prelude, signalling the solemn, almost inaudible commencement of his narrative. Something magnificent had come into being, and one can understand the enthusiasm that gripped its creator when he saw how his vast design had turned out, full of profound new artistic potentialities. But what exactly was it that had come into being? Aesthetic theorists have from time to time rejected the dramatic cycle as a legitimate form. Grillparzer was one of them. He argued that the interrelationship of the various parts gives the whole thing a certain *epic quality*, which admittedly enhances its grandeur. But with that he has defined the effect of the *Ring*, the nature of its greatness; and what we find is that Wagner's principal work owes its particular grandeur, precisely, to that epic mode in which the subject matter was itself rooted. The *Ring* is a dramatized epic, the product of its creator's distaste for antecedent events that hover unseen behind the action – a distaste that was not shared, of course, by the theatre of the ancients or classical French tragedy. Ibsen is much closer to classical drama in this respect, with his analytical technique and his skill in unfolding the story of past events. There is also a certain irony in the fact that Wagner's theory of sensuous *dramatic* representation should have led him by such an astonishing route, *malgré lui*, to the epic mode.

His relationship with the individual arts from which he created his total work of art [Gesamtkunstwerk] is worth pondering. There is something curiously dilettante about it, as Nietzsche himself points

* Meaning the *texts*, not the music.

out in his remarks on Wagner's childhood and youth in the (pro-Wagner) fourth of his *Unzeitgemässe Betrachtungen* [Thoughts out of Season]:

> His youth was that of a dilettante all-rounder who didn't seem to know where he was going. He was not confined by any inherited family tradition to one particular artistic discipline. Painting, poetry, acting and music were as much a part of his life as a scholarly upbringing and an academic future; a casual observer might well have supposed that he was born to play the dilettante.

And not just the casual observer, in fact: observing him with passion and admiration one might say, at the risk of being misunderstood, that Wagner's art is a case of dilettantism that has been monumentalized by a supreme effort of the will and intelligence – a dilettantism raised to the level of genius. There is something dilettante about the very idea of combining all the arts, and without his success in subjugating them all, by a supreme effort, to his own immense expressive genius, the whole notion would never have got beyond the dilettante stage. There is something dubious about his relationship with the arts; absurd though it sounds, there is an element of the philistine about it. At bottom, Italy and the visual arts left him completely cold. To Mathilde Wesendonck in Rome he writes:

> Look around and see the sights for me too: I need somebody to do it for me ... I am rather peculiar in that way, as I have repeatedly had occasion to realize – and most clearly of all in Italy. For a while I am much excited by some lively impression made upon my eye; but it never lasts for long ... It seems that the eye as an organ for perceiving the world is simply not enough for me.

And understandably so. He is, after all, a man who lives through his ears, a musician and a poet; but it is strange, for all that, that he can write to the same correspondent from Paris in these terms:

> Oh, how the child revels in Raphael and painting! How lovely, delightful and reassuring! But as for me – *it leaves me totally unmoved*. I am still the same old heathen who has lived in Paris for a year and never yet set foot in the Louvre. Doesn't that tell you everything??

Not everything, but quite a lot that is curiously revealing. Painting is a great art, as great as the total work of art. It existed in its own right before the latter and continues to exist thereafter; yet it leaves him unmoved. If only he had been a lesser man – the deep slight to painting would not have been so hard to bear! For the fact is that the visual arts had nothing to say to him, either as past history or as living, contemporary work. The great glory of French Impressionist painting, which grew to maturity alongside his own work, he scarcely even noticed: it did not concern him. His only connection with it lay in the fact that Renoir painted his portrait – a picture that does not exactly idealize its subject, and that will not have pleased him greatly. Quite clearly his attitude to literature was very different from his attitude to the visual arts. All his life it gave him endless inspiration, particularly through the works of Shakespeare – even if the theory he used to glorify his own talent caused him to speak almost pityingly of those whom he called 'literary writers'. But what of that, when he himself gave so much to literature, enriching it so immensely by his own works – albeit it should never be forgotten that they are not designed to be read, are not works of language in the normal sense, but a kind of musical exhalation, which needs to be supplemented by images, gestures and music in order to become true poetry through the interplay of all these elements. Considered from a purely linguistic point of view they often seem somewhat overblown and baroque, naive, with an air of grandiose and overbearing ineptitude: yet interspersed with passages of sheer genius, of a power, economy and elemental beauty that banish all doubt – though they cannot efface our awareness that these are creations that stand outside the tradition of great European literature and poetry, blueprints for an expressive theatrical performance that relies on words as one of its resources. When I think of these flashes of linguistic genius scattered in among Wagner's dilettante audacities I think in particular of *Der Ring des Nibelungen* and of *Lohengrin*, which, viewed simply as a poetic creation, is perhaps his purest, noblest and most beautiful achievement.

His genius resides in a dramatic fusion of the arts that constitutes a 'work' in the true and legitimate sense only inasmuch as it *is* a totality, a synthesis. There is a wild, illegitimate quality about the constituent parts, even about the music itself (in so far as it is not a means to the overall end), that disappears only when the parts are united in the sublime whole. That Wagner's relationship to language differs from that of our great poets and writers, that it lacks the rigour and finesse that obtain wherever language is felt to be the highest good, the ordained medium of art, is shown by his occasional verse, those sugary romantic tributes and dedications to Ludwig II of Bavaria, those vulgarly jolly little rhymes he composed for his friends and helpers. The most lightweight piece of occasional verse dashed off by Goethe is solid gold poetry of high literary merit compared with these linguistic banalities, this versified bar-room humour, which cannot raise more than a dutiful smile even from committed Wagner admirers. Better to turn instead to his prose essays, those manifestos and self-commentaries which set forth his aesthetic theories and his critique of culture – artistic writings of astonishing perspicacity and intellectual vigour, although admittedly they cannot compare for style and intellectual content with Schiller's works on the philosophy of art – his immortal essay *Über naive und sentimentalische Dichtung* [Discourse on Spontaneous and Reflective Poetry], for example. There is something difficult to read about them, a certain woolliness and stiffness, and again that same sense of random, unkempt amateurism; they do not really belong to the great tradition of German and European essay-writing, are not really the works of a born writer, but the incidental products of necessity. For Wagner every thing of itself was a product of necessity. Happiness, a sense of vocation, fulfilment, legitimacy and greatness – these he achieved only through the sum of all the parts.

And was not his musicianship likewise the product of necessity, a great act of will designed to serve the overwhelming whole? Nietzsche once observed that so-called talent cannot be the essence of genius. 'See how little talent Richard Wagner had, for example,' he exclaims. 'Was there ever a musician so impoverished as he at the age of 27?' True enough, Wagner's music sprang from beginnings that were timorous, meagre and derivative, and those beginnings came much later in his life than in the lives of other great musicians. He himself writes:

I can remember still being assailed with doubts around the age of 30 and wondering whether I really had the makings of a unique artistic talent. In my works I could still detect other people's influence and my own imitativeness, and it was only with apprehension that I dared to contemplate my future development as a truly original creative artist.

This retrospect dates from 1862, when Wagner was at the height of his powers. But only three years previously, at the age of 46, he had written to Liszt from Lucerne, at a time when work on *Tristan* was not going at all well:

> I cannot find the words to tell you how wretched I feel as a composer; from the bottom of my heart I regard myself as a complete bodger. You should just see me sometimes, sitting there and saying to myself 'it *must* work' – and then going over to the piano and scraping together some feeble rubbish, before finally giving up with my brains in a stew. What a dreadful feeling that is – what a profound inward conviction of my own musical shoddiness! And then *you* come along, you from whose very pores music seems to gush forth like a spring, a cascade, a torrent – and I'm supposed to listen to the kind of things you say about me. I find it very hard not to think they were meant as pure irony ... It's a curious business, my dear fellow, and I tell you now: there is less to me than meets the eye.

Clearly this was the voice of depression, and not a word of it was to be taken seriously. Liszt responded accordingly, accusing Wagner of being 'insanely unfair' on himself. Besides, every artist knows that feeling of sudden shame when he contemplates the masterpieces of his own and an earlier age: it stems from the fact that every artistic venture represents a new and in itself highly 'artistic' assimilation of the personal and the individual to art *per se*, and every artist, even one with several acknowledged successes to his name, can suddenly find himself wondering, as he compares his work with the masterly achievements of others: 'How is it possible even to mention a personal interpretation of mine in the same breath with those other things?' But in the man who came to a halt in the third act of *Tristan*, such a degree of depressive self-abasement and desperate inner doubt in the face of the musical challenge does seem rather strange – and psychologically curious. In truth, the dictatorial self-assurance of

Wagner's old age, when he scornfully dismissed much of beauty (including Mendelssohn, Schumann and Brahms) in the pages of the *Bayreuther Blätter*, all to the greater glory of his own art – that self-confidence was purchased at the price of much self-doubt and despondency in the face of art during those earlier years! And where did these feelings spring from? Surely it was only the fact that in such moments he made the mistake himself of looking at his musical talent in isolation, measuring it against the highest musical achievements – whereas in fact it ought to be judged only in relation to his poetic talent, and vice versa. This same mistake has been chiefly responsible for the fierce resistance with which his music has had to contend. We who derive so much joy and rapture from this miraculous world of sound and its peculiar intellectual magic, so much profound amazement at the spectacle of such immense, self-made ability – we find it difficult to understand this resistance, this aversion; the kind of expressions used to describe Wagner's music – words like 'cold', 'algebraic', 'shapeless' – seem to us appallingly misleading and obtuse, indicating an insensitive poverty of understanding and lack of appreciation, and we tend to think that such judgements can have come only from the ranks of uncultured philistines, forsaken by God and music alike. But this is not the case. Many of those who judged thus, who could not but judge thus, were not narrow-mindedly bourgeois; they were artistic spirits and thinking men, makers of music and lovers of music, people who cared about the fate of music, and who rightly claimed to be able to distinguish between music and non-music: and it was their view that this was *not* music. Their assessment has been completely overturned, and its defeat has been final and enduring. But although it was wrong, was it also inexcusable? Wagner's music is not wholly and entirely music, any more than the dramatic text that it turns into poetry is wholly and entirely 'literature'. It is psychology, symbolism, mythology, emphasis – all of these things; but it is not music in the purest and fullest sense as understood by those confused art critics. The texts around which it is woven, which it thereby makes into drama, are not literature – but the music is. It seems to shoot up like a geyser from the precivilized bedrock depths of myth (and not only 'seems': it really does); but in fact – and at the same time – it is carefully considered, calculated, supremely intelligent, full of shrewdness and cunning, and as literary in its conception as the texts are musical in theirs. Resolved into its primal elements, the music is designed to throw into high relief philosophical propositions that have been embodied in myth. The insatiable chromaticism of the *Liebestod* is a literary idea. Likewise the deep, elemental flow of the Rhine, the seven primitive blocks of chords on which Valhalla is built. A famous conductor once said to me, on his way home after conducting a performance of *Tristan*: 'This is no longer music.' He was voicing the emotional shock and excitement we both felt. But what we now intend as an expression of admiring approval is bound to have sounded initially like an angry rejection. Music such as that which accompanies Siegfried's Rhine journey, or the lament for the slain hero, pieces of unspeakable splendour to our ears and our minds, had never before been heard; they were 'unheard of' in the most scandalous sense of the term. That critics should regard this concatenation of symbolic motif-quotations, standing out like rocky outcrops in the torrent of primordial musical processes, as 'music' in the sense of Bach, Mozart and Beethoven was too much to ask. It was too much to ask that they should give the name of 'music' to the E flat major triad that shapes the *Rheingold* Prelude. Nor indeed *was* it music. It was an acoustic idea: the idea of the beginning of all things. Music has here been pressed into service in imperiously dilettante fashion to portray a mythical concept. Psychoanalysis tells us that love is just an amalgam of perversions. But it is still love, for all that – the most divine phenomenon in the world. By the same token, Richard Wagner's genius is just an amalgam of dilettante accomplishments.

But what accomplishments they were! He is one of those musicians who can persuade even the unmusical to listen to music. That may be an argument against him in the eyes of esoterics and élitists: but what if the unmusical number among their ranks men and artists like Baudelaire? For Baudelaire the encounter with Wagner was the discovery of music *tout court*. He himself was unmusical; he told Wagner in a letter that he understood nothing about music, and had known nothing beyond a handful of charming pieces by Weber and Beethoven. And now this rapturous enthusiasm, which fired him with the ambition of making music with language, of emulating Wagner with language alone – an undertaking that had far-reaching consequences for French poetry as a whole. A music that is not really music, a music for the layman, can afford to welcome such converts and proselytes; many a more orthodox composer might well envy it on that account – and not only on that account. This exoteric music contains things of a brilliance and splendour that make such distinctions seem merely ridiculous. The 'swan' motif from *Lohengrin* and *Parsifal*; the sounds of a moonlit summer's night at the end of Act II of *Die Meistersinger*, and the quintet in Act III; the passage in A flat major in the second act of *Tristan und Isolde*, and Tristan's vision of his beloved walking on the waves; the Good Friday music in *Parsifal* and the mighty transformation music in the third act; the glorious duet between Siegfried and Brünnhilde at the beginning of *Götterdämmerung*, with the folk-song-like intonation of 'Willst du mir Minne schenken' [If thou wouldst give me love] and the thrilling 'Heil dir, Brünnhild', prangender Stern!' [All hail, Brünnhilde, resplendent star!]; certain passages from the Venusberg adaptation of the *Tristan* period – these are inspirations that could make even absolute music pale with envy or blush with delight. And yet I have picked these out at random. I could just as easily mention others, or point to the astonishing artistry that Wagner displays in redirecting, changing and reinterpreting a motif that has already been introduced earlier in the music – as he does, for example, with Hans Sachs's shoemaking song in the prelude to Act III of *Die Meistersinger* – a piece we have already heard in comic vein as a rough workman's ditty in the second act, and which now recurs quite transfigured in the prelude, invested with unimagined poetic beauty. Or what about the many rhythmical and tonal transformations and reinterpretations that the so-called 'faith' motif in *Parsifal*, familiar to us from the first bars of the overture, undergoes in the course of the work, beginning with Gurnemanz's great narration? It is hard to speak of these things when words are all one has to evoke them. Why is it, even as I speak of Wagner's music, that I can hear in my mind such a small detail, a mere arabesque, as the horn figure in the lament for Siegfried that prepares us harmonically for the 'love' motif of his parents – so easily described in technical terms, yet in essence indescribable? At such moments it is difficult to say whether it is Wagner's own special and particular art or music *per se* that one admires and that affects one so deeply. In a word, it is heavenly – and one uses the word without embarrassment, unmanly and gushing though it may be, in the knowledge that music alone can elicit such an epithet.

The general spiritual tenor of Wagner's music is marked by a certain pessimistic heaviness and measured yearning, a sense of fragmentation in its rhythms, of forces struggling out of dark confusion to find deliverance in beauty; it is the music of an oppressed soul, not a music that speaks dancingly to our muscles, but the toiling, heaving and struggling of northern drudgery, which Lenbach* summed up with characteristic mother wit when he remarked one day to Wagner: 'Your music is like a carter's wagon bound for the kingdom of heaven.' But it is more than that. For all its spiritual weightiness one should not forget the dash, the splendour and the serenity of which it is also capable – in the knightly themes, for instance, the motifs composed for Lohengrin, Stolzing and Parsifal; nor the delightful unspoiled-elfin teasing of the Rhinemaiden tercets, the burlesque humour and scholarly frivolity of the *Meistersinger* overture, or the rustic merry-making of the folk dance in the third act. Wagner can do it all. As a portrayer of character he is without peer, and to comprehend his music as an instrument of characterization is to admire it beyond all measure. It is a picturesque art, grotesque even, conceived slightly larger than life, as the theatre demands, yet at the same time distinguished by an inventiveness in matters of detail, an agile capacity for entering into outward forms and speaking, gesticulating from *within* them, that had never before been equalled. Its greatest triumphs are celebrated in individual characters – in the musical-poetic figure of the Dutchman, for example, with that encompassing aura of desolation and damnation, yielded up in despair to the wild raging of the seas ... In Loge's elemental incalculability and treacherous charm. In the blinking and fawning of Siegfried's dwarfish foster father. In Beckmesser's fatuous malice and folly. This omnipotence and ubiquity of transformation and representation reveals the Dionysian actor and his art – or arts, if you will; not only does he change his human face, but he also enters into the natural world, speaking out of the storm and the tempest, the rustling of the leaves and the sparkling of the waves,

---

* Franz von Lenbach (1836–1904), fashionable Munich artist who painted a number of portraits of Wagner.

the dancing flames and the rainbow's arc. Alberich's magic hood is the universal symbol of this genius for masquerade, this infinite capacity for imitation, which is truly just as much at home in the crawling and hopping of the bloated, earthbound toad as it is in the carefree cloudland existence of the Aesir. It is this infinite power of characterization that can unite such spiritually disparate works as *Die Meistersinger*, with its bluff, Lutheran-Teutonic jollity, and the death-sick, death-drunk world of *Tristan*. It distinguishes each work from the next, develops each from its own unique tonal beginnings, so that each individual work is like a self-contained galactic entity within the personal cosmos of the total *oeuvre*. Between the works there are musical points of contact and links that indicate the organic unity of the whole. In *Parsifal* we can still hear strains of *Die Meistersinger*; in the music of *Der fliegende Holländer* there are already elements that anticipate *Lohengrin*, while the text already contains such premonitions of the highly wrought religious language of *Parsifal* as the lines: 'Ein heil'ger Balsam meinen Wunden / Dem Schwur, dem hohen Wort entfliesst' [A holy balsam for my wounds / Flows from your oath, your lofty words]; and in the Christian world of *Lohengrin* the remains of paganism personified in the figure of Ortrud lend a certain *Ring*-like quality of sound to the whole ambience. But each work as a whole remains stylistically distinct from all the others in a way that makes us vividly aware of the secret of *style* as the essence of all art, if not indeed its very substance: the secret (that is) of wedding the personal to the objective. In each of his works Wagner is wholly himself, and there is not a bar in them that could have been written by anyone else, that does not bear the unmistakable stamp of his hand. Yet at the same time each is distinctive, a stylistic world of its own, the product of a capacity for objective empathy that counterbalances personal individuality and is perfectly subsumed therein. Perhaps the greatest miracle in this regard is *Parsifal*, the work of the 70-year-old, which, as an exploration and articulation of remote, hideous and sacred realms, stands at the very limits of achievement – despite *Tristan und Isolde* the most extreme of Wagner's works, and testimony to a capacity for matching style to psychological nuance that surpasses at the last even what we have come to expect from him, filled with sounds in which one immerses oneself each time with renewed disquiet, curiosity and enchantment.

'A sorry business indeed,' wrote Wagner from Lucerne in May 1859, in the midst of his exhausting labours on the third act of *Tristan*, which renewed his interest in a figure he had long since conceived and sketched out in his mind – the figure of Amfortas. 'A sorry business! Just imagine what had happened! I had suddenly realized, with awful clarity, that Amfortas is my Tristan of Act III intensified to an inconceivable degree.' This 'intensification' is the involuntary and ultimately self-indulgent law by which all his work lives and grows. He laboured all his life to perfect those accents of torment and contrition that we hear in Amfortas. They are already present in Tannhäuser's 'Ach, schwer drückt mich der Sünden Last!' [Right heavy weighs my burden of sin!], and in *Tristan* they have seemingly attained the ultimate heights of shattering expressive force; but in *Parsifal*, as he realizes with horror, they will have to be surpassed, to undergo that 'inconceivable intensification'. He is unconsciously searching for situations and occasions of increasing power and intensity in order to carry certain accents to their ultimate limit. The individual themes and works are a series of stages, progressively more extreme variants of the basic unity underlying his perfectly consistent and fully rounded life's work – a work that 'develops', but in a sense is all there right from the beginning. This in turn relates to that interlocking and overlapping of creative ideas which means that an artist of this type and intellectual cast is never just involved with the particular work or project on which he happens to be engaged at the time, but feels simultaneously the weight of all his other creative concerns bearing down upon him as he works. There is an apparent air (and more than just apparent) of conscious strategy, of a whole career carefully mapped out in advance – to the extent that in 1862, while working on *Die Meistersinger*, Wagner can announce with all certainty in a letter to Bülow from Biebrich that *Parsifal* will be his last work – some twenty years before it is actually written down. Before that, of course, he had to finish off *Siegfried* – with interruptions while he wrote *Tristan* and *Die Meistersinger* – and the whole of *Götterdämmerung*, in order to fill in the gaps in his grand design. He was preoccupied with the *Ring* throughout the whole of his work on *Tristan*, in which the voice of *Parsifal* is audible right from the beginning. The latter was also present during the robustly Lutheran *Meistersinger* phase, and had in fact been waiting in the wings ever since the Dresden première of *Tannhäuser* in 1845. The year 1848 produced the prose sketch that condensed the Nibelung myth into dramatic form, the first draft of *Siegfrieds Tod*, from which *Götterdämmerung* would subsequently develop. In between, however – in 1846-7 – he had written *Lohengrin* and sketched out the plot of *Die Meistersinger*, which of course serves as a satyr play and humorous counterpart to *Tannhäuser*. In fact the 1840s, whose half-way point marked his thirty-second birthday, actually produced the entire programme for his remaining life's work, from the *Holländer* right through to *Parsifal* – a programme that will be carried into execution over the next four decades, up until 1881, while his mind is at work on every project at once, each nesting in the other like a set of Chinese boxes. Strictly speaking his work has no chronology. It unfolds through time, but is essentially present *in toto* right from the very beginning. His last work, which he knew to be his last many years before he finally wrote it at the age of 69, was a kind of deliverance inasmuch as it signified an end, a conclusion, a completion, after which nothing more would follow; and the labour that he devoted to it as an old man, as an artist who had lived out his potential to the full, was really no more than tinkering. It is finished, the vast undertaking; and the heart that has stood up to the most punishing demands for seventy long years can come to its rest in one last paroxysm.

This enormous creative burden was laid upon shoulders that were by no means those of a St Christopher, upon a constitution so frail – as it appeared, and as it was felt to be by Wagner himself – that nobody would have ventured to predict that it would hold out for long and carry such a load to its journey's end. His was a constitution that felt itself to be constantly on the edge of exhaustion, and knew the sensation of well-being only as a rare exception. Constipated, melancholy, insomniac, afflicted in every kind of way, this man was in such a state by the age of 30 that he would frequently sit down and cry for a quarter of an hour at a time. He could not believe that he would live long enough to complete *Tannhäuser*. To undertake the execution of the Nibelung project at the age of 36 seemed to him temerity, and when he was 40 he was 'thinking daily of death' – and this from the man who was to write *Parsifal* at the age of nearly 70.

It was a nervous affliction that so tormented him, one of those medically indeterminate ailments that mock the sufferer over the years and threaten to make life unbearable, while never actually putting life at risk. To believe that they do *not* put life at risk is very hard for the victim, and understandably so; and more than one passage in Wagner's letters testifies to his conviction that he is destined for an early death. 'My nerves', he writes to his sister at the age of 39,

> are already in an advanced state of decay; perhaps some outward change in my fortunes will contrive to keep death at bay for a few more borrowed years: but only my actual death – my dying has already begun.

And in the same year:

> I am extremely ill with my nerves, and after trying all kinds of drastic cures I have no more hope of recovery ... My work is the only thing that sustains me: but the nerves of my brain are already so far gone that I can never work for more than two hours in a day – and even then only on condition that I lie down afterwards for another two hours and eventually manage a little sleep.

Two hours in a day. From such brief bouts of labour (on occasion, at least) was this gigantic *oeuvre* gradually heaped up, battling with a strength that was quickly exhausted each time, the gift of a resilient tenacity on which his rapidly depleted energies could always draw for temporary renewal – and which is known in moral terms as *patience*. 'True patience is a sign of great resilience,' observed Novalis; and Schopenhauer praises patience as the truest form of bravery. It was this physical-moral union of resilience, patience and bravery that enabled this man to accomplish his mission; and it is hard to imagine another artist whose life reveals so clearly the characteristic and vigorous constitution of genius, that blend of sensitivity and strength, delicacy and stamina – that blend of 'despite the odds' and self-surprises from which the greatest works spring, and which in time generates an understandable feeling of having been sacrificed to an undertaking with a will of its own. It is indeed difficult not to believe that the work of art has a metaphysical will of its own as it strives to come into being, regarding the life of its creator as a mere tool and sacrificial victim, half willing, half unwilling. 'To tell you the truth, I feel wretched – but at least I feel.' A typical outburst of desperate, head-shaking self-mockery from Wagner's correspondence. And he does not omit to establish a causal connection between his sufferings and his practice of art, viewing art and disease as one and the same affliction – with the result that he sought escape, naively enough, in a cold-water cure. 'A year ago,' he writes,

> I was at a hydrotherapy centre, with the intention of becoming a completely healthy person in body and senses. My secret wish was that the attainment of physical health would enable me to rid myself entirely of art, the bane and torment of my life; it was a last desperate bid for happiness, for true, pure enjoyment of life, such as only the consciously healthy man can know.

What a childishly confused and touching confession! With cold water he thinks to cure himself of art – which is to say, of the disposition that makes him into an artist. His relationship to the art that was his destiny is almost too complex to unravel, entangled in all kinds of contradictions; at times he seems to wriggle and twist within it, as if enmeshed in a net of logic. 'And now I'm supposed to produce *that*?' exclaims the 46-year-old, after an excited discussion of the psychological and symbolic aspects of the *Parsifal* plan. 'And write the music for it into the bargain? No thank you. Let someone else do it, if they've a mind to; I shall have nothing to do with it!' Note the unmistakable tone of feminine coquetry in these words, full of trembling desire for the work, full of the knowledge 'You must' and of exquisitely pleasurable resistance! The dream of escaping from art, of being free to live instead of obliged to create, of being *happy*, is one that recurs constantly in his letters; words like 'happiness', 'pure happiness', 'pure enjoyment of life' run through them like a thread, always as the antithesis to a life of art – and together with the notion of art as a substitute for any immediacy of enjoyment. At the age of 39 he writes to Liszt:

> With every passing day I fall into a deeper decline: the life I live is *indescribably worthless*! Of life's real enjoyment I know absolutely nothing: for me the 'enjoyment of life, of *love*' [Wagner's own emphasis]* is merely something to be imagined, not

* TM's interpolation.

experienced. So my heart was forced to enter my brain, and my life became a wholly artificial affair: only as an 'art-ist' can I live my life henceforth, now that my 'person-ality' has been wholly subsumed into that function.

It must be said that art has never been characterized more bluntly or with more desperate candour as narcotic, hashish, *paradis artificiel*. And we find outbreaks of furious rebellion against this artificial existence, as when he writes to Liszt on the occasion of his fortieth birthday:

> I think I'll be rebaptized: wouldn't you like to be godfather? If only we could *both* then depart from here forthwith and get out into the world! ... Come with me into the great wide world – even if only to perish in style, to dash ourselves blithely to pieces in some abyss!

One thinks of Tannhäuser, clasping Wolfram in his arms to drag him along into the Venusberg: and indeed, in Wagner's fantasy of privation the world and 'life' are conceived wholly as a kind of Venusberg, as the locus of a radical devil-take-the-hindmost irresponsibility, where people perish in frenzied enjoyment – all the things, in fact, for which a 'worthless' life of art must serve as surrogate.

In contrast to this – but yet in a curious way connected with it – art also appeared to him in a very different light: as a source of release, a quietive, a state of pure contemplation and will-lessness. For thus had philosophy taught him to view it; and with the intellectual complaisance and readiness to learn of the artist-child he was anxious to follow where philosophy directed. Oh yes: he was an idealist all right! The meaning of life lay not in itself but in something higher, in the appointed task, in creative work; and 'to be eternally caught up in the struggle for life's necessities', as he was,

> to have to spend long periods of time thinking about nothing else other than how I can contrive to secure a brief respite and provide for my immediate and essential needs, and to be obliged, to that end, to step right outside my real character and appear a totally different person to those from whom I would seek assistance – it really is outrageous ... All these cares are very well suited to the

person for whom life is an end in itself, and for whom the care of providing for life's needs lends a particular spice to the pleasure he looks forward to taking in those acquisitions: consequently nobody can really understand why all that is so utterly abhorrent to the likes of us, given that such is the common lot and condition of mankind. That somebody can look upon life not as an end in itself, but as the means to a higher end – how many people truly understand that? (From a letter to Mathilde Wesendonck, written from Venice in October 1858.)

Indeed, it *is* shameful and degrading in the extreme to have to struggle and beg for a living when a living as such is not what one desires, but that higher purpose above and beyond life itself – namely art, creative work, for which one must fight to secure the necessary peace and repose, and which itself appears suffused with the light of peace and repose. But once the freedom to attend to the real business of work has been laboriously won (and the terms are fairly exacting), then the real toil is only just beginning – the higher toil of the will to produce and create, the struggle with art, about whose true nature one has cherished a number of philosophical illusions during the lowly struggle for a living: for by no means is it redemptive knowledge and pure 'idea', but a supreme convulsive effort of the will – in very truth the fiery wheel of Ixion.

Purity and peace: for these he cherished within his breast a profound longing, complementary to his thirst for life; and as soon as that longing came to predominate, following the failure of his attempts to enjoy at first hand, art came to appear, by yet another complicated twist, as the obstacle to salvation. In this we see an affinitive repetition of Tolstoy's rejection of art, of his cruel denial of his own natural gift in the name of the 'spirit'. Ah yes: art! How right the Buddha was when he called it the surest way to miss the path of salvation! It was in a long, stormy letter written to Mathilde Wesendonck from Venice in 1858 that Wagner expounded this to his friend, after telling her of his plans for a Buddhist drama to be called *Die Sieger* [The Victors]. 'Buddhist drama': there's the rub, for this is nothing less than a contradiction in terms – as he realized when he faced the problem of turning a man who is perfectly liberated and released from all passion – the Buddha himself – into suitable material for dramatic (and more specifically, musical) representation. That which is pure, holy, pacified through knowledge is artistically defunct: sanctity and drama are quite clearly incompatible. So it was a happy chance that Sakyamuni Buddha (according to the sources) was confronted with one last problem, entangled in one last conflict: he has to wrestle with the difficult decision whether to admit the chandala girl Savitri to the holy order, contrary to his earlier principles. Here – thank heavens – he becomes a possible subject for art. Wagner is delighted – but in the same instant his conscience is burdened by the guilty realization of art's dependence on life, and of its power to lead men astray. Has he not caught himself desiring drama instead of sanctity? Without art he could be sanctified, a holy one; with art that can never be. The highest knowledge, the most profound insight – were they to be vouchsafed him – would only ever serve to make him into a poet, an artist; they would appear to him with moving visual immediacy as an entrancing *image* that he could not but choose to execute in creative form. Worse still – he even takes pleasure in this devilish antinomy! It is abominable: but it is also fascinatingly interesting. One is tempted to make a psychological-romantic opera out of it – which is more or less what Wagner does in that letter to Frau Wesendonck. The letter is the draft of such a work. Goethe observes: 'There is no surer way of avoiding the world than through art; and there is no surer way of attaching oneself to it than through art.' Just look what happens to those serenely thankful words in the mind of a Romantic!

But whatever the truth about art, however it may cheat us both of true sensuous joy and of salvation – Wagner's work advanced without pause, thanks to powers of resilience that he secretly had to admire. The musical scores were piling up, and that was the main thing. This man knew as little as the rest of us about how life should be lived; it is *he* who is lived by *life*, which extorts from him what it will (in this case his musical *oeuvre*) without the least concern for the mental toils in which he has to struggle:

My dear! This *Tristan* is turning into something *terrible*! And as for the last act!!! I fear the opera will be banned – unless a bad performance turns the whole thing into a parody; my only salvation lies in mediocre performances! Thoroughly *good* ones would make people quite mad, I am sure of it. To think that I've had to come to this!! Oh Lord! I was just now in full flight! Adieu!

A note to Mathilde – and a distinctly un-Buddhist note it is, filled with weird, frightened laughter at the reckless infamy of what he is doing. He was endowed with vast resources of good temper and inexhaustible resilience, this dispirited melancholic, whose illness was simply a socially unconventional form of health. What vibrant magic must have emanated from a man whose society Nietzsche never ceased to extol as the one great happy experience of his life! Above all he possessed the inestimable gift of being able to cast aside lofty concerns and give himself up to the banal and the commonplace – to declare the time come, after a day of hard, concentrated work, for simple human good cheer, which he did in Bayreuth with the habitual cry of 'Not another serious word!' to his fellow artistes, that little band of theatre folk whom he needed in order to realize his works, and with whom he got on so splendidly despite the enormous difference in intellectual stature, being himself a child of the theatre well acquainted with the makeshift world of players and actors. His unassuming friend Heckel from Mannheim, the first Bayreuth shareholder, has a marvellous story to tell. 'Very often,' he writes, 'Wagner's personal relations with his artistes were enlivened by a mood of exuberant merriment. At the last piano rehearsal in the salon of the Hotel Sonne he was in such high spirits that he actually *stood on his head!*' That too reminds one of Tolstoy – and specifically of the time when the aged prophet and troubled Christian leapt on to the shoulders of his father-in-law Behrs out of sheer bubbling high spirits. Wagner was an artiste himself, just like the tenors and virtuosos who called him 'maestro': in other words, a man who was *genuinely* amusing and desirous of amusing others, an organizer of entertainments and celebrations of life – in profound and very healthy contrast to the man of perception and knowledge who sits in judgement, the man of absolute earnest, like Nietzsche. It is wise to recognize that the artist – even the one who inhabits the most solemn realms of art – is never an absolutely earnest person, that he is concerned with creating effects, with providing entertainment of the highest order, and that tragedy and farce both spring from one and the same root. A slight change in the lighting is enough to transform one into the other; farce is a secret tragedy, and tragedy, ultimately, is a sublime joke. The earnestness of the artist: now *there* is food for thought. Some may find the thought offensive, in so far as the intellectual earnest of the artistic individual, his serious commitment to the truth, are at issue: for his artistic earnest – that celebrated 'playful earnest', the purest and most touching form of human high-mindedness – is not for a moment at issue. But what are we to make of that other kind of earnestness, as displayed, for example, by that seeker after truth, thinker and confessor, Richard Wagner? For quite clearly the sensuous, revolutionary spirit of Wagner's younger years, which shapes the atmosphere and mental climate of *Siegfried*, was utterly disavowed, cancelled out and revoked by the ascetic-Christian ideas and doctrines of his old age, that eucharistic philosophy of sanctification through abstinence from 'fleshly enjoyment' in every sense of the word – by those attitudes and perceptions of which the Parsifal theme is the 'expression', and indeed by *Parsifal* itself. It was gone, that youthful spirit – it could no longer be allowed to exist. If the artist had been in intellectual earnest about those new, late, but surely definitive truths, then the works of his earlier period, now recognized as mistaken, sinful and pernicious, must needs have been repudiated and destroyed, cast into the flames by their creator's own hand so that mankind might never again be exposed to their effects, so inimical to salvation. But he would not think of doing so. The thought, quite literally, never entered his head. Who would wish to destroy such beautiful works? Each stands alongside all the others, continuing to be performed; for the artist honours his own biography. He surrenders himself to the changing physiological moods of each period in his life, representing them in works that contradict each other intellectually, but that are all beautiful and worthy of preservation. To the artist, new experiences of 'truth' mean new stimuli to play, new expressive possibilities – nothing more. He believes in them – takes them seriously – only to the degree that is necessary in order to bring them to the highest pitch of expression and make the deepest possible impression with them. Consequently he is very much in earnest about them, earnest to the point of tears – but then again, not totally, and therefore not *at all*. His artistic earnest is 'playful earnest', and absolute by nature. But his intellectual earnest is not absolute, for it serves as a means to the end of play. Thus it is that the artist is so ready, among his familiars, to make fun of his own solemnity – to the point where Wagner could send Nietzsche the text of *Parsifal* with a note signing himself 'Richard Wagner, Elder of the Church'. But Nietzsche was no artist's familiar; and this kind of good-humoured, eye-twinkling complaisance failed to appease that deadly-sullen, absolute earnest of his, which disapproved of the Romish Christianity of a repertoire that he none the less described as a supreme challenge to music. When Wagner behaved childishly, hurling a Brahms score from the piano in an access of rage, Nietzsche was deeply pained by such a display of artistic jealousy and obvious desire for sole supremacy, and he remarked: 'In that moment Wagner was not great!' When Wagner took relaxation in trivial things, acted the goat and told earthy anecdotes, Nietzsche blushed for him – and we can understand his shame at this abrupt change of tone, although something in us (our artistic side, perhaps) counsels us not to understand it *too* well.

The discovery of the philosophy of Arthur Schopenhauer was *the* great event in Wagner's life. None of his earlier intellectual encounters – such as that with Feuerbach – can compare with it in personal or historical significance: for it meant supreme consolation, profound reassurance and intellectual deliverance to the one whom it so perfectly befitted, and it undoubtedly gave his music the liberating courage to be itself. Wagner had little faith in the reality of friendship; in his eyes – and in his experience – the barriers of individuation that separate human souls make solitude insuperable and total understanding impossible. Here he felt himself understood by one whom he understood perfectly in his turn: 'My friend Schopenhauer', and 'a gift from heaven in my solitude'. 'But I have one friend', he writes,

of whom I am growing more and more fond: and that is my dear old Schopenhauer, who looks so grumpy, but is really so profoundly amiable. When I am feeling at the end of my tether emotionally, how uniquely refreshing to open that book and suddenly to find myself so wholly once again, to see myself so fully understood, so clearly expressed – only in a completely different language which swiftly transforms suffering into an object of cognition ... There occurs a most wonderful interaction, a meeting and exchange of the very happiest kind: and always this effect is new, because it is growing constantly stronger ... How nice to think that the old man has absolutely no idea what he means to me, *what I have come to mean to myself through him.*

The joy of thus recognizing oneself in another is possible between creative individuals only if they speak different languages; otherwise it becomes a disaster, a fatal case of 'him or me'. In a relationship like this, which bridges the gap between two different categories, between plastic creation and philosophical thought, there is none of that jealousy which is generated between similar psychological types who overlap and duplicate each other. The dictum *Pereant qui ante nos nostra dixerunt* no longer applies, nor Goethe's question for artists: 'Can one live while others live?' On the contrary, the fact that the other lives is a help in times of need, a glorious, unlooked-for confirmation and elucidation of one's own being. Probably never in all the history of the human psyche has the need of the dark, tormented spirit, of the artist, for intellectual support, for justification and instruction through the philosophical idea, been so wonderfully answered as Wagner's was by Schopenhauer.

Die Welt als Wille und Vorstellung [The World as Will and Idea]: how my mind fills with memories of my own youthful intellectual fervour, my own joy in conception, full of melancholy and thankfulness, when I think of the rapport between Wagner's *oeuvre* and this world-critical, world-ordering book, this poem of knowledge and artistic metaphysic compounded of compulsion and intellect, of will and contemplation – this miraculous edifice of ideas, at once ethical, pessimistic and musical, which exhibits such a profound historical and human affinity with the score of *Tristan*! The old words come back to me with which this young man in his novel described the impact of Schopenhauer on his middle-class hero:*

> He was filled with a great and unknown sense of thankful contentment. He experienced the incomparable satisfaction of seeing how a mind of towering superiority seized hold of life – life in all its strength, cruelty and mockery – in order to subdue it and condemn it ... the satisfaction of the sufferer who has always

* TM is referring to Thomas Buddenbrook's discovery of Schopenhauer in the novel *Buddenbrooks* (1901).

hidden his sufferings away, with feelings of shame and bad conscience, in the face of life's coldness and harshness, and who suddenly receives a full dispensation from the hands of a great and wise man to be afflicted by this world – this best of all possible worlds, which has been unmasked with sovereign contempt as the worst of all possible worlds.

They rise up again, those old words of thanks and celebration, which tell of an intellectual joy reverberating without end, of that nocturnal awakening out of brief, deep sleep, a sudden and delicious arousal, when the slumberer felt within his heart the germ of a metaphysic that revealed the ego as an illusion, death as the means of escape from its inadequacy, the world as the creation of the will and as its eternal possession – so long as the will does not deny itself in knowledge and emerge from illusion into peace. This is the rider, the doctrine of wisdom and salvation added on to a philosophy of the will that has little enough to do, in its conception, with the wisdom of peace and quietus – a conception that could be grasped only by a personality of powerful will and drives, tormented by its own ungovernability, but in which the drive for purity, spirituality and knowledge was just as strong as the dark compulsive drive – a *world-erotic* conception, which expressly identifies sexuality as the focus of the will, and would have us understand the aesthetic condition as that of pure and disinterested contemplation, as the only – and only temporary – possibility of escaping from the torture of compulsive drives. It is born of the will, of the desire that runs contrary to better judgement, this philosophy which is the intellectual denial of the will; thus did Wagner perceive it, as a fellow spirit profoundly akin to the philosopher, and thus did he seize upon it with supreme gratitude as his own, as the complete expression of his own nature. His too, after all, was a nature compounded of the dark, compulsive and agonizing will to power and pleasure and the urge for moral purification and redemption, of passion and the longing for peace; and a system of ideas that represents the most bizarre blend of pacifism and heroism, that declares 'happiness' to be a chimera and implies that the highest and best available to man is a life cast in the *heroic* mould – what a joy it must have been to a nature like Wagner's, as though patterned on himself and created for him alone!

In some of the orthodox studies of Wagner it is alleged in all seriousness that *Tristan* was not influenced by the philosophy of Schopenhauer. Such a view testifies to a curious lack of perception. Of course, the quintessentially Romantic glorification of the night that we find in this sublimely morbid, consuming and magical work, thoroughly initiated into all the direst and noblest mysteries of Romanticism, is not something that is uniquely Schopenhauerian. The sensuous-suprasensuous intuitions of *Tristan* have a more distant origin in that fervent consumptive Novalis, who writes: 'A marriage that gives us a companion for the night is also a union concluded unto death. In death is love most sweet; for the lover, death is a bridal night, a secret full of sweet mysteries.' And who in *Hymnen an die Nacht* [Hymns to the Night] laments: 'Must the morning always come again? Shall the power of this earthly life never end? Shall love's secret sacrifice never burn for all eternity?' Tristan and Isolde call themselves 'children of the night' – which is a verbatim echo of a phrase in Novalis. An even more remarkable literary antecedent, which tells us even more about the true origin, the emotional and intellectual basis of Wagner's *Tristan*, is that little book of ill repute by Friedrich von Schlegel, *Lucinde*, which contains these words:

> We are immortal, like love itself. No more can I say 'my love' or 'your love', for both are identical and perfectly at one, love met with love in equal measure. It is a marriage, an everlasting union and conjoining of our souls, not merely for that which we call this world or the world to come, but for a true, indivisible, nameless, infinite world, for our entire life and being throughout all eternity.

Here we find the image of the lovers' fatal potion:

> And so too, when I thought the time had come, I would drain a cup of laurel water with you as merrily and lightly as the last glass of champagne we drank together, when I spoke the words: 'Even so let us drink out the remainder of our days!'

Here too we find the idea of the *Liebestod*:

> I know that you too would not wish to outlive me, that you would follow your too-hasty husband even unto the grave, and

would descend with ecstasy and love into the flaming abyss to which a savage law condemns Indian wives, desecrating and destroying the most tender and sacred preserves of free will by brute design and commandment.

Here we read of the 'rapture of sensual delight', which is a genuinely Wagnerian concept. Here, in prose form, is an erotic-quietistic paean to sleep, the paradise of rest, the holy stillness of passivity, which in *Tristan* becomes the somnolent horn motif and the melody shared among the violins. And it was nothing more or less than a literary find when, as a young man, I came across this ecstatic rejoinder in the love dialogue between Lucinde and Julius: 'O eternal longing! Yet at the last the fruitless longings and vain illusions of the day shall fade and die, and a great night of love shall feel at peace for ever' – and noted in the margin: 'Tristan'. I do not know to this day whether anybody else has noticed this verbal parallel, this recurrence of the same idea as an unconscious reminiscence – any more than I know whether scholars have realized that the title of Nietzsche's book *Die fröhliche Wissenschaft* [The Gay Science] likewise comes from Schlegel's *Lucinde*.

By its cult of the night, its execration of the day, *Tristan* reveals itself as a Romantic work, deeply rooted in Romantic thought and sensibility, which as such had no need of Schopenhauer to stand godfather. The night is the true domain and dwelling place of all Romanticism, its real discovery, which it invariably presents as the truth in contrast to the vain illusions of the day – the realm of sensibility contrasted with reason. I have not forgotten the impression made upon me by my first visit to Linderhof, the castle built by the sick King Ludwig with his craving for beauty, where I found this primacy of the night expressed in the very proportions of the rooms. The living rooms and day apartments of the little summer residence, situated in its glorious mountain fastness, are small and comparatively unimposing, nothing more than closets. There is only *one* room in the building that has been executed on a vast scale by comparison, furnished in gold and silks with heavy, elaborate splendour: the bedroom, with its bed of state beneath a spreading canopy, flanked by golden candelabra – the real stateroom of the royal residence, consecrated to the night. This pronounced ascendancy of the day's 'more lovely half', the night, is archetypally, quintessentially Romantic; in this, Romanticism is closely allied to the whole mythical complex of mother-moon cults, which have always been contrasted, since the beginnings of civilization, with sun worship, the religion of light as the male-paternal element; and it is within the general orbit of this world that Wagner's *Tristan* is firmly located.

But when Wagner scholars tell us that *Tristan und Isolde* is a love drama, which as such implies the supreme affirmation of the will to life, and consequently has nothing to do with Schopenhauer; when they insist that the 'night' celebrated in that work is the night of love, 'where love's pleasures delight us', and that if this drama contains any philosophy at all, then it is the precise opposite of the doctrine of the denial of the will, which means that the work is quite unconnected with Schopenhauer's metaphysic – then we are dealing with an astonishing lack of psychological sensitivity. The denial of the will is the moral-intellectual component of Schopenhauer's philosophy, which is of little essential significance. It is merely secondary. His system is a philosophy of the will that is fundamentally erotic in character: and in so far as it is *that*, *Tristan* is replete with it, steeped in it. The torch whose extinction at the beginning of Act II of this mystery play is pointed up by the death motif in the orchestra; the enraptured cry of the lovers 'Selbst dann bin ich die Welt' [Then I, I am the world!], with the 'longing motif' rising up from the depths of a music that underscores the psychological and metaphysical meanings – are we to believe this is *not* Schopenhauer? In *Tristan* Wagner is no less a creator of myths than in the *Ring*: his love drama, too, is essentially concerned with a myth of the world's creation. 'I frequently gaze with longing towards the land of Nirvana,' he writes to Mathilde Wesendonck from Paris in 1860. 'But Nirvana soon turns into Tristan again – you know the Buddhist theory about the origins of the world. The merest breath troubles the heavenly clarity' – and he writes down the four chromatically ascending notes with which his *opus metaphysicum* begins and on which it expires, the sequence G sharp, A, A sharp, B – 'it rises and swells, takes on solid shape, and in the end the whole world stands before me again in all its impenetrable vastness.' This is the symbolic musical idea that is normally known as the 'longing motif', and which, in the cosmogony of *Tristan*, signifies the beginning of all things, like the E flat major Rhine motif in the *Ring*. This is Schopenhauer's 'will', represented by that which Schopenhauer termed 'the focus of the will' – love's desire. And this mythical equation of the irksome-sweet cosmogonical principle – which first troubled the heavenly clarity of the void – with sexual desire is so thoroughly Schopenhauerian that the denial of the adepts is a perverse eccentricity.

'How could we die?' asks Tristan in Wagner's first draft, the as yet unversified predecessor of the final text, 'What in us could be slain that were not already love? Are we not but wholly love? Can our love ever end? Could I ever wish to cease loving love? Were I to die now, would love also die, since love is all we are?' This passage demonstrates the unequivocal poetic equation of the will with love. The latter stands quite simply for the will to life, which cannot end in death, but is liberated from the binding constraints of individuation. At the same time it is very interesting to note how the love myth in the drama is presented in purely spiritual terms, untainted by any distracting historical-religious associations. Expressions such as 'if he go to hell or to heaven', which are still there in the first draft, have been dropped from the final version. Clearly this was a conscious decision to eliminate historical colour – but only in respect of the work's intellectual-philosophical content, and only for its sake. This dehistoricization, remarkably enough, is accompanied by the most vivid and colourful treatment of topographical, ethnic and cultural aspects, by a stylistic discrimination that testifies to his incredibly unerring powers of empathy and artistry. Nowhere is Wagner's art of mimicry more enigmatically triumphant than in the shaping of the style of *Tristan*, which is not just a matter of the language as such, not limited to turns of phrase borrowed from the ethos of courtly epic, but which in some intuitively brilliant way knows how to imbue the whole complex of words and sounds with a thoroughly Celtic flavour, an atmosphere compounded of the English, the Norman and the French – and all done with a power of imaginative identification that shows how totally at home in mind and spirit Wagner is in a European locale that predates the emergence of separate national states. That dehistoricization and concentration on the universally human obtain *only* in the intellectual-speculative sphere, in the service of the erotic myth. For its sake, heaven and hell have been shut out. There is no Christianity, although it would have been a natural part of the historical background and ethos. There is no religion of any kind. There is no God – nobody mentions Him, nobody invokes Him. There is only erotic philosophy, atheistic metaphysics, the cosmogonical myth in which the longing motif summons the world into being.

Wagner's healthy brand of sickness, his diseased brand of heroism, are just one instance of the contradictions and convolutions inherent in his nature, its ambiguity and equivocality, which we have already seen in the union of two apparently so contradictory aptitudes as the gift for myth and the gift for psychology. The concept of the 'Romantic' is still the most useful as a means of classifying his character: but that concept is itself so complex and elusive that it represents not so much a definition as the abandonment of any attempt to define.

Only in Romanticism is it possible to create means and effects that combine popular appeal *and* exquisite refinement, over-stimulated 'infamy' (to use a favourite expression of E. T. A. Hoffmann's): only Romanticism makes possible that 'double focus'* of which Nietzsche speaks in relation to Wagner, and which knows how to accommodate the finest and the coarsest at one and the same time – quite unconsciously, of course: it would be facile to infer any self-serving motive in this – with the result that creations like *Lohengrin* can delight the minds of men such as the author of *Les Fleurs du Mal* while furnishing simple edification at the popular level, leading a Kundry-like double life as relaxing operatic entertainment and the passionate love of sophisticated, suffering and fastidious minds. The Romantic – particularly when it is allied with music, to which it aspires with all its being, and without which it could not achieve fulfilment – has no truck with exclusiveness, with the 'pathos of distance', nor does it say to any man, 'This is not for you'; with part of its being it speaks to the very least among us – and it is no use saying that this is true of *all* great art. Other great art, it may well be, has succeeded in combining the childlike with the sublime; but the combination of fairy-tale artlessness with wily shrewdness, the trick of embodying the most sophisticated intellectual ideas in an orgy of sensual intoxication and making it 'popular', the ability to clothe the profoundly

* *doppelte Optik*: in TM's letter to the editor of *Common Sense*, presumably written in English either with or without assistance, this phrase is somewhat curiously rendered as 'twin optics' (see p. 198).

grotesque in eucharistic solemnity and the tinkling mysteries of trans-
substantiation, to couple art and religion in a sexual opera of
supreme audacity, and to set up such holy artistic profanity in the
heart of Europe as a kind of theatrical Lourdes, a grotto of miracles
for a weary twilight age that lusts after some kind of faith – all this
is *uniquely* Romantic, and in the classical-humanist tradition of art
(which is the truly aristocratic tradition) this would be wholly unthinkable. The cast list for *Parsifal* – what a bizarre collection, at
bottom! What an assemblage of extreme and repellent oddities! A
sorcerer emasculated by his own hand; a desperate woman of split
personality, half corrupter, half penitent Mary Magdalene, with ca-
taleptic transitions between these two states of being; a love-sick high
priest, who awaits redemption at the hands of a chaste boy; this boy
himself who brings redemption, this guileless fool, so very different
from the awakened youth who wakes up Brünnhilde, and in his own
way another case of remote peculiarity: together they remind one of
that motley bunch of freaks packed into Achim von Arnim's famous
coach – the ambivalent gypsy witch, the dead layabout, the golem in
female shape and the field marshal Cornelius Nepos, who is really a
mandrake root grown beneath a gibbet. The comparison seems blas-
phemous, and yet the grave characters of *Parsifal* derive from the
same Romantic penchant for extremism as Arnim's scurrilous crew.
Had they been presented in the guise of a novella, this would have
been more obvious; only the mythicizing and sanctifying powers of
the music mask the affinity, and it is from the solemn spirit of the
latter that the whole thing emerges not as gruesome-facetious nonsense, as it does with the literary Romantic, but as a deeply religious
sacred drama.

A susceptibility to the *changeant* problem of art and the artist, a
melancholy grasp of the ironies that divide art's true nature from its
effects – these are typical of youth, and I can recall many an observation on this theme from my younger years, indicative of a passion
for Wagner that had passed through the school of Nietzsche's
critique, and dictated by that 'disgust for knowledge' which one
imbibed from him as the most appealing part of his philosophy for
young minds. Nietzsche said that he would not touch the score of
Tristan unless he was wearing gloves. 'Who dares to speak the word,'
he exclaims, 'the *real* word to describe the *ardeurs* of the *Tristan*

music?' The rather old-maidish tone of this question strikes me as much funnier now than it did at the age of 25. For what is there to 'dare'? Sensuality, unbounded, spiritualized sensuality, raised to a mystical order of magnitude and portrayed with the utmost naturalism, sensuality that will not be appeased by *any* gratification – this is the 'word' he means; and one wonders how it is that Nietzsche, that 'free, superlatively free spirit', has suddenly developed the rancour towards sexuality that is suggested in such a psychologically accusing manner by his question. Has he not forgotten his accustomed role as the defender of life against morality? Is this not Nietzsche the arch-moralist, the pastor's son, whom we see before us? He describes *Tristan* in a phrase borrowed from the mystics as 'the lust of hell'. All right – and one needs only to compare the mysticism of *Tristan* with that of Goethe's 'Selige Sehnsucht' [Blissful Yearning], with its reference to 'higher union', to realize how remote we are from Goethe's world in Wagner. But then Nietzsche himself, ultimately, furnishes as good a measure as Wagner of how much more *afflicted* the spiritual condition of the West had become in the course of the nineteenth century, compared with the age of Goethe. The kinds of effects brought forth by Wagner, at once numbing and stirring, are like those engendered by the sea – yet nobody would dream of engaging in psychological analysis while standing on the seashore. What is good enough for nature in her grandeur ought to be good enough for great art, and when Baudelaire speaks with a complete absence of sanctimonious criticism and with innocent artistic enthusiasm of the 'ecstasy of joy and understanding' that the *Lohengrin* Prelude has excited in him, and raves about 'opium trances', the 'extraordinary pleasure that moves in the high places', then he displays considerably more spirit and independence of mind than Nietzsche, with his dubious 'caution'. On the other hand, his observation about the whole Wagner cult is still valid – that it is a 'mild epidemic of sensuality that does not know it'; and it is only this phrase 'that does not know it' which may irritate and frustrate a certain desire for clarity in the face of Wagner's Romantic popularity. It may be one reason why some 'prefer not to be part of it'.

Wagner's dramatic ability to unite the popular and the intellectual in a single figure is most perfectly revealed in the hero of his revolutionary period, Siegfried. The 'breathless delight' that the future theatre director of Bayreuth felt one day as he watched a puppet show – and which he describes in his essay 'On Actors and Singers' – is turned to practical, productive purpose in the dramatization of the *Ring*, that supreme piece of popular entertainment, with its uncomplicated hero. Who can deny the striking resemblance between this Siegfried and the little fellow who wields the slapstick in the fairground booth? Yet at the same time he is the son of light, Nordic sun myth – which does not prevent him, thirdly, from being something very modern and nineteenth-century: the free man, the breaker of old tablets and renewer of a corrupt society – or 'Bakunin', as Bernard Shaw's cheery rationalism always terms him. Harlequin, god of light, and anarchistic social revolutionary, all in the same person: what more could the theatre possibly ask for? And this art of commingling is only an expression of Wagner's own commingled and thoroughly equivocal nature. He is neither poet nor musician, but a third kind of being in which these two attributes are fused together in a unique way: a Dionysus of the theatre, who knows how to underpin the most extravagant expressive processes with poetry and in a certain sense to rationalize them. But to the extent that he *is* a poet after all, he is not a poet in the modern, cultural and literary meaning of one who creates from the mind and from consciousness, but in an altogether more religious and profound sense: it is the soul of the people that speaks from him and through him, and he is only its mouthpiece and instrument – only 'God's ventriloquist', to quote Nietzsche's *bon mot*. This at least is the accepted and orthodox interpretation of his poetic gift; and there is a certain element of gigantic amateurism about it, measured by cultural and literary standards, which appears to support this interpretation. Yet at the same time he is capable of writing in a letter: 'Let us not underrate the power of reflection. The work of art that is produced unconsciously *belongs to periods of history remote from our own*: the work of art that belongs to an age of high cultural refinement can only be a product of the conscious mind.' This is a slap in the face for the theory that imputes a wholly mythical origin to his work; and in fact, alongside those elements which bear the stamp of inspiration and blind-beatific rapture, there is so much in it that has been cleverly thought out, so much that is richly allusive and carefully structured, so much thoughtful spadework to set beside the giant sweep of god-like creation, that it is impossible to suppose it the product of some dark, irrational trance. The extraordinary discernment he displays in his critical writings is not in fact in the service of the mind, 'the truth', or abstract understanding, but of his own creative *oeuvre*, which it seeks to explain and justify, and for which it aims to prepare the ground in both a private and a formal sense: but it is no less real for all that. The other possibility is that he himself was totally excluded from the creative process, that he yielded entirely to the promptings of the popular soul. But our own feeling that it cannot have been like this is confirmed by all kinds of more or less authentic reports from his immediate circle, suggesting that sheer staying power often had to take the place of spontaneous inspiration with him; that on his own admission he was able to do his best work only with the aid of reflection; and by such remarks attributed to him as: 'I tell you I have tried and tried, thought and thought, until I finally found what I was looking for.'

In short, his poetic and artistic gifts are linked on the one hand to periods of history 'remote from our own', while on the other they belong to those in which the evolution of the human brain towards modern intellectualism has long since been accomplished; and this is reflected in the indissoluble blend of the daemonic and the bourgeois in Wagner's nature – very similar to the case of Schopenhauer, who in this respect is closely akin to him as a contemporary and as a personality. The decidedly unbourgeois extremism of his character, which he attributes to the influence of music – 'It simply turns me into a thoroughly exclamatory person,' he said, 'and the exclamation mark is really the only adequate form of punctuation for me once I have left my notes behind!' – this extremism is expressed in the enthusiastic nature of all his mental states, particularly the depressive ones; it emerges in his outward fortunes (fortune being but the consequence of character), in his troubled relationship with the world, in a life filled with conflict and rejection, persecution and turmoil, summed up by him in dramatic verse through the mouth of his Woeful-Siegmund:

I sought out menfolk and women: whomever I found, wherever I found them, whether man or woman I sought to win – always I was an outcast, misfortune lay upon me. Whatever I thought right, others rejected as wrong; whatever I thought wrong, others favoured as right. Wherever I was, there was strife; anger followed me wherever I went; though I sought pleasure, I found only pain.

Every single word is born of experience; there is not one that could not be said to describe his own life exactly, and these lovely lines simply say in verse what he puts into prose in a letter to Mathilde Wesendonck: '... since the world, properly speaking, really doesn't want me', or again to her husband:

> ... that it is so hard to find a place for me in this world, so that I am bound to go astray at every turn. I am in a parlous state ... So we stand opposed, the world and I, like two battling rams, and obviously the one with the thinner skull is going to be crushed – which probably explains where I get most of my nervous head-aches from.

This desperate levity is all part of the general picture. Sometimes – when he was around the age of 48 – he spoke of the 'crazy moods' with which he used to entertain everybody in Weimar, and only because he dare not risk becoming serious, not ever again, lest he fall prey to an almost crippling emotional vulnerability.

> This is a failing in my temperament which is now coming increasingly to the fore. I try and control it as best I can, for I fear that one day I might cry myself to death.

What intemperate weakness! What Hoffmannesque eccentricity! The violent ups and downs of his nature, its tempestuous, tragic pathos, stylized into a black, accursed restlessness and yearning for peace and redemption, are most forcefully portrayed in the *Holländer*, where they are used to marvellous effect to animate and colour the central character: just by his use of large intervals in the rise and fall of the Dutchman's vocal part Wagner manages (in a particularly clear example of his technique) to create this impression of furious unrest.

Clearly he was not bourgeois in the sense of one who subscribes to convention and conformity. But for all that he breathes the air of the bourgeoisie, the air of his age – the same air that is breathed by Schopenhauer, the capitalist philosopher: a moralistic pessimism, a mood of decline set to music, which are archetypally nineteenth-century, and which that epoch combines with monumentality, with outsize form, as though size in itself were the natural attribute of morality. He breathes, I say again, an atmosphere of the bourgeois, not only in this general sense, but in a much more personal sense as well. I do not propose to make much of the fact that he was a revolutionary of 1848, a champion of the middle classes, and therefore a politically-minded citizen; for he was political in his own special way, as an artist and in the interests of his art, which was revolutionary in character, and which he thought would benefit in some intangible way, in terms of gaining a better hearing, from the overthrow of the existing order. But some more private aspects of his personality seem distinctly bourgeois amidst all the brilliance and creative fire, as when he writes to Liszt in a mood of comfortable contentment after moving into the *Asyl* on the green hill near Zurich:

> Everything has been disposed and furnished for a long-term stay, in accordance with my wishes and needs; everything is in its rightful place. My study has been disposed *with that fastidious care and elegant comfort which you know of old in me*; my desk is positioned under the large window ...

The fastidious tidiness and bourgeois elegance of the surroundings that he needed for his work are of a piece with that element of reflectiveness and assiduous craftsmanship which his daemonic creativity does not eschew, and which represents, precisely, its bourgeois aspect: his subsequent self-dramatization as 'German master craftsman', complete with Dürer headgear, had its own innate and natural justification, and it would be wrong to see only the white-hot eruptive fire in his work and to ignore the element of traditional Old-German craftsmanship – that honest perseverance, pride in workmanship and ingenious diligence which are an integral part of it. To Otto Wesendonck he writes:

> Let me tell you briefly about the current state of my work. When I took it up, I had every hope of being able to complete it at great speed ... Partly I was so beset with cares and worries of every kind that there were often long periods when I simply couldn't work at all; but partly too I soon learned to recognize my own characteristic approach to my present works with such clarity and

certainty – realizing that I *cannot* produce them in a hurry, and that I can be satisfied with them only to the extent that every last detail is based on a good idea, properly elaborated – that I could never accept the kind of sketchy, slapdash work that can only result from spending too little time on it.

This is that 'loyalty and honesty' which Schopenhauer claimed to have inherited from his mercantile forbears and translated into the intellectual sphere – the thoroughness and bourgeois meticulousness that are mirrored in his musical scores, not dashed off on to the page, but written with the utmost care and neatness – particularly the score of his most rapturous work, *Tristan*, which is a model of clear and painstaking penmanship.

But at the same time it cannot be denied that Wagner's fondness for middle-class elegance shows a tendency to degeneracy, a strong tendency to assume characteristics that no longer have anything to do with the German sixteenth century, with master craftsman status and Dürer headgear, but which represent the nineteenth century at its international worst – in a word, the characteristics of bourgeois vulgarity. His private and artistic persona contains elements that are not only traditionally and solidly middle-class but also 'bourgeois' in the modern sense – a taste for the opulent, for luxury and wealth, for velvets and silks and lavish Wilhelminian splendour: a private, personal trait in the first instance, but one that reaches deep down into his intellectual and artistic being. Ultimately Wagner's art is a product of the same historical and aesthetic milieu as those elaborate dried-flower arrangements (complete with peacock feathers) by Makart which used to grace the padded and gilded salons of the bourgeoisie; and we know for a fact that he planned to commission Makart to paint some sets for him. To Frau Ritter he writes:

> I've recently developed a passion for luxury again (although any-one who realizes what it is meant to replace in my life will think me exceedingly frugal): in the mornings I sit down in this luxury and I work – that is the most important thing, and a morning without work is a day spent in hell ...

It is hard to say which seems more bourgeois – the love of luxury, or the fact that a morning without *work* appears so utterly intoler-able. But here we approach the point where the bourgeois suddenly turns into the disturbingly artistic, outrageous and disreputable, acquiring a stamp of touching and venerably interesting morbidity for which the term 'bourgeois' suddenly no longer seems appropriate – and we enter the strange realm of *stimulation*, to which Wagner alludes in very reticent terms in a letter to Liszt:

> It is only with real desperation, in fact, that I keep on returning to art. When this happens and I am compelled to renounce reality once more – when I am compelled to plunge once more into the waters of artistic imagination in order to gratify myself in a world of fantasy – then my imagination must at least have some help, and my powers of fantasy be given some assistance. I cannot then live like a dog, bedding myself down on straw and drinking rough liquor: I must feel myself cosseted somehow, if my mind is to succeed in the bitter and onerous task of creating a world that does not exist ... When I recently took up the *Nibelungen* project again and resolved to carry it into execution, many things had to conspire to create in me the requisite mood of artistic sensuality: I had to be able to live better than I did latterly!

His special 'passion for luxury' – the particular form of cosseting that his powers of fantasy needed – is well known: the down-lined silk dressing gowns in which he wrapped himself, the satin counterpanes with their rich braiding and rose garlands under which he slept – these palpable intimations of a lavish extravagance for which he incurred debts running into thousands. The brilliant satin robes are the luxury in which he sits down to work in the mornings, to perform his bitter and onerous task. Decked out in these, he acquires the 'mood of artistic sensuality' he needs in order to summon up the world of ancient Nordic heroes and the sublime symbolism of nature, to fashion the young, golden-locked hero forging the sword of victory on the anvil while the sparks fly – scenes and images that cause the hearts of German youth to swell with lofty feelings of manly pride.

The contradiction proves nothing at all. Nobody takes the rotten apples in Schiller's desk, whose smell nearly caused Goethe to faint, to be an argument against the true sublimity of Schiller's works. Wagner's working conditions happened to be more extravagant, and of course one could easily imagine more appropriate forms of costume than silk dressing gowns to aid the stern labours of artistic creation – a monkish habit, for example, or the uniform of a soldier. But in both cases this is merely an instance of standard artistic pathology, bizarre but innocuous, to which none but the philistine could take exception. And yet there *is* a difference between them. Schiller's work contains no hint of the rotten apples whose odour of decay so stimulated him. But who can fail to see that Wagner's satins are in some way still there in the finished work? It is quite true: Schiller's idealistic will is more purely and unequivocally embodied in the impact of his work, in the way in which it conquered mankind, than Wagner's moral convictions are expressed in the manner of *his* work's impact. His beliefs as a cultural reformer were directed against the idea of art as luxury, against luxury in art; he believed in the cleansing and spiritualization of operatic drama, which for him was synonymous with art itself. Rossini he referred to contemptuously as the 'sensual son of Italia, wallowing blithely in the lap of luxury', while dismissing all Italian opera music as a 'whore' and its French counterpart as a 'cold-smiling coquette'. But are his moral hatred and rejection of such an art revealed as felicitously as they might be in the character and resources of his own art, in the means whereby it came to captivate and subjugate bourgeois society throughout Europe and the world? Was it not that element of the delicious, the sensual-pernicious, sensual-consuming, heavily intoxicating, hypnotically caressing, the thickly and richly padded – in a word, that supremely luxurious element in his music – which drew the bourgeois masses into its arms? In his poem about the two jolly journeymen*, of whom one wastes his life in dissipation, Eichendorff speaks of the element of seduction as 'buhlenden Wogen' [caressing surge], as 'der Wogen farbig klingendem Schlund' [the surge's gorgeous-sounding chasm]. Wonderful words. Only a Romantic poet could evoke sin in such powerfully suggestive language: and in *Tannhäuser* and *Parsifal* Wagner has equalled the poet's achievement. But then, is not his orchestra just such a 'farbig klingender Schlund', from which one awakes 'müde und alt' [tired and old], like Eichendorff's young fop?

If the answer to these questions is in any sort 'yes', then we are dealing with what is called a 'tragic antinomy', one of those contra-

---

* 'Frühlingsfahrt' (1818). TM omits the adjective 'buhlend' in his citation of the second phrase from the poem.

dictions and paradoxical inconsistencies in Wagner's character that are the subject of our present enquiry. There are many of them; and since a good number of them are concerned with the relationship between intention and effect, it is most important to insist on the total and admirable purity and idealism of his artistry, and to safeguard it against any misunderstandings to which the sheer scale and the mass audience appeal of Wagner's success might give rise. Every critic, including Nietzsche, tends to impute the effects of an art to conscious and calculating intent on the part of the artist, and to imply the notion of a planned strategy – quite wrongly and mistakenly, as though any artist could do other than create precisely what he himself *is*, what seems right and proper to him: as though there could exist an artistry whose effects he himself scorns, and that are not first and foremost effects on him, the artist! 'Innocence' may be the very last word that can be applied to any art: but the artist himself is innocent. The enormous popular success 'won' by Wagner's musical drama has never been vouchsafed to great art either before or since. Fifty years after the master's death, his music is played night after night in the four corners of the earth. This art of theatre and mass popular appeal contains elements of imperialist world-domination, of powerful provocation and despotic, demagogic incitement, which might lead one to suppose that its underlying motive force was ambition, a monstrous, overbearing will-to-power. The truth is very different. 'I will tell you this much,' writes Wagner in a letter to his mistress from Paris, 'that only the feeling of my own *purity* gives me this strength. I feel myself to be *pure*: I know in my heart of hearts that I have always laboured for others, never for myself; and to that my constant sufferings bear witness.' If that is not entirely true, it is at least sufficiently truthful to silence all scepticism. He was a stranger to ambition. 'I care nothing for greatness, renown or popular influence,' he assures Liszt. Not even for popular influence? Perhaps in the benign, paternalistic form of popularity that speaks to us with such worthiness and heartfelt pomp from *Die Meistersinger* – an ideal, a fantasy, an attitude to art and the artist that is typically Romantic-democratic. For the popular appeal of Hans Sachs, against whom 'the whole guild' cannot prevail because the people are ready to do anything for him, is indeed a fantasy. In *Die Meistersinger* Wagner flirts with the notion of the people as the supreme judge of art – the antithesis of all élitist exclusivity in art, and wholly characteristic of Wagner's democratic-revolutionary aesthetic, his view of art as a direct appeal to the hearts of the people: in sharp contrast to that aristocratic, classical-courtly concept of art which had once prevailed, and which prompted Voltaire's dictum: 'Quand la populace se mêle de raisonner, tout est perdu.' And yet, when this artist reads his Plutarch, unlike Karl Moor* he feels an aversion for these 'great men', and the very last thing he desires is to be like them.

> Ugly, petty, violent natures, insatiable – for the simple reason that they are empty within, and must be forever gorging themselves on the outside world. You can keep them, your 'great men'! I hold with what Schopenhauer said: 'Not he who conquers the world, but he who overcomes the world is worthy of our admiration'! May God preserve me from these 'mighty' individuals, the Napoleons and all the rest of them.

Which was he – one who overcame the world, or one who conquered? Which of the two is summed up in his formula 'Then I, I am the world!', underscored by the theme of world-eroticism?

But in any case the insinuation of ambition in any normal worldly sense can be dismissed for the simple reason that Wagner was working initially without any hope or prospect of making an immediate impact, which actual circumstances and conditions would not allow – working in a vacuum of his own invention, towards an imaginary, ideal theatre that could not possibly be realized for the present. There is certainly no hint of cool calculation or the ambitious exploitation of existing opportunities in words such as these, addressed to Otto Wesendonck:

> For I see clearly that I am fully myself only when I create. The actual performance of my works belongs to a purer age, an age for which I must prepare the way by my own sufferings! My closest artistic friends are filled with amazement at my new works: but none who is better acquainted with the official art world of our day feels strong enough to hope. All I meet with are sympathy and sadness. And of course they are right. Nothing shows me more clearly how frighteningly far ahead I have moved of all that surrounds me.

* Karl Moor, a character in Schiller's *Die Räuber*.

Never has the loneliness of genius, its alienation from reality, found more moving expression. So are we who span the last few decades of the nineteenth century and the first third of the twentieth, with the World War and the incipient breakdown of late capitalism – we in whose lifetime Wagner's art has conquered the great theatres and triumphed in perfect performances throughout the civilized world – are we that 'purer age', for which he had to 'prepare the way by his own sufferings'? Are the generations of mankind between 1880 and 1933 the ones best qualified to attest, by their overwhelming acclaim of one man's art, the true stature and quality of that art?

Let us not ask. Let us note, rather, how his greatness proves itself in the way it tries to accommodate itself to the world – but without success! A comic little opera, a satyr play to *Tannhäuser*, something for him and the public to relax with, the sincere desire to produce an accessible entertainment in lighter vein – and the result is *Die Meistersinger*. Or what about something in the Italian manner, melodious, lyrical and tuneful, with a small cast, simple to stage – now *that* ought to be possible: and what emerges is *Tristan*. A man cannot make himself smaller than he is, and he cannot make himself different; a man creates what a man is, and all art is truth – the truth about the artist.

So the enormous universal impact of this art springs from personal roots that are conspicuously intellectual and pure, not only in terms of its sheer high standards, which despise nothing more than the 'mere' effect, the effect without a cause, but also because all the imperialist, demagogic and crowd-swaying elements in it are to be interpreted in the first instance in a wholly hypothetical and ideal sense, having reference to conditions that must first be transformed by revolution. And this artistic innocence obtains pre-eminently where a richly instrumented will-to-inspire expresses itself in the *appeal to nationalism*, in the celebration and glorification of things German – seen at its most obvious in *Lohengrin*, when King Henry invokes 'the German sword', and in *Die Meistersinger*, through the worthy sentiments of Hans Sachs. It is thoroughly inadmissible to ascribe a contemporary meaning to Wagner's nationalist gestures and speeches – the meaning that they would have today. To do so is to falsify and abuse them, to sully their romantic purity.

When Wagner introduced the national concept into his work as a familiarly potent theme – before, that is, it had been realized in practice – it was still in its heroic, historically legitimate era, the time when it was valid, fully alive and authentic, when it was pure poetry and spirit, an ideal aspiration. It is nothing but demagogy when today the 'German sword' lines – or indeed that key statement at the end of *Die Meistersinger*: 'Zerging' in Dunst das Heil'ge Röm'sche Reich, uns bliebe gleich die heil'ge deutsche Kunst' [And were the Holy Roman Empire to fade away, Holy German Art is here to stay!] – are thundered tendentiously into the auditorium by the basses, in order to achieve an added patriotic effect. It is these very lines – the first to take firm shape, and already there at the end of the earliest sketch, the Marienbad draft of 1845 – that prove how totally intellectual and apolitical Wagner's nationalism was: for they speak of a downright anarchic indifference to political structures, as long as German intellectual and spiritual values – 'German Art' – are preserved intact. That what he had in mind was not actually German art, but his own brand of musical drama, which is by no means exclusively German, having assimilated not only Weber, Marschner and Lortzing, but also Spontini and grand opera – that is another question altogether. At bottom he may well have thought as Goethe, the greatest non-patriot of them all, was accused of thinking by Börne: 'What do the Germans want? They have me, after all.'

All his life Richard Wagner was more of a socialist and cultural utopian in his political beliefs – looking to the kind of classless society, freed from luxury and the curse of gold and founded on love, that he saw as the ideal audience for his art – than a patriot in the aggressive, nationalistic sense. His heart was on the side of the poor against the rich. He did his level best, later on, to play down his involvement in the revolutionary disturbances of 1848, which cost him twelve years of painful exile, looking back with shame on such 'detestable' optimism and equating the *fait accompli* of Bismarck's Reich, as well as he was able, with the realization of his own dreams. He went the way of the German middle classes: from revolution to disillusion, and finally to pessimism and a resigned turning-inwards under the protection of a powerful state. Yet his writings contain what is, in a way, a highly un-German dictum: 'The man who seeks to evade politics only deceives himself.' Such a lively and radical mind was naturally aware of the underlying unity of the human dilemma, the inseparability of mind and politics; he did not subscribe to the self-delusion of the German middle classes that one can be cultivated and unpolitical – the delusion that has been the cause of Germany's wretchedness. Before the foundation of the Reich and before he made his home in Bayreuth, Wagner's relationship to his fatherland was that of a man isolated, misunderstood and rejected, full of hostile criticism and contempt. 'How filled I am with enthusiasm for the Confederation of German Nations!' he writes from Lucerne in 1859. 'By heavens, that evil scoundrel Louis Napoleon had better not lay a finger on my beloved German Confederation! I should be too, too distressed if anything were to change in that quarter ...' The longing for Germany that so consumed him in his exile was replaced by bitter disappointment at the reality he found when he did return home. 'This is a wretched land,' he cries, 'and a certain Herr Ruge was right when he said: "The Germans are despicable."' It should be noted that such malicious sentiments are elicited solely by the lack of response in Germany to his works; their tone is one of childish pique. Germany is good or bad to the extent that it believes in him or falters in its belief. As late as 1875, when some well-wisher observed in company that nobody had ever been so enthusiastically received by the German public as he, Wagner could still reply with bitter humour: 'Oh yes! The Sultan and the Khedive of Egypt have taken up subscription bonds.'

It does credit to his artist's soul that he was able none the less (unlike Nietzsche) to discern the fulfilment of his patriotic wishes in the re-creation of the German Reich through Bismarck's wars, and was able and willing to recognize, in the Reich that Nietzsche never tired of vilifying, the right and proper soil for his cultural undertaking. The resurrection of the German Reich – without Austria – was a staggeringly successful historical achievement, which reinforced Wagner's belief (as his friend Heckel tells us) in the evolution of a truly German art and culture – which is to say, in the receptive possibilities for his own artistic work, the sublimated opera. Out of that confidence was born the 'Kaisermarsch', and the poem addressed to the German army before Paris, a work that only proves the point that Wagner without music is no poet; out of it too came 'Eine Kapitulation', that unbelievably tasteless satire on the death throes of Paris in 1871 – a self-betrayal in every sense of the word. But the principal fruit of this confidence was his manifesto, 'On the Staging of the Festival Drama *Der Ring des Nibelungen*', which elicited one solitary offer of support from the aforementioned Heckel, who was a pianoforte dealer in Mannheim. Opposition to Wagner's ambitions and claims, and a reluctance to take his part, remained considerable; but the year that saw the proclamation of the new German Reich also saw the foundation of the first Wagner Association and the issue of subscription bonds for the Festival Drama cycle. The process of becoming established, of carrying ideas into practice – full of compromises, as such things always are – had begun. Wagner was enough of a politician to ally his own cause with that of Bismarck's Reich: he recognized an unparalleled success, yoked his own to it, and the European hegemony of his art became the cultural appurtenance to Bismarck's political hegemony. The great statesman to whose work he wedded his own understood nothing of the latter, never took the slightest interest in it, and dismissed Wagner as a crackpot. But the ageing Kaiser – who also understood nothing of it – came to Bayreuth and said: 'I never thought you'd bring it off!' The Wagnerian *oeuvre* had been recognized as a matter of national importance, part of the official life of the Reich, and it has always been associated, in a sense, with the Imperial black, white and red – little enough though it has to do in its deepest essence, or even in the manner of its Germanness, with any authoritarian or martial conceptions of empire.

Any discussion of the contradictions and intertwined complexities of Wagner's character must take account of that magnificent blend of the German and the cosmopolitan which is part and parcel of that character, and which distinguishes it in an absolutely unique and thought-provoking way. There has always existed – there exists still – a German art of great distinction (and I am thinking particularly of literature) that belongs so wholly to the Germany of quiet inwardness and domesticity, that is so peculiarly and intimately German, that it can achieve its effects and inspire admiration – in the worthiest possible manner – only in the domestic sphere, lacking any wider European or international appeal. Such art has its place just like any other, and the question of merit does not enter into it. Far lesser material – staple, run-of-the-mill stuff to suit the popular taste – is instantly exportable, and, being common, is only too well understood everywhere; but other works, which are not a whit inferior to that exclusively domestic art in terms of quality and stature, have manifestly been anointed with that drop of democratic-European oil which gives them an entrée into the world at large and assures them of an international reception.

Wagner's art is of this type – except that in his case one cannot very well speak of a 'drop' of anointing oil: his art positively drips with it. Its Germanness is profound, potent and beyond all doubt. The birth of drama out of the spirit of music, as it is accomplished in pure and enchanting form at least once, at the height of Wagner's creative powers, in *Tristan und Isolde*, could only have come out of the German experience; and we may properly regard as 'German' in the highest sense of the word its colossal ingenuity, its penchant for myth and its metaphysical drive, but more than anything else its deeply serious self-awareness as art, that lofty and solemn conception of art (or rather, of the theatre) with which it is imbued and which it communicates to its audience. Yet at the same time it is made for the larger world, and accessible to the larger world, as no other German art of this rank ever has been, and to infer its 'will', its character, from its empirical manifestation is to think very much along the lines favoured by its creator. I referred once before to a book written by a non-German, by the Swede Wilhelm Peterson-Berger – *Richard Wagner als Kulturerscheinung* [Richard Wagner as Cultural Phenomenon] – which has some very perceptive observations on this point. The author writes of Wagner's nationalism, of his art as a national German art, and observes that the only genre *not* absorbed into his great synthesis is German folk music. Although he is capable of sounding a folksy German note from time to time for purposes of characterization, as in *Die Meistersinger* and *Siegfried*, this never constitutes the keynote and starting point of his musical writing – is never the *source* from which it wells up spontaneously, as in the work of Schumann, Schubert and Brahms. There is a necessary distinction to be made, he argues, between folk art and national art; the former is aimed at a domestic audience, the latter at an international one. Wagner's music is more national than popular; to the foreigner as such it may appear typically German in many respects, but at the same time – as the Swedish writer puts it – it has an unmistakably cosmopolitan cachet.

Here, it seems to me, Wagner's peculiar brand of Germanness has been analysed with remarkable subtlety and sensitivity. Wagner is indeed 'German' and 'national' to an exemplary - perhaps all too exemplary - degree. For *as well as* being an eruptive revelation of the German character, this *oeuvre* is also a theatrical representation of it - and a representation whose intellectualism and brash force-fulness of impact extend to the point of caricature and parody, and appear destined to elicit from an international audience tremoring with horrified curiosity a cry of: 'Ah! ça c'est bien allemand par exemple!' True and potent though it is, then, this Germanness is refracted and fragmented in the modern mode, is decorative, analyti-cal and intellectual - hence its powerful fascination, its innate capa-city for cosmopolitan, not to say planetary influence. Wagner's art is the most sensational self-portrayal and self-critique of the German character that could possibly be imagined; as such it is calculated to make German culture interesting even to the most doltish foreigner, and a passionate preoccupation with this art is necessarily and always a passionate preoccupation with that selfsame Germanness which it glorifies in a manner both critical and decorative. Therein lies its nationalism; but that nationalism is steeped in a European artistry to a degree that renders it profoundly unsusceptible to any simplifica-tion - especially of the simple-minded variety.

'You will be serving the cause of one whom the future will single out as the most illustrious among all the masters.' These words were written in 1849 by Charles Baudelaire to a young German music critic who was an ardent admirer of Wagner. This prediction, aston-ishing in its accuracy, was born of ardent love, kindred passion, and it is a mark of Nietzsche's critical genius that he was able to recog-nize this kinship without knowing of its utterances. 'Since Baudelaire was the first in his day to champion the unknown Delacroix,' he writes in the sketches for *Der Fall Wagner* [The Case of Wagner], 'perhaps he would now be the first "Wagnerian" in Paris. There is a lot of Wagner in Baudelaire.' It was not until years later that he saw the letter in which Wagner thanks the French poet for his words of tribute; and he enjoyed his triumph. Yes, Baudelaire, the earliest admirer of Delacroix - that Wagner of painting - was indeed the first Wagnerian in Paris, and one of the first genuine, deeply affected and artistically sympathetic Wagnerians to be found anywhere. His

Tannhäuser essay of 1861 was the first crucial and epoch-making discussion of Wagner, and it has remained the most significant in historical terms. The joy of rediscovering himself in the artistic intentions of another, such as Wagner's music afforded him, was something he only ever knew on one other occasion, when he made the literary acquaintance of Edgar Allan Poe. These two, Wagner and Poe, were Baudelaire's gods – a strange-sounding combination to German ears! The propinquity with Poe suddenly places Wagner's art in a new light, transposing it into a psychological context in which its patriotic interpreters have not accustomed us to seeing it. A brightly coloured and fantastic world opens up before us at the mention of his name, the world of Western Romanticism in its high and late periods, intoxicated with death and beauty – a world of pessimism, of intimate acquaintance with exotic drugs and an over-refinement of the senses that indulges rapturously in all manner of synaesthetic speculation, the dreams of Hoffmann/Kreisler of the correspondences and intimate relations between colours, sounds and perfumes, of the mystical transformation of the interfused senses . . . Such is the world into which Richard Wagner must be projected, in which he must be imagined: as the most illustrious confrère and comrade of all these symbolists for whom life was an affliction, who espoused compassion and sought after ecstasy, blenders of the arts and worshippers of 'l'art suggestif', impelled by the need 'd'aller au delà, plus outre que l'humanité', as Maurice Barrès put it – the last of that brotherhood, the lover of Venice, city of *Tristan*, the author of *Du sang, de la volupté et de la mort*, nationalist at the end and Wagnerian from beginning to end.

> 'Sind es Wellen / sanfter Lüfte?
> Sind es Wogen / wonniger Düfte?
> Wie sie schwellen / mich umrauschen,
> soll ich atmen / soll ich lauschen?
> Soll ich schlürfen / untertauchen,
> süß in Düften / mich verhauchen?
> In des Wonnemeeres / wogendem Schwall,
> in der Duftwellen / tönendem Schall,
> in des Weltatems / wehendem All –
> ertrinken – / versinken –
> unbewußt – / höchste Lust!

Are they breezes / gently wafting?
Or perfumes sweet / and scents so soft?
How full they flow / to fill my senses,
Shall I breathe / or shall I hearken?
Shall I drink / and sink below,
In scents of sweetness / breathe my last?
In the sea of bliss / the billowing surge
In the flood of scent / the sound's sweet urge,
In the universal breath / where all things merge –
Drowning – / sinking –
All sense benighted – / bliss requited!

This is the ultimate, the supreme statement of that world, its culmination and triumph, stamped and imbued with its spirit, whose European, mystical-sensual artistry was stylized by Wagner and the young Nietzsche into an improving German idiom and related to tragedy, with Euripides, Shakespeare and Beethoven as their major points of reference. In his irritation at a certain characteristic German vagueness in matters of psychology, Nietzsche subsequently revised his views, overemphasizing Wagner's European artistry and pouring scorn on his German master craftsman image. He was wrong. Wagner's commitment to German culture was genuine and profound. That Romanticism should have attained its climax and won universal acclaim in German, and under the guise of trusty Teutonic craftsmanship, was foreordained in its very nature.

A final word about Wagner's intellectual position, about his relationship with the past and the future. Here again his character exhibits a dualism, an interweaving of seeming contradictions, corresponding to the antithesis between Germanism and Europeanism. There are *reactionary* elements in Wagner, elements of backward-lookingness and obscurantist worship of the past; his fondness for the mystical and the ancient mythic-legendary, the Protestant nationalism of *Die Meistersinger* and the Catholicizing in *Parsifal*, his predilection for the Middle Ages, for the world of knights and princes, for miracles and burning religious faith – all this could be interpreted in this sense. And yet every instinct for the real and true nature of this artistic enterprise, directed wholly as it is towards renewal, change and emancipation, strictly forbids us to take its language and mode of expression literally, instead of for what it really is: an artistic idiom of a highly figurative kind, whose real purport at every turn is quite different and entirely revolutionary. This creative mind, charged with life and vehemently progressive for all its melancholia and attachment to death; this glorifier of the world-destroyer who was born of the most sensual union; this audacious musical innovator, who in *Tristan* already stands with one foot on atonal soil, and whose like would assuredly be branded a *Kultur*-Bolshevist today; this man of the *people*, who all his life set his face resolutely against power, money, violence and war, and who thought to build his Festival Theatre for a classless society (whatever the times may subsequently have turned it into): let no spirit of pious or brutal regression claim him for its own – but all those whose endeavours are directed towards the future.

But it is futile to invoke the spirits of departed great men in order to ask them their opinions – if any – on problems of contemporary life with which they were not confronted as such, and which are alien to their intellectual experience. What view would Richard Wagner take of our present problems, needs and tasks? That 'would' is empty and chimeric, a conceptual nonsense. Opinions are of secondary importance, even in their own day; how much more so in a later age! What endures is the man himself, and the fruit of his struggle, his work. Let us be content to honour Wagner's work as a powerful and complex phenomenon of German and Western European life, which will ever continue to serve as a profound stimulus to art and knowledge.

A Protest from Richard Wagner's
Own City of Munich*

Now that the uprising of Germany as a nation has assumed stable institutional form, it can no longer be regarded as an unwarranted diversion if we now address the public at large in order to protect the memory of that great German Master, Richard Wagner, against defamation. We regard Wagner as the musical-dramatic embodiment of the deepest German sensibilities, which we will not permit to be insulted by the kind of aestheticizing snobbery that finds such arrogant and pretentious expression in the commemorative addresses on the subject of Richard Wagner delivered by Herr Thomas Mann.

Having had the misfortune to forfeit his one-time national sentiments at the time of the establishment of the Republic, exchanging them for cosmopolitan-democratic views, Herr Mann has failed to draw from this the lessons of a modest and decent reticence, but has elected to make a name for himself abroad as a spokesman for the German spirit. In Brussels and Amsterdam and elsewhere he has described Wagner's figures as a 'fertile field for Freudian psychoanalysis', and characterized his work as 'a case of dilettantism that has been monumentalized by a supreme effort of the will'. His music, we are told, is not music in the pure sense, nor are the texts of his operas pure literature. It is 'the music of an oppressed soul, lacking the élan of dance'. At bottom (he says) there is an element of the philistine about him.

If this in itself must be accounted ignorant presumption in the context of a commemorative address, the critical affront is made quite insufferable by the lukewarm and patronizing praise that Wagner's music is accorded on the grounds that it is 'made for the larger world, and accessible to the larger world', and represents a blend 'of the German and the modern'.

* 'Protest der Richard-Wagner-Stadt München', *Münchner Neueste Nachrichten*, 16/17 April 1933. TM's reply to the 'Protest', which he believed had been initiated by the conductor Hans Knappertsbusch, follows on pp. 151-3.

We are not disposed to tolerate such disparaging treatment of our great German musical genius from anyone – and most certainly not from Herr Thomas Mann, who has furnished the most telling critique and revelation of his own true nature by revising his *Reflections of a Non-political Man* after his conversion to the republican system in such a way that the meaning of the key passages was completely reversed. Any man who has shown himself to be so completely unreliable and unknowledgeable in his published works has no right whatsoever to criticize German intellectual giants of enduring merit.

Max Amann, publisher and Member of the Reichstag

Dr Arthur Bauckner, Director of the State Theatre

Prof. Hermann Bauer, President of the United Patriotic Associations of Bavaria

Dr Alexander Berrsche, musicologist

Prof. German Bestelmeyer, Privy Councillor and President of the Academy of Fine Arts

Prof. Bernhard Bleeker, sculptor

Prof. Gottfried Boehm

Prof. Reinhard Demoll, Privy Councillor

Max Doerner, Full Academic Professor

Prof. Friedrich Dörnhöffer, Privy Councillor and former Director General of the Bavarian State Gallery (retired)

Friedrichfranz Feeser, Major General (retired)

Karl Fiehler, Chief Burgomaster

Clemens von Franckenstein, General Manager of the Bavarian State Theatre

Prof. Walther Gerlach

Hermann Groeber, Full Academic Professor

Olaf Gulbransson, Full Academic Professor

Hermann Hahn, Privy Councillor and Full Academic Professor

Prof. Siegmund von Hausegger, Privy Councillor and President of the Academy of Music

Julius Hess, Full Academic Professor

Dr Ludwig Hoeflmayr, Senior Public Health Officer

Angelo Jank, Privy Councillor and Full Academic Professor

Franz Klemmer, Full Academic Professor

Prof. Hans Knappertsbusch, Director of the Bavarian State Opera

Dr Hans Küfner, Privy Councillor and Burgomaster elect

Friedrich Langenfass, Dean

Wilhelm Leupold, publisher of the *Münchener Zeitung*

Carl von Marr, Privy Councillor, former Director of the Academy (retired) and painter

Wilhelm Matthes, musicologist

Karl Miller, Full Academic Professor

The Board of the Musical Academy: Eduard Niedermayr, Michael Uffinger, Hermann Tuckermann, Emil Wagner

Fred Ottow, Editor of the *München-Augsburger-Abendzeitung*

Josef Pschorr, Privy Councillor of Commerce and President of the Chamber of Industry and Commerce

Prof. Hans Pfitzner, Musical Director

Christoph Röschlein, First President of the Upper Bavarian Chamber of Trades and Crafts

Hans Schemm, Minister in the Bavarian State Government

Adolf Schiedt, Editor of the *Münchener Zeitung*

Adolf Schinnerer, Full Academic Professor

Dr Hans Schmelzle, Councillor and President of the Bavarian Higher Administrative Court

Prof. Georg Sittmann, Privy Councillor

Dr Richard Strauss, Musical Director

Adolf Wagner, Minister in the Bavarian State Government

Fritz Westermann, First Chairman of the Bayreuth League

Reply to the 'Protest from Richard Wagner's Own City of Munich'*

As we reported on 18 April, a number of eminent persons associated with the artistic life of Munich – including such figures as Richard Strauss, Hans Pfitzner and Olaf Gulbransson – have issued a public statement against Thomas Mann in which they charge him with

* Letter dated 19 April 1933, Lugano, published in the *Vossische Zeitung* (Berlin), 21 April 1933.

having insulted the name of Richard Wagner by 'aestheticizing snob-
bery' in his recent address to commemorate the Master. We imme-
diately pointed out that such an accusation against an avowed ad-
mirer of Wagner was bound to affect Thomas Mann deeply, both as
a man and as an artist. Today we print the author's reply to that
accusation.

'A passion for Wagner's enchanted *oeuvre* has been a part of my life
ever since I first became aware of it and set out to make it my own,
to invest it with understanding.' That sentence is a quotation from
an extended critical essay which I published in the April number of
the *Neue Rundschau* under a title that says a good deal about the
approach and spirit of the work – 'The Sorrows and Grandeur of
Richard Wagner'. The piece contains many such sentences; but this has
not prevented it from becoming the target of a violent protest, the
which, issued in the name of a large number of Munich dignitaries,
has not only been published in the *Münchner Neueste Nachrichten*,
but also broadcast over the Munich radio station.

The text of this document, filled as it is with grave slurs on my
character and my opinions, does not refer explicitly or directly to the
original essay. It does not quote it by name, nor does it state where
it was published, thus making it difficult for the reader to check the
validity of the charges made against me. The protest speaks of lectures I have given in a number of foreign cities, in which I have
allegedly disparaged the name of the German Master abroad. To prove
his point, the author has taken a number of quotations out of their
original context in the *Rundschau* essay and dished them up to a mass
radio audience in a manner calculated to jeopardize a just appreciation
of my intentions and stir up the wrath of the nation against me.

The truth of the matter is that I drew on that fifty-two page essay,
which is a passionately written summary of all that Wagner has come
to mean to me, for the substance of a public lecture that I have so
far delivered on four separate occasions in connection with the recent
anniversary. While the original essay was conceived as a definitive
literary statement, full of nuances and shades of meaning, the lecture
was intended for a specific festive occasion, and as such, of course,
it eschewed a good deal of psychological cut and thrust that might
have run counter to the spirit of such an occasion. I delivered it for

the first time on 10 February in the Great Hall of the University of Munich, at the invitation of the Munich Goethe Society – to enthusiastic applause from an audience of some 500 persons, and without exciting any hint of protest or disagreement. I delivered it again on the fiftieth anniversary of Wagner's death in the Concertgebouw in Amsterdam, and then again, in French, in Brussels and Paris. On each occasion it was followed with the most attentive interest by an audience of ardent Wagner lovers. The official representatives of the German Reich in the various capitals were present at these gatherings, and they expressed to me their thanks for the service I had thereby rendered the German name. Yet the protest issued by 'Wagner's Own City of Munich' – as the signatories collectively describe themselves – accuses me of the exact opposite.

I owe it to the German public and to myself to state that this protest proceeds from a gross misunderstanding, and that its content and tone do me a grave and bitter injustice. Hardly any of the honourable, not to say highly distinguished men who appended their names to this document can even have read my essay 'The Sorrows and Grandeur of Richard Wagner', for only a complete ignorance of the role that Richard Wagner's gigantic *oeuvre* has always played in my life and work could have persuaded them to associate themselves with this malicious attack on a German writer.

I therefore urge all those in Germany who look with quiet favour on my work not to doubt for one moment my loyalty to German culture and tradition – or my loyalty to them.

To Willi Schuh*

Villa Castagnola, Lugano
21 April 1933

Dear Herr Schuh,
You must allow me to express my heartfelt thanks to you for the kind and forceful things you have said in connection with the Munich

* Willi Schuh (b. 1900), music editor of the *Neue Zürcher Zeitung* and prolific author on musical subjects.

'Case of Wagner'. Your article* in particular is to me a sign and surety that the discredit in this sad and foolish affair will one day redound on its authors and their more or less orchestrated band of followers. I am delighted that this wretched episode has given me an opportunity of making the acquaintance, in you, of one who understands my work so well and takes such a kindly interest in it. What began as a truly alarming business is now turning out to be nothing but gain for me.

Yours sincerely,

THOMAS MANN

* 'Thomas Mann, Richard Wagner, und die Münchener Gralshüter' [Thomas Mann, Richard Wagner and the Munich Guardians of the Holy Grail], *Neue Zürcher Zeitung*, 21 April 1933.

Reply to Hans Pfitzner*

On 2 July Hans Pfitzner published an article in the *Frankfurter Zeitung* entitled 'On the Public Statement Denouncing Thomas Mann's Wagner Lecture', which has induced me to break the silence I have observed since my letter from Lugano of 19 April and ask once again for a hearing in this painful affair, which has been attended with such serious consequences for my life and livelihood.

A quarter of a year has passed since that ferocious campaign to defame a German writer was conducted in the press and radio with massive support from eminent public figures: yet still, it seems, the controversy about that campaign and its object – my contribution to the Wagner anniversary celebrations – will not be laid to rest. Is it too fanciful to see some connection between this undeniably remarkable phenomenon and the question posed as long ago as April by a

* Written in Sanary-sur-mer in July 1933, but not published until 1974 in Vol. XIII of *TM: Gesammelte Werke* as *Die Neue Rundschau* refused to print it at the time.

Swiss critic* of the Munich enterprise: 'I wonder if the more thought-ful among these protesters will feel a certain disquiet in a couple of years' time, when they think back to their signature appearing at the foot of this cultural statement?' – a question that was echoed only a few days ago in the *Berliner Tageblatt* as a conjecture about what is already the case: 'Even those who signed the declaration have doubt-less turned aside in the end with feelings of disquiet . . .' No, I believe I am not mistaken: the anniversary has left a mild 'disquiet', a kind of moral uneasiness, at least in the minds of the more sensitive among the signatories – even if all this does not find direct expression in any retraction or qualification, but rather in the form of self-justification and 'attempts to make the facts clear'.

The statement by Hans Pfitzner contains remarks that suggest that in some particulars the attack against me was not entirely to his own taste – although I would certainly not make the mistake of inter-preting the sense of his statement as favourable to me. That sense is clear enough. The composer of *Palestrina* still feels the need to rebut a charge made against him as soon as the Munich manifesto appeared: the charge that, by appending his name to the letter of indictment, he was guilty of an act of ingratitude. I am not at all inclined to share this view. Pfitzner is right when he says that one must put principle before personality: on this point there is no quar-rel between us. But the widespread feeling expressed in that charge – which recurred almost without fail in every counter-statement pub-lished – was very human and very pardonable, and I myself would be guilty of ingratitude if I did not attempt to defend those who have lent me moral support in such difficult and dangerous circumstances against the harsh names that Hans Pfitzner has called them.

'Hangers-on and riff-raff', 'a pack of lackeys' he calls them angrily – but why? The article by Willi Schuh in the *Neue Zürcher Zeitung*, one of the first and most vigorous published replies to the 'Protest from Wagner's Own City of Munich', was sent to him anonymously. The woman who sent it was evidently concerned that the maestro should read the article, and feared that he might miss it (which he probably would have done had it not been for her, since this particular issue of the *Neue Zürcher Zeitung* was not widely circu-lated in Munich); and she would assuredly have remained no less

* Willi Schuh, see p. 153.

'anonymous' if she had put her name to the lines she enclosed with the article. Anonymity can be a very mean subterfuge. But when its motive is modesty, there is no cause for reproof. It sufficed the sender to think of herself and identify herself as one of many – 'one of tens of thousands', as she writes with touching faith. How can such sufficiency be offensive in an age when all happiness and honour are sought and found in being One among Many?

Furthermore, the piece that she sent – 'Thomas Mann, Richard Wagner and the Munich Guardians of the Holy Grail' – cannot remotely be described as anonymous. It was published by the *Neue Zürcher Zeitung* because 'to all those beyond the frontiers of the German Reich who take an active part in German intellectual life the Munich manifesto appears unworthy and damaging to the standing of the new Germany, and should not be allowed to go unchallenged in a country that enjoys freedom of thought and speech'. Now the *Neue Zürcher Zeitung* is no provincial rag, and its music critic, Willi Schuh, is not some plodding hack. His article, which Pfitzner describes as 'workmanlike' (as though anyone could ever point to anything *un*workmanlike in his writing), is journalism of a very high order, which counters the mass attack launched against me and my work with great dignity and firmness; and it brought me too much comfort, in days when I looked with horror upon so much hatred and blood-lust, for me now to stand aside in silence while Hans Pfitzner treats it like dirt – simply because it notes the fact of *his* signature with particular distaste.

But was this writer alone in professing his sympathy for the position I took and his repugnance toward the spirit of the protest campaign? Hans Pfitzner has seen very little if this is the only one of all the 'workmanlike newspaper articles' prompted by the affair that he has seen – and it was only thanks to somebody else, of course, that he even saw this one. All the leading Swiss journals – the *Berner Bund*, the Basle *National-Zeitung* – indeed, the whole of the informed German-language press beyond the frontiers of the Reich, in Vienna, Prague, not to mention the foreign-language press – all have commented on the incident in a manner very similar to that of the Swiss critic (except that some have condemned it even more strongly): and if all this went unnoticed in Germany – and more especially in Munich – then I cannot help but see in this the workings of a self-protective instinct that may well be convenient and conducive to the maintenance of a 'good conscience', but is not without its dangers. To shield oneself against the feeling and judgement of the world with the armour of ignorance, simply because one cannot afford to have one's illusions shattered, is not a wise course of action for any nation to pursue. Let people do what they must, defying what they may call the incomprehension of the foreign mob: but let them *state* their defiance. Let them at least take cognizance of what others are thinking, lest they run the risk of losing touch with reality, with the forces that are actually shaping our intellectual and moral world.

Wilfully ignorant of all that has been said in the educated outside world against the campaign in which he took part; embittered, indeed, by the single sample of world opinion that was sent to him personally; and evidently ignorant, too, of the statements I myself made in April in my letter to the German press, Hans Pfitzner repeats his claim, in his communication to the *Frankfurter Zeitung*, that I disparaged the German Master abroad in my Wagner lectures, thereby dishonouring the name of German culture, and that by such disgraceful conduct I positively invited the 'Protest from Wagner's Own City of Munich' – primarily for the benefit of the foreign public. How can he continue to maintain this fiction, when the record clearly shows that I delivered the lecture for the first time on 10 February in Germany, at the University of Munich, in a longer version than the one I subsequently used abroad, and without encountering the slightest protest – and that the three repeat readings before foreign audiences were extremely well received in a manner that did honour to the name of German culture? 'One was recently made acutely and profoundly aware in Paris', reports the *Baseler Nachrichten*,

of the depth of Franco-German appreciation for Wagner when Thomas Mann delivered a brilliant lecture on 'The Sorrows and Grandeur of Richard Wagner' to a packed theatre auditorium. His interpretation of Wagner as a man of his times and a timeless phenomenon, pointing the way both back to the past and forward to the future, made a profound impression on all those present at this solemn occasion. Thomas Mann's performance was in the starkest possible contrast to the pretentious exhibitions all too often indulged in by many Germans (mostly of the lesser sort) in

France, or indeed wherever they address themselves to the intelligentsia of other nations. For this reason it deserves to be recorded with gratitude as one of the most significant tributes paid by a living German artist of stature to a dead predecessor – a tribute that made a lasting and indelible impression in Paris and France as a commendation of 'Holy German Art'.

What is the point of insisting that foreign audiences 'must have misunderstood' my lecture, or certain parts of it, and that it is for their sake that the voices of true Wagner lovers have had to be raised in loud protest – when demonstrably those foreign audiences have understood my lecture very well indeed, while failing altogether to understand the 'Protest'? Hans Pfitzner concedes that much of what I said might well lend itself to discussion among artists of discernment, among 'cognoscenti' – but it is irresponsible, he adds, to say that kind of thing in front of Dutchmen, Belgians or Frenchmen. Are there no men of discernment among the Dutch, the Belgians or the French? The art of psychology enjoys a high standing among the nations of Western Europe – eminent Germans, indeed, have found its standing there to be higher than in our own country – and when a distinguished German writer addresses audiences abroad he is not normally besieged by a chauvinist mob intent on 'misunderstanding' every little delicate or bold nuance in his talk and using it to dishonour the name of Germany ... Instead the hall is filled with people who have learned how to read and how to listen, people who love ideas, and are accustomed to following them along paths that are personal, less well trodden, perhaps – and even a little perilous.

I spoke of art as being entire and perfect in each of its manifestations, and of the curious dilettantism – a monumental dilettantism raised to the level of genius – that underlies the notion of the total work of art [Gesamtkunstwerk]. Then somebody who has never heard such a thing in his life gets up on his feet, points an accusing finger and cries: 'He called our German intellectual giant of enduring merit a dilettante!' Whereupon they all scream 'Treason!' and hurl themselves upon me. Shame on you all!

Seemingly it is because Hans Pfitzner lent his name to this mindless act of lynch law that the intellectual world is not disposed to forgive him. It regards his involvement as precisely the kind of 'aberration' that he claims to see in my Wagner essay. What people are ultimately prepared to overlook in Kapellmeister Knappertsbusch, the instigator of the protest, and in a collection of born-again cartoonists, burgomasters, bureaucrats of the art world and worthy brewers – not to mention such a blithe spirit as Richard Strauss – they are not prepared to overlook in the artist and writer Hans Pfitzner; and the day is perhaps not far off that will find him more sensible of the honour that this distinction does him. For he (so the intellectual world esteems) ought to have sensed the rich fulfilment and the passion of a lifetime in my essay, ought to have understood a love that was deep enough to be hurt by its object – and ought to have been sympathetically disposed towards an attachment to the truth that differs (and not to its discredit) from the high-minded clichés and orthodox blatherings of the kind of Wagner literature dismissed by Nietzsche in his phrase 'Nohl, Pohl, Kohl and Co., *ad infinitum*'. It was his place to defend a work born of passionate commitment and understanding, whose analyses are in the service of a higher synthesis, and of which it has been said that it 'raises up once more the Wagner altars overturned by Nietzsche, decking them with *fresh* garlands' – to defend it, if only by default, if only by keeping quiet, against the insults of the agitators: not out of gratitude for any past critical services, of which he hardly stood in need, but out of artistic feeling – and plain, old-fashioned courage. He would have esteemed himself a 'coward', says Pfitzner, if he had refused his signature. My dear maestro! Have you not considered the possibility that the greater personal courage was shown by those Munich notabilities (and they do exist) whose names do *not* appear under the notice of excommunication?

In an open letter on the subject of this affair, which the young German-Bohemian music critic Walter Seidel addressed to Richard Strauss, the writer states:

Wagner's enormously pervasive influence is clearly documented in the fact that the historical debate about the 'Case of Wagner' is still going on today. By the same token (he writes) the artist Richard Strauss could wish for no better fate than to attract the attention of a distinguished German writer fifty years after his death, who would address himself with similar warm feeling to the work of this Herr Strauss and declare his faith in it.

This is true, and it holds equally good for Hans Pfitzner. For that very reason his attitude ought not to have been altogether immune to this consideration: that there might be some positive value, while trying to get at the critical truth, in resurrecting a problem that showed every sign of passing decently away at any moment, of being laid to rest in some remote hall of historical fame – resurrecting it in its first exciting and perplexing piquancy, bringing it once again (and possibly for the last time) within the orbit of passionate concern, and speaking of it in words that are *alive* – not in the tired clichés of an academic lip service. This must call for a writer who by tradition and by his own mental affiliations maintains a living link with the marvels of the late-Romantic world of the nineteenth century, the world of Wagner and Schopenhauer – and with the heroic spectacle of that world's vanquishment by Nietzsche. It really needs a man in his late fifties to know the way, still, to that citadel; for the younger generation it has all long since sunk below the horizon. 'Wagner's Own City of Munich', which thrust the great artist from its bosom in 1865 – thanks to the efforts of the very same sort of person who is today the fanatical guardian of Wagnerian orthodoxy and the scourge of heretics – is scarcely aware of the fact that since it had a change of heart over Wagner all kinds of things have happened in the intellectual and musical world, and new generations have arisen whose mental affinity with the world of Wagner is so slight that one would like to describe their attitude to his work as 'hostile', were one not obliged to call it merely apathetic. Perhaps it was not given to any emptily fulsome *Festschrift* to win converts here, however few – perhaps that was to be achieved only by an avowal of admiration deepened by scepticism; and for the sake of such advocacy people ought to be prepared to make certain allowances. In a letter to me the young curator of a museum in northern Germany wrote:

> For my own part, belonging as I do to a generation that has been brought up on the conventional objections to Wagner's work and thereby denied access to his genius, I freely confess that it was your essay that first equipped me to overcome those prejudices.

It has been said – notably by critics in France – that the piece has a certain refreshing quality, and that it is calculated to 'revive an issue that had appeared to be thoroughly exhausted'. But this has more to do with a certain directness of tone than with any substantive originality, and anyone familiar with the subject can see at once that the essay has its cultural antecedents in 'Nietzsche's immortal critique of Wagner'. It might provide the reflective reader with material and inspiration for this or that observation on the interrelationship and compatibility of culture and spontaneity. But any claim to 'originality' needs to be further qualified still; for virtually nothing in the essay is new even in terms of my own production. It is little more than a vessel in which I have collected together my various thoughts, feelings and statements – many of them already published – on the subject of Wagner over a period of many years – material, indeed, that spans my entire writing career. It is a 'composition' as much in the mechanical as in the organic sense of the word. It brings together and develops these scattered pieces at greater length, and what I now find so remarkable is that the combined whole succeeds in scandalizing people who either ignored the individual pieces or acknowledged them as valuable contributions. I recall a letter of congratulation that one of the signatories to the Munich manifesto, Herr von Hausegger, President of the Academy of Music, was kind enough to write to me on some occasion or other, in which that distinguished musician thanked me on behalf of many for the work I had done to further the cause of Wagner. Now that work was *identical* to the offending essay in its ideas and content, and even in its actual wording. Specifically, one of its 'most provocative' passages – the discussion of Wagner's decorative Germanness and his nationalism – may be found, verbatim and *in toto*, in the *Reflections of a Non-political Man.**

This is curious, but it leads inevitably to one conclusion. That conclusion is that the effect produced by a given statement depends not on *what* is said, but on *when* it is said. I should have known this, and I should have been prepared for a 'vigorous protest', as Hans Pfitzner puts it. Nor will I seek to take refuge behind the fact that the invitation to speak was naturally extended long before the event, and that my work on the essay, from which the lecture was

---

* This book is TM's long confession of his German patriotism and conservatism, on the writing of which he spent almost three years during the First World War. It contains (in the chapter 'On Virtue') the highest praise and most intelligent appreciation that Pfitzner's opera *Palestrina* ever received. See also the extracts from it about Wagner on pp. 51-66.

subsequently taken, was done back in the weeks of winter – far removed from that German springtime whose many side effects included such a drastic curtailment of public receptivity to the work. It is not my intention to offer apologies, but to ask a question. And the question is this: shall a writer who, in the finer moments of his youth and manhood, had something of value to say to the young people and the culture of his nation, to whom was even vouchsafed the honour of representing that nation's culture abroad – shall such a writer be accorded the right to have his say even when the times and the political climate have changed, to finish his life and work in the manner in which he began – or shall he not? The second answer would be tantamount to a demand for enforced retirement, which, given that life and self-expression are indissolubly one for the artist, would mean the surrender of life itself and voluntary physical withdrawal from this earth – a course of action, indeed, that is by no means uncommon in the Germany of today.

Such a demand would be unprecedented. We are getting older, and our particular sensibility (which at one time, according to how 'significant' we were, was representative of its age) is being superseded by a very different consciousness, albeit one that embraces elements to which we were already sensitive, which were already contained in our knowledge and experience – by a humanity 'après nous', which, taken as a whole, is no longer our own, and whose voice we can no longer claim to be. Hans Pfitzner, to whom these remarks are addressed, fully understands this fate, which none can escape. In his *Palestrina* he has portrayed the melancholy and resignation of ageing genius, which asks itself uncertainly 'whether the world is not now moving along unimagined paths, while all that seemed to us eternal is passing away as the wind' – and portrayed it in a profoundly conservative spirit in that he allows his seemingly *passé* artist hero to become 'the saviour of music' in the course of one great creative night. This was poetic fiction, a sublime fantasy. But for the sake of his past contribution to the enrichment of life and culture the artist who has found his own identity has always been granted the privilege – out of respect, good manners, gratitude or whatever other human reasons – of playing out his life's melody to the very end, even though times have changed, and speaking his truth, finishing his work. And rightly so. For the gift of art is a gift from the hand of life itself – or better still, perhaps, it is the gift *of* life itself, which dates less rapidly than some fresh young generation that believes it holds the key to the entire present and future would like to suppose; and he who has once been on good terms with life will never ever, as I believe, fall out with life altogether. Although his mental and spiritual make-up are determined by his historical experience, such a man will still be able to place his creative powers in the service of an age and a world that are no longer strictly speaking his own, simply by virtue of those elements within the new order which his own sensibility (as I said earlier) has anticipated tentatively from afar.

Why should I not state here and now (for example) that my thought and writing are by no means wholly divorced from that contemporary form of heroism which opposes the enfeebling and life-abasing obsession with psychology with such disdain and such a surfeit of historical consciousness? Just twenty years ago now, in a story called *Death in Venice*, which many a young man is said to have packed in his kit when he went to war in 1914, I wrote about an artistry that has 'found dignity', that, weary of its own 'sympathy for the abyss', has set itself up as the didactic model for a morality that is resolved 'to deny knowledge, to reject it, to pass it by with averted gaze', lest it contrive in any sort to weaken or paralyse the artist's will, his power of action, his creative impulse. The fact that things ended badly, that the 'mature resolve' turned out to have been foolhardy, is no indication that the author was unsympathetic to these ideas. But is it surprising if, at a time when such things have become the currency of mass slogans, he finds himself unable to join in with quite the same gusto as one to whom they appear as the fresh, new-minted wisdom of the day? Herr von Hausegger merely allowed himself to be carried away by fashionable commonplace when he wrote an open letter to the Editor of the *Neue Rundschau* declaring that my portrayal of Wagner offended against the ethos of our age – 'an age that is casting off the shackles of materialist hair-splitting analysis'. I am tempted to contradict him. It seems to me that his delight in the casting-off of shackles is an expression of that same dangerous and peculiar warping and perverting of the libertarian ideal whereby Germany (not for the first time) is now confusing and alarming world opinion. One should not countenance any criticism of 'materialist hair-splitting analysis' – particularly when it is having a hard time. It has helped to cast off many a shackle itself, and has served the cause of human freedom well. It represents truth – only one side of the truth, if you will, the pessimistic-naturalistic side, but truth all the same, radiant and valiant to boot, and by no means unheroic, let me add; and there ought to be room for its democratic spirit to live and survive alongside the autocracy that is currently in vogue.

'The men of the new regime', wrote that young custodian of the arts from northern Germany,

> will have to learn in time that your work contains infinitely more courage, more desire for truthfulness, more clarity of thought (all qualities of a heroic nature, of course!) than all this noisy parroting of the latest party line on culture. Things cannot and shall not come to such a pass in Germany that the serious intellectual efforts of a lifetime are despised, while the art of forming one's opinions via the path of least resistance is highly prized.

These are fine words, full of hope; but unfortunately things have already come to such a pass – and in more ways than one. The contemptuously hectoring tone of the Munich manifesto gives me to understand that I ought never to open my mouth again, that eternal silence should be my lot – and all because I made a well-meaning but unsuccessful attempt to relate the republican idea to the intellectual history of my countrymen, to reconcile them with freedom in the traditional sense – traditional in some sort even in Germany – and with a Europe united under the banner of that freedom which then seemed to me to be taking shape. Was that so pernicious that the only viable course of action now open to me is to commit hara-kiri? It is fair to say that this is very much a local point of view, which is not shared by broad sections of the German public – and I will not speak about reactions abroad for fear of provoking anyone unnecessarily. In short, my lengthy reflections on this home-grown counsel have been punctuated by so much friendly advice to the contrary, earnestly exhorting me to a higher duty, that I shall probably refrain from following that counsel, resigning myself instead to waiting upon the naturally appointed hour that will release me from the imperfections of my earthly existence.

But all this is not the main reason why many people find it offensive, not to say intolerable, that civilized persons should have been party to the Munich kangaroo court. Let me quote one response – not, I hasten to add, because I am captivated by a description of my person whose effusiveness plainly derives from the writer's sincere disapproval of the treatment meted out to an intellectual. The following passage appeared in one of Prague's German-language newspapers a week after the Munich bombshell:

> What really appals the impartial observer about the notorious indictment of Thomas Mann by distinguished representatives of German intellectual life is the *modus operandi* whereby a man of lofty and superior intellect, who has been a credit to German letters for the past thirty years, is handed over for sentencing by the mob, by all the hangers-on, the little men consumed with envy and jealousy, the sycophants and the yes-men who have no opinions of their own, who have no right to pass judgement in matters of the intellect – and this at a time of enormous political and social upheaval, and in the context of a mass popular movement to which the intellectual leaders of the nation – they of all people – would be better advised not to submit so readily and meekly.

If this last observation seems too sweeping and unkind, one must remember that the writer is viewing these events from a foreign perspective – and make allowances accordingly. For the rest he has hit the nail on the head, echoing what thousands of others have felt – and none more deeply or bitterly, of course, than myself, the victim of the attack.

If one of my Munich judges, or indeed several of them – if Hans Pfitzner, whose sharp polemical sting Busoni and others have already had occasion to fear, or President von Hausegger or my Rotarian friend, Generalmusikdirektor Knappertsbusch – if any one of them had sat down and written an article for a journal or newspaper, giving public voice to his honest outrage at my manner of commemorating a great man, then all would have been well, and I could have had no possible objection. My presentation of Wagner was open to debate, open (indeed) to criticism of the strongest sort; of its many champions I would be the very last to deny that. I am painfully, not to say paralytically aware of my own shortcomings as a writer, and all I can claim for myself are honesty and the famous will to truth – the personal and historically determined truth of my own experience. Did none of them feel strong enough to tackle me alone, man to man? Was it really necessary to assemble so many big guns in order to overpower me? It is their manner of going about it that cries out to heaven, and that should have repelled the finer spirits among them. To carry the protest on to the streets, to trumpet my offence up and down the country, to cast an intellectual and artistic issue, delicate by its very nature, before the ignorant and already inflamed masses, to rouse their blood with disconnected quotations couched in a sea of invective: this was – to put it prudently – imprudent.

A 'vigorous protest'? This was no vigorous protest, but a lethal act of denunciation, social ostracism and national excommunication. Since this incident my person and my property have become the object of increasing harassment by local officialdom, making it perfectly plain to me that in the Germany of today I would be a fourth-class citizen, proscribed and outlawed. When a German writer who has always endeavoured to serve his countrymen according to his lights and to the best of his ability, and who has enjoyed widespread support from these same countrymen not just for 'fourteen years',* but for a whole generation; a writer, moreover, who is far too conscious by nature of his debt to the classical Goethean tradition to feel really cut out for martyrdom – when such a writer is no longer able, in this day and age, to complete his life's work without appealing to the protection and the civilized indulgence of a foreign land, more clement than his own and a friend, still, to freedom of thought, then the gentlemen who sounded the call to arms in Munich should at least know that they are directly responsible for this grotesque and unnatural state of affairs, from which nobody can derive any real satisfaction.

The time will come, whether I live to see it or not, when the summary expulsion of Germans who have been profoundly instrumental in maintaining and upholding their country's traditions will be recognized and regretted as a pernicious and shameful act of madness. But those among the Munich protesters who have any kind

---

* Meaning the duration of the Weimar Republic. Hitler's rhetoric turned the 'fourteen years' into a powerful symbol of the 'dark night' from which Germany had, of course, triumphantly emerged in January 1933.

of affinity for things intellectual and for the written word, for knowledge and personal revelation and the linguistic discipline organically connected with them – in a word, for literature – may well be asking themselves already whether a writer who puts his trust in German liberty and culture and freely offers up a work of the mind written with love, but ill suited (as it happens) to the current climate of official thought, deserves to be punished by the loss of his home and fatherland.

To René Schickele*

Küsnacht
16 May 1934

[...] Excellent – your observation on the novel as the total work of art! It's something I've always thought myself. Wagner's notion of it was ludicrously mechanical. [...]

* René Schickele (1883–1940), German writer who emigrated to France in 1933. His works include a novel in the form of a trilogy, *Das Erbe am Rhein* (1925–31).

To Karl Vossler*

Küsnacht
4 May 1935

Dear Councillor,
I was delighted by your letter and by your amusing and friendly comments on the essays.† You are quite right: I don't think I was really cut out to be a satirist or a rationalist, although I often find refreshment and relaxation in these dry realms. But I freely admit

* Karl Vossler (1872–1949), professor of romance languages in Heidelberg, Würzburg and Munich. His works include studies of Dante and Racine, and translations of their writings.
† *Leiden und Grösse der Meister*, Berlin, 1935, the last work by TM to be published in Germany until 1946. It includes the essay translated here as 'The Sorrows and Grandeur of Richard Wagner', pp. 91–148.

that with the passing years I think of myself more and more as an Apollonian, while the Dionysian appeals to me less and less. Just consider R. Wagner as an intellectual and a human being. Confused, helpless and at a loss, full of longing in every direction, longing for life and longing for death – dreadful, when you think about it. Too much a passive *object* of life for my taste. It grips him tightly and squeezes works out of him like so many enormous bubbles. But have you ever read anything by him that showed him as an intellectual lord and master of life? It is not fair to think of Goethe. But I can't help thinking of him, because he has reason as mankind's crowning glory, and yet could write the lines 'Sagt es niemand, nur den Weisen …' [Tell it to none save only the wise …] [. . .]

To Willi Schuh

Schiedhaldenstrasse 33,
Küsnacht-Zurich
28 June 1936

Dear Dr Schuh,

Last night I read through your Wagner book [Richard Wagner's Letters to Judith Gautier]* at a single sitting – for me the most interesting thing that has been published in a long time. It is the Wagner I know who lives in these pages – both in these extraordinary letters and in your splendid introduction, whose whole approach to the subject I find extremely congenial. Indeed, I think I am right in feeling that this publication serves in a sense to confirm and justify the picture of Wagner I myself attempted to present.

Is it not painful in the extreme to witness the degeneracy both intellectual and moral brought about by war, as seen in the letters written to Mendès† in 1870? The helplessly enthusiastic capitulation of such a mind before the historical deeds of a captain of state – a man no less sophisticated than himself in his own way – is shameful

---

* *Die Briefe Richard Wagners an Judith Gautier*, ed. Willi Schuh, Zurich, 1936.
† Catulle Mendès, Judith Gautier's husband at this time.

to behold. What a corrupting effect war has on culture and things of the mind! It is some consolation to read his comment in a letter eight years later: 'I feel myself to be the only true German amidst this dull-witted race of people they call the Germans!' Doubtless this will always be the collective national sentiment of more cultivated Germans.

Many, many thanks for your splendid gift!

Yours,
THOMAS MANN

To Stefan Zweig*

Schiedhaldenstrasse 33
Küsnacht-Zurich
14 November 1937

Dear Herr Zweig,

The new volume† is full of splendid things, and *Renan* in particular seems to me a masterpiece of compassion. I am delighted – and most grateful. For the past week I have been working like a Trojan: a lecture on Wagner's *Ring* suddenly had to be got ready for a performance of the whole cycle at the Stadttheater. On revient toujours ...

With warmest regards,
THOMAS MANN

* Stefan Zweig (1881-1942), prolific Austrian writer and dedicated pacifist. Emigrated to England in 1938 and in 1940 to Brazil, where he later committed suicide.
† *Begegnung mit Menschen, Büchern und Städten*, Vienna, 1937.

Richard Wagner and *Der Ring des Nibelungen**

Ladies and Gentlemen:

In the lecture on Richard Wagner that I delivered in the Great Hall at the University of Munich nearly five years ago, and that was to be (though I did not know it at the time) my farewell to Germany, I spoke these words:

> A passion for Wagner's enchanted *oeuvre* has been a part of my life ever since I first became aware of it and set out to make it my own, to invest it with understanding. What it has given me in terms of enjoyment and instruction I can never forget, nor the hours of deep and solitary happiness amidst the theatre throng, hours filled with frissons and delights for the nerves and the intellect alike, with sudden glimpses into things of profound and moving significance, such as only this art can afford.

These words express an admiration that has never been in the least diminished, or even tinged, by any scepticism, nor by any of that mischievous abuse to which its great object can easily lend itself. Fortunately so: for admiration is the finest gift we have. Indeed, if anyone were to ask me which emotional response to the phenomena of our world and the manifestations of art and life I regard as the most noble, felicitous, wholesome and essential, then I should reply without hesitation that it is admiration. How could it be otherwise? What would man be – what would the artist be – without admiration, enthusiasm, rapture and a sense of surrender to something other than himself, something far greater than himself – but something with which he feels a supreme affinity, which holds a powerful appeal for him, and which he ardently desires to assimilate, to 'invest with understanding', to make fully his own? Admiration is the wellspring of love, nay, love itself – a love that would lack depth, passion, and

* A lecture given on 16 November 1937 at the University of Zurich on the occasion of a performance of *The Ring* at the Zurich Stadttheater. Published in *Mass und Wert* (Zurich), Vol. I, No. 3, 1938.

above all intellectual awareness if it did not also know how to doubt and suffer at the hands of its chosen object. Admiration is both humble and proud, proud of itself; it knows the meaning of jealousy, the youthful defiance of the question: 'What can *you* possibly know about it?' It is at once the most pure and the most productive of emotions, looking up to its object and spurring the admirer on to emulation: it inculcates high standards, and acts as the most powerful and sternly exacting stimulus to one's own intellectual endeavours. It is the root of all talent. Where it is absent, where it withers and dies, there nothing can grow; and all that remains is impoverishment and wilderness.

I must tell you, ladies and gentlemen, that in my strong belief in admiration as a productive force I am but a disciple and follower of that mighty artist of whom I spoke on that occasion in Munich, and of whom I wish to speak again today. In the celebrated 'Mitteilung an meine Freunde' [Communication to my Friends] Wagner makes no bones about attributing all artistic ability to the gift of admiration – or, as he puts it, the 'power of receptivity'. 'The initial artistic resolve', he writes, 'is simply the satisfaction of the involuntary urge to imitate whatever appeals most strongly to our fancy' – a proposition wholly characteristic of the man himself and his personal genius, which is rooted in theatrical representation, yet at the same time a proposition that contains a large measure of objective truth. The one thing that determines the artistic temperament, he says – in complete contrast to the political temperament, which always subordinates the outside world to itself and its own advantage, never itself to that world – is that the artist surrenders himself without reserve to those impressions which impinge favourably on his sensibility, impressions of life, and above all impressions furnished by art; for the artist as such is always motivated in the first instance by purely artistic impressions. But their impact is governed by that selfsame power of receptivity, which must be filled to exquisite overflowing with these impressions before the artist feels the urge to communicate them. The fullness of this overflowing, this enthusiasm, is the measure of artistic power; it is nothing more nor less than the need to communicate this rich abundance of received impressions to others. Power, the power of life and of love, the power to assimilate whatever is cognate and needful: this is the essence of genius, of that receptive power which, at its most consummately strong, must necessarily be transformed into productive power.

Let me say again that the objective truth of this profession is beyond dispute. It is a fine and high-minded observation, and a wholly accurate one, that the gift of admiration, the ability to love and to learn, the power to assimilate, absorb, transform and develop as a person are the source of every great talent. How fitting, then, that we who have come together to admire a great work, and to prepare our minds for a festive performance of the same, should begin by paying sincere homage to admiration itself.

He himself was a great admirer, the maestro who created this work – and not only in his youth, the traditional season of enthusiasm, but (such was his tremendous vitality) all the way through into old age and until the very last. We are told how, during the final months of his life in the Palazzo Vendramin in Venice, and indeed before that in Bayreuth, he used to entertain his family and friends in the evenings by reading aloud or playing music to them: Shakespeare, Calderón and Lope, Indian and Old Norse folklore, Bach, Mozart and Beethoven – the whole enriched by his own observations, words of eulogy, and forceful vignettes full of feeling and insight. One is touched to hear him speak of 'Mozart's delicate genius of light and love', which he had undoubtedly always admired profoundly, but which perhaps only now, in contemplative old age, he is free to honour with a pure and uninhibited devotion, now that his own life's work, so much less ethereal, so much more ponderous and heavy-laden, has been safely accomplished. Indeed, it seems that the capacity to admire the things of beauty created by others, far from being the prerogative of the busy years of struggle, may be at its least constrained and its most purely disinterested in old age, when the artist has completed his own work, and when the ego no longer needs to view the works of others in relation to itself, seeking reflections of itself, comparing itself with them. 'Beauty', said Kant, 'affords pleasure without self-interest.' Now it may well be that only he who has been appointed to bring forth great beauty of his own can truly take a 'pleasure without self-interest' in the beautiful creations of others. The praise that he bestows upon them no longer needs to flatter himself, to affirm and defend his own status. The aged maestro admired *Felix Mendelssohn*, calling him 'the model of a thoughtful, temperate and subtle artistic sensibility'. These are words of praise that could hardly be said to describe Wagner himself; this is objective, unselfish admiration. *Beethoven* was always the ultimate, the supreme genius: 'One cannot speak of him', he was still saying in his old age, 'without adopting the accents of rapture.' But after playing the 'Hammerklavier' Sonata, transported by these 'pure spectra of human existence', he suddenly came out with these curious words: 'Something like that will work only for piano – it would be quite absurd to perform it in front of a large audience.' So says the great practitioner of theatre and mover of the masses, the giant of the orchestra, who always appealed to the crowd on a lofty plane – and who always needed the crowd for the fulfilment of his artistic mission. Is not his comment on the Beethoven piano sonata an open, self-forgetful concession to an emotional intimacy and exclusivity that was not his own forte, the affectionate, even jealous defence of a standing with which he does not desire to compete? Is this not a totally unselfish admiration?

The only other figure that he ranked alongside Beethoven was *Shakespeare* – the supremely real, the fearsome parable of life, alongside the supremely idealized. He read the royal tragedies to his family, *Hamlet* and *Macbeth*, and on occasion the creator of *Tristan* would have to pause in his reading, with tears of artistic rapture in his ageing eyes. 'The things that man saw!' he cried. 'And *such* things he saw! He is absolutely unique – a sheer miracle: he cannot be comprehended in any other terms!' But are we then to understand that mere spoken drama – 'literary writing', as he had sometimes termed it disparagingly in his younger years – gave birth in this instance to the unique, the miraculous? What had become of the message of salvation contained in the 'total work of art', said to be the only viable instrument for the realization of art, and to which the future supposedly belonged? That had been fighting dialectics, passionate and necessary propaganda in his own behalf. What he had written he had written. But in conversation this man who had fulfilled himself completely, and who could now allow himself to be fulfilled by other things, paid homage to masterpieces in which the world and mankind are portrayed by the word alone, and which he undoubtedly ranked as high above himself as Goethe claimed to rank them above himself throughout his life.

And what about *Goethe*, indeed? We find him too at these Venetian soirées, and to him also the old maestro extends his unstinting admiration – and in an area that is wholly characteristic: for the scene that the great creator of myths most loved to read in that intimate circle, commenting upon it in terms of wonderment and affection, was the 'Classical Walpurgis Night' from *Faust* Part II. 'This is probably the most original and artistically perfect of Goethe's creations,' he used to say. 'Such a totally individual resurrection of classical antiquity in the freest of forms, brought vividly to life with such masterly humour and brilliance of observation, in a highly-wrought language of extraordinary artistic refinement', as he was constantly reiterating, was something quite beyond compare.

It gladdens our hearts to see the genius of Wagner inclining itself here in private before that of Goethe – something that never occurs in his writings, so far as I know; and it is a highly remarkable occurrence, this meeting of two spheres that are normally diametrically opposed and poles apart – an experience both reassuring and uplifting to behold, this sudden coming together in friendship of two mighty and contradictory manifestations of the eclectic German spirit – the Nordic-musical versus the Mediterranean-sculptural, the lowering-moralistic versus the sunny-inspired, the primevally folk-based and mythological versus the European, Germany as all-powerful feeling and Germany as mind and civilization perfected. For we, of course, are both: Goethe and Wagner, Germany is both of these. Theirs are the ultimate names for the two souls within our breast, which seek to separate one from the other, but whose clash and conflict we must ever learn to perceive anew as eternally fruitful, as a wellspring of inner richness – the ultimate names for that German duality, that German schism which runs through the hearts and minds of all sensitive, thinking Germans, and which we, with profound pleasure, here see transcended for a moment by the ageing Wagner's selfless admiration for Goethe's Greek phantasmagoria.

It is no coincidence, of course, that this meeting should have taken place on the common ground of *myth*. The old fashioner and interpreter of myths, who announced as soon as he had finished *Der fliegende Holländer* that from now on he wanted only to tell fairy stories, is delighted to encounter his supremely urbane counterpart in these primeval regions, his very own territory; and he never ceases to rejoice and marvel at the sovereign ease and sophisticated grace with which he moves therein. What a contrast indeed between the Wagnerian and Goethean treatments of myth – even disregarding the differences in their respective mythical spheres, the fact that Goethe peoples his theatre of the mind not with dragons, giants and dwarfs, but with sphinxes, griffins, nymphs, sirens, Psylli and Marsi: creatures not of Old-Teutonic but of ancient European origin – and certainly not archetypally German enough, in Wagner's eyes, to be suitable for musical treatment. But in other ways too – what a clash of artistic attitudes and temperaments! Each is equally great in its way, beyond a doubt. 'Great the figures, great likewise the memories.' But the grandeur of Goethe's vision carries no hint of pathos or tragedy; instead of celebrating myth, he jests with it, treating it with a fond and familiar playfulness, mastering it in every last detail and portraying it in amusing, witty language with a precision that suggests humour and affectionate parody rather than sublimity. The whole episode is a mythological entertainment, fully in keeping with the general feel of the *Faust* poem as a kind of world revue. But nothing could be less Wagnerian than Goethe's ironical manner of invoking myth, and the 'Classical Walpurgis Night' will have appealed little, if at all, to the youthful Wagner, the Wagner who was still completely bound up in his own work. Only later, when he had become detached enough for genuinely objective artistic appraisal, was he able to admire it.

Wagner's own discovery of myth – which is to say, his growth from traditional opera composer to artistic revolutionary and pioneer of a new form of drama born of myth and music, calculated to enhance the intellectual standing and artistic dignity of the operatic stage enormously and endow it with a truly Germanic seriousness – that process of growth and discovery will always repay fresh study, and will always remain a most remarkable and noteworthy chapter in the history of art and the theatre. But its human interest is also considerable, for its aesthetic and artistic motivation is conjoined with social and ethical impulses and a concern for the morality of art, which are the ultimate source of its pathos. It was a cathartic process, a process of cleansing, purification and spiritualization, which is to be esteemed all the more highly in human terms in that the personality that took it upon itself, and in which it was accomplished, was intensely passionate, torn by dark and violent appetites for popular acclaim, power and pleasure.

We all know how this perilously multi-talented artist began by flinging all his energies into the grand historical opera, and how, in that established form familiar to audiences, he achieved a triumph, with *Rienzi*, that would have persuaded anyone else to pursue this well-worn path for the rest of his life. What prevented Wagner from doing so was the depth of his intellectual conscience, his capacity for disgust, his instinctive and as yet unexplained abhorrence of the role played by the musical theatre in the bourgeois society of his day, where it served as an insipid and opulent diversion; but above all it was his attitude to music itself, which he viewed with too pious, too traditionally and loftily Teutonic a feeling for him not to regard grand opera as an abuse of its inmost soul. Plainly put, he thought music too important to serve as a mere tinkling accompaniment to some overblown bourgeois entertainment. In him it yearned to find more pure, more fitting dramatic embodiment; and in *Der fliegende Holländer*, *Tannhäuser* and *Lohengrin* we see him striving with growing success to develop the forms that would embody music more worthily. His creative involvement in the Romantic world of legend was effectively his way of mastering the purely human dimension, which he regarded as the true home of music – in contrast to the historical-political dimension. At the same time, however, that involvement signified for him a turning-away from a bourgeois world of decaying values, fake culture, plutocracy, sterile academicism and bored materialism – towards a culture of the people, a 'popular' culture in that sense, which increasingly came to appear to him as the shape of things to come, both socially and artistically, and as the instrument of redemption and purification.

Wagner experienced modern culture, the culture of bourgeois society, through the medium and in the image of the operatic theatre of his day. The status of art – or of that art, at least, which appealed to his taste – in that contemporary world became the criterion by which he judged bourgeois culture as such: so it was hardly surprising that he should learn to despise and hate it. He saw art reduced to the level of an extravagant consumer product, the artist degraded to a slave of money; he saw superficiality and dull routine where he longed for holy earnest and beauteous solemnity; he watched with fury while vast resources were squandered, not for the attainment of high artistic purpose, but for that which he despised above all else as an artist: the easy, cheap effect. And because he saw that none of this offended anyone else as it offended him, he concluded that the political and social conditions that could bring forth such things, and to which they properly belonged, were utterly vile – and must be changed by revolutionary means.

And so it was that Wagner became a revolutionary. As an artist he became a revolutionary because he thought that sweeping changes in society would bring about better conditions for art – for his art, the drama of the people, compounded of myth and music. He always denied being a political animal as such, and never concealed his distaste for the doings of the various political parties. Although he welcomed the revolution of 1848 and took part in it, he acted out of vague revolutionary sentiment, not because he believed in the concrete objectives of that particular revolution: his own inmost dreams and ambitions far transcended those objectives, *for they transcended the bourgeois age itself*. It is important to realize that a work like *Der Ring des Nibelungen*, which Wagner planned after *Lohengrin*, was written essentially as an attack on the bourgeois civilization and culture that had reigned supreme since the Renaissance – that its blend of primitivism and futurity was aimed at a non-existent world of classless populism. The opposition that it encountered, the outrage that it excited, were directed not so much against the revolutionary aspects of its form or the fact that it broke with the rules of an artistic genre – the opera – from which it had manifestly departed. For that was by no means the only thing from which it had departed. Germans raised in the tradition of Goethe, who knew their *Faust* by heart, were moved to angry and contemptuous protest – a respectable protest, the product of their continuing attachment to the cultural milieu of German Classicism and humanism, which this work of Wagner's had repudiated. Cultivated middle-class Germans laughed at all that *Wagalaweia* stuff and all that alliteration, as if it were some barbarous whimsy; if the term *Kultur*-Bolshevist had existed in Wagner's day they would undoubtedly have applied it to him – and not without reason. The vast, not to say planetary success subsequently accorded to this art by the middle classes, the international bourgeoisie, who found it a source of stimulus to their senses, their nerves and their intellect, is a tragi-comical paradox, which should not blind us to the fact that it was intended for a very different public, with a social and moral message aimed far beyond the confines of any capitalist-bourgeois system to a world freed from power-mania and plutocracy, a world founded on justice and love, where all men would be brothers.

For Wagner, myth was the language of the enduringly poetic and creative *people*. This is why he loved it, and why he surrendered himself to it so completely as an artist. Myth, to him, signified simplicity, the absence of cultivation, nobility, purity – in short, what he termed the 'purely human', and what for him was the only truly musical. Myth plus music equals drama, equals art itself, for only the purely human seemed to him a fit subject for art. It was only when he was confronted by the choice between two subjects that had taken hold of his imagination during the composition of *Lohengrin – Friedrich der Rotbart* and *Siegfrieds Tod* – that he fully realized how ill-suited to art (or art as he understood it) was all historical formalism and relativism, in contrast to the unadulteratedly and eternally human. It took a long struggle and a good deal of theoretical rumination before he was able to decide between these two rival subjects; and the story of how the archetypal hero myth won out over the history of the Emperor is told by Wagner himself in the great 'Mitteilung an meine Freunde' [Communication to my Friends], which he wrote later in Switzerland, and which is one of the most revealing documents to have come to us from the confessional pen of this great artist. There he explains how he could have treated the subject matter of Barbarossa – which appealed to him as a part of the German past – only in the form of a spoken drama, precisely because of its politico-historical character; and how he would have had to dispense altogether with the music that was essential for the full realization of his poetic gifts. At the time of *Rienzi*, when he was still a composer of operas, he could no doubt have entertained the notion of setting a drama about the Emperor Barbarossa to music. But he was no longer a composer of operas, and it was not possible for him to desire a return to that stage of his career – not least because he always naively equated his own private artistic destiny with art *per se*, and was quite convinced that both the opera and the spoken drama, once outgrown by him, must needs disappear for good, while the new form that he created – the musical theatre of myth – would be the art of the future. But the only fit subject matter for such an art was the purely human and ahistorical, freed from all conventions: how happy, then, was Wagner to find that as he worked his way into his chosen material, the Siegfried saga, he was able to separate out more and more of the historical dross, cleansing the subject matter of subsequent accretions and taking it back to the point where it had emerged, new-born, in its purest human manifestation, from the poetic soul of the people.

This curious revolutionary was just as radical about the past as he was about the future. The saga was not enough for him: nothing less than the primal myth itself would do. Even the medieval *Nibelungenlied* signified modernity, distortion, theatricality, historicity – it was nowhere near primitive or musical enough for the sort of art he had in mind. He had to go all the way back to the ultimate source and origin, to the ancient Norse and Germanic foundations of the myth in the *Edda*; that was the kind of sacred historical depth he needed for his art of the future. As yet he did not know that even within his own work he would not be able to bring himself to stop and begin at some point already burdened with a past – to make his entry *in medias res*: that here too he would be compelled, magnificently, to go back to the first source and origin of all things, the primeval cell, the first E flat of the prelude to the Prelude; that it would fall to him to construct, by himself, a musical cosmogony, indeed, a mythical cosmos, and to endow it with a profoundly meaningful life of its own: the ringing pageant of the world's beginning and end.

But what he did know was that in his tireless backward journeying to find the ultimate depths and origins he had discovered the man and the hero that he was looking for, the hero whom he, like Brünnhilde, loved before he was born – *his* Siegfried, a figure who in his timelessness delighted and satisfied his passion for the past no less than his yearning for the future: man – and here I quote Wagner's own words – 'in the most natural, sunny fullness of his physical manifestation, the male-embodied spirit of the One eternal creative purpose, the doer of real deeds, filled with supreme, naked power and indisputable charm'. This, then, was the mythical figure of light, bounded and restricted by nothing, man unprotected, totally self-reliant and self-sufficient, resplendent in freedom, the fearlessly innocent doer of deeds and fulfiller of destiny, who through the sublime natural phenomenon of his death heralds the twilight of old and outmoded world forces and redeems the world by raising it to a new plane of knowledge and morality – he it was whom Wagner made into the hero of the drama intended for music that he drafted, not in modern verse, but in the alliterative language of his ancient Scandinavian source, and that he called *Siegfrieds Tod*.

He was not destined to complete the project on his native soil. Implicated in the Dresden uprising of 1849, Wagner became a political refugee overnight, and found himself in a foreign land – which is to say, in misery (the two words are cognate in German). But the source of his misery and heartache was not that foreign land – Switzerland – where he soon found friends such as he had never found in Germany, under whose patronage all his future works, right the way through to *Parsifal*, were to evolve: not Switzerland, but Germany itself, and he was saddened by the failure of the revolution as he would later be saddened by Prussia's victory over Austria and the establishment of a Prussian hegemony in Germany. The whole course of German political history up to 1870 – and very possibly beyond – turned out contrary to his wishes, which suggests that his wishes were misguided. But a worship of facts is not a very high-minded approach to take to history, and history is not something so splendid that one need feel obliged to pity those minor nations who take no part in it (or only the smallest possible part) – or that one should not esteem the wishes cherished by sensitive, thinking individuals, simply because those wishes have been thwarted by history. Perhaps – who knows? – Germany would be in a better state, and Europe would be in a better state, if German history had developed in accordance with Wagner's wishes, which is to say, in the direction of freedom – wishes that were shared by many other thinking Germans, and whose abortive failure it was that drove the author of *Siegfrieds Tod* to seek refuge in Switzerland.

Not that we have any cause to regret it. Nowhere, not even at home, would his life's work have been free to unfold more gloriously than it did here, and there is plenty of documentary evidence to show that he was gratefully conscious of the fact. 'Let me now go to my work with a will,' he writes to Otto Wesendonck in the autumn of 1859. 'Let me now write the works that I conceived there, in the tranquil, magnificent land of the Swiss, looking out upon those sublime, gold-capped mountains. They are miracles, and I could not have conceived them anywhere else on earth.' 'Miracles': one is touched to hear him say it so openly, in his tragic, costly good fortune, simply because it is the plain truth. No term better fits these unexampled manifestations of art; and nothing in the history of artistic creation does it fit better than these – with the possible exception of a few major achievements in architecture, such as some of the Gothic cathedrals. Not that this is necessarily meant, in the final analysis, as some kind of supreme accolade. After all, we would not be tempted to apply the term 'miracles' to other precious and indispensable cultural landmarks, such as *Hamlet*, *Iphigenie*, or even the Ninth Symphony. But the score of *Tristan* is a miracle, especially in its irksome affinity with *Die Meistersinger*, which almost defies mental grasp – and also because both these works were undertaken as mere relief from the painstaking, gigantic intellectual edifice of the *Ring*. It is the product of a quite unparalleled eruption of talent and genius, the profoundly serious yet enchanting work of a sensuous sorcerer intoxicated with his own finesse.

It must mean a great deal to the Swiss that they looked after and played host to this extraordinary man for so long, and a complete performance of *Der Ring des Nibelungen*, such as the Zurich Stadttheater is now proposing to stage, is a timely reminder of the close associations between that work and this city, such as no other city can boast. If this is mere chance, it is a chance charged with significance and deserving of our applause. For it is only right and proper that this bold work of the German mind, which was destined to conquer the world, should have come into being in the free and congenial atmosphere of this city: a truly international city, not in terms of its size, but by virtue of its situation and function, and one that has always looked with kindness on the innovative endeavours of the European avant-garde – and will, I hope, continue to do so. Here it was that Wagner made his home in the 1850s, years that saw the detailed working-out of the text and the completion of much of the musical score. It was here, in the 'downstairs room of the Dependance Annexe of the Hôtel de Baur', that the first public reading of the dramas was given by the author before an invited audience on four successive evenings in 1853, from 16 to 19 February. And it was from here that Wagner wrote many letters telling of the progress of the work, the frustrations and hold-ups, the exultant struggles – letters optimistically setting forth his plans, like the one addressed to his niece, Clara Brockhaus, in March 1854:

> *Das Rheingold* was not begun until November, and is now fin-ished: it's only a matter of completing the orchestration. In the summer I shall write the music for *Die Walküre*; next spring I shall start work on *Der junge Siegfried*, which means that by the sum-mer of the year after next I should have finished *Siegfrieds Tod*
> . . .

That proved to be a miscalculation. We must look to the commem-orative plaque on the house at Triebschen to discover where and when *Götterdämmerung* was finally completed. The master craftsman who wrote the *Ring* was a highly critical and finicky artist, who, as he puts it in another letter, 'can be satisfied with his works only to the extent that every last detail' – and his vast opus is rich in such detail – 'is based on a good idea'. And that takes time. But as Zurich now prepares to stage the *Ring* cycle in its entirety once more, it may justly echo the words of Goethe's Duke, who says of Tasso's poem: 'And I call it, in a certain sense, mine own.'

It was from Zurich – or more precisely, on an excursion to Albis-brunn – that Wagner wrote his great letter to Liszt of 20 November 1851, in which he first unfolds and explains the plan of his mighty undertaking to his Weimar friend and patron. 'Let me now relate,' he solemnly begins, 'in all honesty and truth, the story of the artistic undertaking in which I have been engaged for some time past, and the turn that it perforce had to take.' And then he tells that extra-ordinary, and for him ecstatically bewildering story, which one must relive in the imagination in order to discover how little an artist knows of his own work at the outset, how poorly, to begin with, he understands the inherent self-will of the enterprise on which he is embarking – with no idea of what the work itself aspires to become, of what it must become inasmuch as it is uniquely *his* work, and which the artist himself often views with the feeling: '*That* wasn't what I intended, but now I *must* do it, God help me!' The source and origin of great works is not the pallid ambition of the ego: the driving ambition belongs not to the artist but to the work itself, which aspires to be much greater than he ever dared to hope (or feared), and which imposes its will upon him. Wagner did not set out to astonish the world by writing a world epic that would take four evenings to stage. That this was what he must do he learned with horrified – and proud – delight from his own work. He had done *Lohengrin*, and now he wanted to do *Siegfrieds Tod*. He had already written the libretto, or half written it; now he wanted to finish it off by writing the music. But he could not do it – or rather, he could not do it just yet. It was not enough simply to go ahead and stage the work before the audience of his dreams: it was his duty to prepare that audience in advance. But how? By writing another drama. This one was overburdened with antecedent events. In effect, it was only the final chapter in an extended myth that had gone before; and either he would have to tell the whole story in narrative form in the course of the drama, or he would have to assume that his audience already knew it. The first solution was artistically unsatisfactory; the second implied certain cultural pretensions. And Wagner loathed cultural pretensions. He was not a man to make such demands. Wherever he went to work the world began anew, and nobody should have need of any previous knowledge in order to understand. Perhaps he already had an inkling that this time the world really would have to begin anew; but he would not admit as much to himself. What he did admit to himself, to begin with, was simply this: that to take too much for granted and expect too much of the spectator's powers of deduction would undermine that primal simplicity, the simplicity of myth, which he saw as the work's essential characteristic; and that he must first write a *Junge Siegfried*, in which those earlier events would be brought to life as far as possible on the stage, making them directly accessible to the audience.

He wrote the forest drama, and found it enchanting. He immediately started to set it to music, and all went smoothly with the work of composition. But then it suddenly occurred to him that he ought to attend first of all to his health, and he took himself off to a clinic for cold-water cures. What he was really doing was escaping into illness, escaping from the work in hand. He was in great heart for his work; and then again, his heart was not really in it – not yet.

Something was not quite right here, and that something was not his health (which, delicate though it was, he would not have given a second thought under other circumstances) but his conscience. It was time for another confession: *Der junge Siegfried* would not suffice, and he could not begin here either. Far too many vital links – everything that gave moving and far-reaching significance to the plot and characters of the two existing dramas – were still not physically present on the stage, and had to be left to the audience's imagination. This did not accord with the will of the work, even though it might have accorded with the desires of the artist, timorous creature that he is, whose secret, inmost wish is always that the cup might pass from him. But this particular cup was intent on being drained to the last drop. Mental images of things unseen and past were all well and good; they could even be intensely moving and full of significance – he would see to that. But that which was past must at some stage have been made present: the audience must be placed in a position to remember for themselves – to remember because they had actually *been* there, and now needed only to be reminded by his music. The story of Siegmund and Sieglinde, Wotan's plight and Brünnhilde, who defies him by acting in accordance with his own true will – all that had to be put on to the stage first in a further evening, no matter how taxing the task or how many years of his life it might cost him. *Die Walküre* had to be written. And no sooner had he realized this than he realized, of course, that even three evenings would not be enough – that a fourth drama would logically have to precede the first, in which everything down to the very last detail – which is to say, everything back to the very earliest beginnings, the primal occurrence: the theft of the gold and Alberich's curses, the curse on love and the curse on gold, together with the first glimmering of the sword idea in Wotan's mind – had to be brought before the simple senses of the people. In the beginning was the Rhine.

This was how Wagner described the task laid upon him to Liszt, and he implored him not to think that this mad design was the result of some detached, calculating fancy. Rather, it had been forced upon him as a necessary consequence of the nature and substance of this material, which now filled his whole mind and demanded to be executed in its entirety. 'You will understand', he writes, 'that my latest plan was not dictated to me by reflection alone, but by enthusiasm.' Nothing could be more plausible when we consider what came into being over the next two decades: a *ne plus ultra* of almost unfathomable ingenuity and overpowering richness of meaning. From the enthusiasm it engenders, the sense of grandeur that so often seizes us in its presence – which can be compared only to the feelings excited in us by nature at her noblest, by evening sunshine on mountain peaks, by the turmoil of the sea – we can well imagine the enthusiasm that accompanied its conception.

What part reflection played, and continues to play, in this enthusiasm – both that of the author and that of the spectator – and whether a clear-cut distinction can be drawn here between reflection and enthusiasm, reflection and *feeling*: these are different questions, and in attempting to answer them one should not, I think, rely too much on Wagner's own claims that feeling means everything to him and intellect nothing – that his art addresses itself only to the former, while the latter has no part to play. Artists sometimes fail to understand themselves, and Wagner may well have been closer to self-understanding when he wrote: 'Let us not underrate the power of reflection. The work of art that is produced unconsciously belongs to periods of history remote from our own; the work of art that belongs to an age of high cultural refinement can only be a product of the conscious mind.' Those are his own words. And in fact, alongside those elements which bear the stamp of inspiration and blind-beatific rapture, there is so much in his output – particularly in the *Ring* – that has been cleverly thought out, so much that is richly allusive and carefully structured, so much thoughtful spadework to set beside the giant sweep of god-like creation, that it is impossible to suppose it the product of some dark, irrational trance. His unique fascination rests, precisely, on the fact that his genius is an unparalleled blend of the supremely modern and intellectual with elements of a primitive demotic appeal through myth; and that it would be unwise, in the case of Wagner and his influence, to draw a clear-cut distinction between reflection on the one hand and enthusiasm on the other is shown most clearly by his relationship to music as such, which was conspicuously intellectual, even cerebral, and had a decisive influence on the evolution of the Nibelung project from a single drama to a four-part mythical cycle.

There is no mention of this in the great letter to Liszt. And yet it seems certain that it was the music, and not the drama as such, which was 'to blame' for what happened to Wagner with the material. Why was it that he could not begin with the plot of *Siegfrieds Tod*, but was led back to the beginning of creation? Because the drama would not accommodate accounts of previous events? But the drama as such has nothing against accounts of previous events. On the contrary, the drama often delights in their unfolding, using what is known as the analytical method. This method was practised in ancient Greek and French classical drama, and it was practised by Ibsen, who in this respect was closely akin to the classical dramatists. If Wagner's only artistic resource had been the language of poetry, he could have done what they did. But he was not just a poet – he was a musician as well; and he was not the one separately and in isolation from the other, but both at once, in primal unity. As a poet he was a musician; as a musician he was a poet. His relationship to dramatic poetry was that of the composer; his music forced his language back into a primitive state, so that without their music his dramas were only half poetry. Nor was his relationship to music purely musical; it was literary or poetic to the extent that it was decisively influenced by the spiritual and symbolic content of his music, its richness of meaning, evocative power and allusive magic. It was (after all) his specifically musical poetic gift that had led him gradually to abandon traditional operatic forms, and had suggested to him his new technique of weaving a fabric of themes and motifs – new in so far as it had never before been applied on such a richly allusive scale to an entire dramatic work. It had started with the *Holländer*, whose musical core and seed was Senta's Ballad in Act II – a condensed image of the whole drama, whose themes were then developed into a continuous fabric running right through the work. In *Tannhäuser* and *Lohengrin* this musical-poetic method was further refined and developed, as an increasingly accomplished artistry in the transformation of the thematic material raised it above the level of the simple reminiscence, as already used by earlier composers. (One thinks, for example, of the moving repetition of the waltz theme from the carnival in the closing scene of Gounod's *Faust*.) And now here, in the case of the Nibelung myth, this brilliant and ingenious technique promised delights and effects of unparalleled splendour and solemnity – but subject to certain conditions that forced Wagner to reflect and pause: for as he was proposing to plunge straight into the composition of *Siegfrieds Tod*, these conditions (it seemed to him then) had not been satisfied. The drama he could step into at will; parts of the long epic prehistory (he could assume) were already familiar to his audience, and the rest could be filled in by exposition. But he could not step into the music *in medias res*, for the music required its own prehistory, just as deep-rooted as that of the drama: and this could not be communicated by indirect means. The drama could not derive intellectual sustenance from it, or live, musically, on memories alone, and Wagner's new technique of weaving an interconnected fabric of themes could not celebrate its highest and most moving triumphs unless this primal music had actually been played and heard in present conjunction with the dramatic moment to which it alluded.

It was possible, of course, to write a deeply moving piece of music to accompany the death and funeral cortège of 'the most noble hero in the world', a piece that was born out of the tragic moment and could stand on its own in isolation from everything else. But would that not be just like the old-style operatic composers, who wrote a series of 'numbers', and whose powers of invention were only ever applied to the individual scene, without reference to the whole and its poetic design? What if he were to take his method of sustaining the fabric of themes not only for a single scene but for an entire drama and extend it vastly, applying it not only to one drama but to an entire epic cycle of dramas, in which everything, from the very beginning, was put on the stage? The result would be a veritable feast of associations, a whole universe of brilliant and profound allusions, a structure of musical remembrance so magnificent and moving at times that nobody would be able to hold back tears of enthusiasm – the same enthusiasm that he himself felt at the very idea of it all, and which he described in his letter to Liszt. Then the lament for the death of Siegfried – the *Trauermarsch* [Funeral March], as it is known – would be something more than a conventional operatic *pompe funèbre*, no matter how impressive. It would be an overwhelming celebration of thought and remembrance. The young boy's longing enquiry after his mother; the 'hero' motif of his line, created by a captive god to act in godless freedom; the 'love' motif of his brother-sister parents, rising up so marvellously from the depths; the mighty sword being unsheathed from its scabbard; the great fanfare phrase that signifies his own essential being, first heard long ago on the prophetic lips of the Valkyrie; the sound of his horn, drawn out in vast rhythmic cadences; the sweet music of his love for the once-awakened one; the ancient lament of the Rhine-maidens for the stolen gold, and the dark motif that recalls Alberich's curse: all these sublime reminders, pregnant with feeling and destiny, would pass before us with the body on the bier, while the earth shook and the sky was rent by thunder and lightning. And that was just one example of all the spiritual grandeur and mythical pathos that was to come if the drama were transformed into a theatrical epic. Back to the beginning, to the beginning of all things – and of their music! For the bottom of the Rhine, with the shimmering hoard of gold where the Rhinemaidens delight to sport and play, was none other than the world's original state of innocence, untouched as yet by greed and evil curse – and by the same token it was *the beginning of music itself.* And it was not just the music of myth that he, the poet-composer, would give us, but the very myth of music itself, a mythical philosophy and a musical poem of Creation, the story of its growth from the E flat major triad of the deep-flowing Rhine into a richly structured world of symbols.

And so the giant opus was conceived, a work without parallel, it may be said – without exaggerating or being untrue to works of art from a different, perhaps even purer sphere. For it is truly *sui generis*: a work that seems utterly beyond modernity, yet in the refinement, awareness and deliberate recency of its technique is extremely modern. Again, in its pathos and its romantic, revolutionary urge it is primitive – a world-poem interlaced with music and prophetic Nature, in which the original substance of life interacts, day and night hold colloquy, and the mythical prototypes of man – the fair, blithe, golden-haired and those that brood in hate, grief and rebellion – engage each other in profound fairy-tale plot. Siegfried's antagonist is *Hagen*, a figure whose sombre bulk looms so much larger than any earlier or contemporary variants, the Hagen of the *Nibelungenlied* or the Hagen created by Hebbel. The figure of the demi-goblin, conceived in jealousy, is perhaps the supreme triumph of Wagner's theatrical-poetic powers of characterization, deriving much of its force from the spoken word – as when, for example, Hagen explains with bitter self-mockery why he would not swear the oath of blood brotherhood:

> Mein Blut verdürb' euch den Trank!
> Nicht fliesst mir's echt
> und edel wie euch;
> störrisch und kalt
> stockt's in mir;
> nicht will's die Wange mir röten.
> Drum bleib' ich fern
> vom feurigen Bund.

> My blood would spoil the drink for you!
> For it flows not noble
> and pure, as in your veins;
> sluggish and cold,
> it creeps within my breast,
> and flushes not my cheeks.
> So I'll have no part
> in your fiery union.

These few succinct words create a whole image, a mythical stage-character mask. Hagen talking in his sleep, conversing in the night with Alberich; Hagen guarding the hall alone, while the 'free sons' and 'blithe companions' do his will, bringing him the ring of world mastery; and above all Hagen in grimly humorous mood, summoning the men to Gunther's ill-fated wedding – the theatre knows no more daemonic scenes than these.

It has always seemed to me absurd to question Wagner's poetic gifts. What could be more poetically beautiful or profound than Wotan's relationship to Siegfried, the fatherly-mocking and condescending attachment of the god to the boy who will destroy him, the loving abdication of the old power in favour of the eternally youthful? The composer has the poet to thank for the marvellous sounds he finds here. But then again, how much the poet has to thank the composer for, and how often (it seems) the poet only really understands himself when he enlists the aid of his second language to interpret and amplify, the language that is for him the true repository of subliminal knowledge, beyond the reach of the word. Mime's attempt to teach Siegfried the meaning of fear, his clumsy description of 'shuddering and horror', is underscored by the darkly disfigured music of the burning fire, together with the similarly distorted and refracted motif of the sleeping Brünnhilde. Thus the dwarf's description of fear is accompanied by the very thing which, in the world of the *Ring*, is the symbol of all that instils fear, the fear-inspiring *par excellence*, the ultimate deterrent, the guardian of the rock: the fire, which Siegfried will not fear, the fire that he will break through without learning the meaning of fear. But at the same time, deep down in the depths of the music, there is a shadowy hint of the thing that really will teach him fear: a reminiscence of the sleep-banished maiden, of whom he knows nothing, but whom he is destined to waken. The audience is transported back to the end of the previous evening, and realizes that at the very bottom of Siegfried's soul, so slow to comprehend in matters of fear, there stirs an inkling of what makes men truly afraid: and that is love, of which the dull-witted boy has likewise not learned the meaning, but which he is destined to learn along with fear, for here the two are psychologically and musically one.

Earlier, beneath the linden tree, he dreams of how his mother might have looked – his mother, a mortal woman. The motif of love for woman, the theme of 'woman's priceless delights' from Loge's narration in scene ii of *Das Rheingold*, is recalled here in the music of the orchestra. And that same psychological complex of mother-image and love for woman later finds expression in words when Siegfried releases the Valkyrie from the coat of mail and discovers: 'Das ist kein Mann! ... Feurige Angst fasst meine Augen, mir schwankt und schwindelt der Sinn! Wen ruf' ich zum Heil, dass er mir helfe? Mutter! Mutter! Gedenke mein!' [This is no man! ... Burning fear lays hold of my eyes: my mind grows dizzy and faint! On whom shall I call to succour and save? Mother, O Mother! Think thou on me!]

Nothing could be more Wagnerian than this blend of mythical primitivism and psychological, not to say psychoanalytical modernity. This is the naturalism of the nineteenth century, hallowed by myth. For Wagner is not only an unrivalled master in the portrayal of physical nature, the world of storm and tempest, the rustling of leaves and the sparkling of waves, the dancing of flames and the rainbow's arc: he is also a great explorer and interpreter of psychological nature, of the unchanging human heart. He girds the rock of virginity with burning fear, which the primal male force, driven on by its purpose of arousal and procreation, breaks through, only to appeal for help, at the sight of what it has timorously desired, to the sacred-feminine source from which it sprang – to its mother. Wagner's world and Wagner's work are concerned solely with the primeval poetry of the psyche, with the simplest of beginnings, the pre-conventional and the pre-social: and these things alone seem to him to be fit material for art. His work is the German contribution to nineteenth-century art in the monumental tradition, which in other nations pre-eminently took the form of the great social novel. Dickens, Thackeray, Tolstoy, Dostoevsky, Balzac, Zola – their works, heaped up with the same urge for moralizing grandeur, constitute the wider *European* nineteenth century, the world of literary and social criticism. The German contribution, the form that this greatness took in Germany, knows nothing of the social dimension and desires to know nothing of it: for society is not musical, or indeed accessible to art at all. Art can be created only from the pure humanity of the mythical age, from the timeless, non-historical proto-poetry of nature and of the heart, which furnishes a refuge from the social dimension, a purgative for its depravity; and from its depths the German spirit has created what is perhaps the most sublime, the most compelling work that the century has to offer. The asocial and proto-poetic constitute its own myth, its characteristic and fundamental national identity, which distinguishes it from the spirit and characteristic forms of other European nations. There are many historical parallels, for example, between Wagner and Zola, between the symbolic naturalism of the Rougon-Macquart novels and Wagner's art – and I am not just thinking of the leitmotif device. But the essential and characteristic national distinction is that between the social instinct of the French work and the mythical, primitive, poetic spirit of the German. With the appreciation of this difference the intricate old question – 'What is German?' – finds perhaps its tersest answer. The German spirit is essentially uninterested in the social and the political. Deep down (and since the work of art springs from deep down, one may safely regard it as a reliable yardstick), that sphere is foreign to it. While this is by no means solely a matter for regret, nevertheless one is entitled to speak here of a vacuum, a failure, a deficiency; and it is probably true to say that at a time when social problems are uppermost in our minds, when the ideals of social and economic justice and a more equitable economic order are seen by every thinking man as the most burning issue, and the attainment of such ideals as the most urgent moral priority of the day – that in circumstances such as these this deficiency, at other times so fruitful, does not appear in its most favourable light, and finds itself at odds with the general will and spirit of the times. Confronted with the problems of the day it leads to attempts at a solution that are mere evasions, bearing all the hallmarks of mythical substitutes for genuinely social remedies. It is not difficult to discern just such a mythical substitute in the political and social experiment that is currently being conducted in Germany. The psychological reality underlying today's political jargon can be summed up as follows: 'I am not interested in social solutions of any kind. What I want is the folk tale.' Except that in the realm of politics fairy tales become lies.

When I spoke at the beginning of the mischievous abuse to which the great phenomenon of Wagner lends itself, I knew that I would have to come back to this at some stage; for it seems to me impossible to speak of Wagner today without voicing a protest against such abuse. Wagner as the artistic prophet of a political present that would like to mirror itself in him? Well, more than one prophet has turned away in horror when he saw his prophecies come true, choosing to die in self-imposed exile rather than be buried (let alone live) in the place where his predictions were realized. But it would be an affront to the best that is in us, to our capacity for admiration, to countenance any talk here of 'realization', even in a grotesquely caricatured form. *Volk* and sword and myth and Nordic hero-worship: on certain lips these are despicable plagiarisms, purloined from the vocabulary of Wagner's artistic idiom. By his creation of an art intoxicated with the past and the future, the author of the *Ring* did not transcend the age of bourgeois culture in order to exchange bourgeois values for a totalitarianism that destroys mind and spirit. The German spirit signified everything to him, the German state nothing – as he intimates in those key lines from *Die Meistersinger*:

'Zerging' in Dunst das Heil'ge Röm'sche Reich, uns bliebe gleich die heil'ge deutsche Kunst.' [And were the Holy Roman Empire to fade away, Holy German Art is here to stay!] In the great work that we are now to see again he shows us the evil power of gold, and leads the lust for power to the point where it turns and renounces its ways, so that it cannot choose but love the free spirit who destroys it. His true prophecy is not 'Gut noch Gold noch herrischer Prunk, nicht trüber Verträge trügender Bund' [Goods nor gold nor princely prize, not falsehood's broken word and lies], but the heavenly melody that rises from the burning citadel of worldly dominion at the end of *Götterdämmerung*, proclaiming in musical sounds the same message that speaks to us in words at the end of Germany's other universal poem of life:

> Das Ewig-Weibliche
> Zieht uns hinan.

> The Eternal-Feminine
> Draws us ever on.

From 'Schopenhauer'*

For Richard Wagner, who was first introduced to him by a poet, Georg Herwegh, his [Schopenhauer's] teachings were a 'real god-send', a profound source of blessing, the most illuminating and productively stimulating experience of his life: no more and no less than a revelation. [...]

In this way artists often become the traducers of a philosophy, and thus it was that Wagner 'understood' Schopenhauer when he placed his erotic mystery play *Tristan und Isolde* under the aegis, so to speak, of Schopenhauer's metaphysic. The part of Schopenhauer's teachings that influenced Wagner, and in which he recognized himself, was the explanation of the world in terms of the 'will' or

* A contribution to Bermann-Fischer's series *Ausblicke*, Stockholm, 1938.

instinctive drive, the erotic conception of the world (sexuality as the 'focus of the will'), by which the music of *Tristan* and its cosmogony of longing are shaped. Some have denied that *Tristan* is influenced by Schopenhauerian philosophy – and rightly so, in so far as the 'denial of the will' is concerned. For this, after all, is a love poem; and nowhere does the will affirm itself more powerfully than in love and sexuality. But it is precisely *as* a mystery of love that the work is steeped to the very core in Schopenhauerian ideas. Here the erotic sweetness, the intoxicating essence of Schopenhauer's philosophy has been sucked out, so to speak, leaving the wisdom untouched.

To Karl Kerényi*

Princeton
6 December 1938

[...] The mythological elements in Goethe, particularly in the 'Classical Walpurgis Night', have always furnished a bridge for me between him and Wagner, who was especially fond of this part of *Faust*, and used to read out passages to his family during the last days in Venice, often bursting into cries of admiration. [...]

* Karl Kerényi (1897–1973), Hungarian-born scholar of the history of myth and religion. TM frequently consulted him, particularly when working on *Joseph und seine Brüder*; their correspondence has been published in English, translated by Alexander Gelley, under the title *Mythology and Humanism*, Ithaca and London, 1975.

From an Introduction to *Anna Karenina**

This [*the view that the beginning of Tolstoy's 'venerable but questionable prophetic status' coincides with the arrival of old age*] is the same mistake that is repeated in the popular supposition that Richard Wagner suddenly 'turned religious' in *Parsifal* – whereas in fact it was a progression of magnificently foreordained logic and necessity, whose direction is already clearly indicated in the *Holländer* and *Tannhäuser*.

* Published in English as an introductory essay to an edition of Tolstoy's novel (New York, 1939).

To the Editor of *Common Sense**

Sir:

I am very grateful to you for your kindness in sending me the November issue of your magazine, containing the article on 'Hitler and Richard Wagner', by Peter Viereck. Since I am an avowed admirer of the art of Richard Wagner, you assume that I must have many objections to this essay and might even be minded to protest against it. I must disappoint you. Such is not the case. I read Mr Viereck's piece with very nearly complete approval and regard it as extraordinarily meritorious. For the first time in America, as far as I know, the intricate and painful interrelationships which undeniably exist between the Wagnerian sphere and the National Socialist evil here undergo a sharp and inexorable analysis which will put an end to much sentimental innocence. The dismay, confusion and disillusion this is likely to strike in many well-meaning heads and hearts are no different from the effects that spring from the first impact of knowl-

* Published in English in the January 1940 issue of the New York journal. In parts of this letter TM recycles material from his 1937 lecture 'Richard Wagner and *Der Ring des Nibelungen*', pp. 171–94.

edge generally. They must be accepted for the sake of the service thereby rendered truth.

I can well understand the bitter laughter that overcame your contributor on the occasion of that fashionable Wagner concert, when he heard the speaker solemnly distinguish between the Germany of Hitler and the Germany of Wagner – the latter a Germany of creative freedom, racial tolerance, and democracy. Creative freedom – I can still let that stand. They were indeed exceedingly free, those sensuously intellectual masterpieces by a musician-dramatist, a genius in the art of the theatre. Braving scorn and opposition, they embarked upon their triumphant course in a world still dominated by the classic ideals of humanism. It is certain that, had the word existed in Wagner's time, he should have been called a *Kultur*-Bolshevist.

But racial tolerance? Democracy? There the outlook is gloomy. Nietzsche had not yet openly broken with Wagner – indeed, he may still have believed himself a disciple of Wagner – when he noted down: '*Meistersinger* – a lance against civilization. The German against the French.' That is a mere statement of fact, not yet a taking of issue. But it is a sort of transition from purely critical appreciation to repudiation of Wagner's Germany. It lends significance to the fact that the *Meistersinger* was destined to become the favorite opera of our wretched Herr Hitler.

If two people like the same thing and one of them is inferior, is the object of their affection inferior too? One ought to read the incomparable piece of prose which Nietzsche dedicated to the prelude to the *Meistersinger*. One ought to reread his famous page on *Tristan* in *Ecce Homo*. Baudelaire was one of the earliest Wagnerians. Another favorite of his, aside from the creator of *Lohengrin*, was Edgar Allan Poe. The juxtaposition is bewildering, almost incomprehensible to German ears (if 'German' is taken to be synonymous with a complete lack of psychological insight). Yet it shows who and what Wagner really was – disregarding the fact that he was a 'German master craftsman' and 'against civilization'. He was a European creative artist who knew every last trick of his trade. He had soaked up all the romantic wiles of seduction to console, delight and enchant long-suffering worldly-wise souls. It was no accident that his works had a world-wide effect, such as was never before the lot of any German of stature. The creator of the most overwhelming dramatic spectacles offered by the West in modern times was a shrewd and soul-stirring stage director of ancient legends. His boundless urge and enthusiasm swept into their orbit all the emotional elements of his century – the democratic-revolutionary as well as the nationalist. Later and on a smaller scale, d'Annunzio became an imitator of this system.

Nietzsche spoke of the 'twin optics'* that dominated Wagner's enormous talents – his ambition to win the finest as well as the coarsest. He succeeded, and the result is a certain sense of discomfort felt by the one section of his admirers in the presence of the other. A further consequence of the ambitious ambiguity inherent in this artistry is a corresponding ambiguity inherent in all higher criticism of which it becomes the object. Such criticism will always have an element of discord and passionate irony. It will be a curious blend of abandon and distrust, calling to mind the philosopher's love of 'life' which Nietzsche called the love for a woman who 'fills us with doubt'.

Wagner is one of the most complex phenomena in the history of art and intellect – and one of the most fascinating, because he offers the most profound challenge to one's conscience. I am somewhat taken aback by the fact that Mr Viereck, in his excellent article, gives the impression that I had proved rather unresponsive in the face of the gravity of this phenomenon, as though I had contributed to the over-simplified notion that Wagner is an unmistakable representative of the 'good' Germany, in contrast to the 'evil' of Herr Hitler. He quotes a lecture of mine on Wagner's essays on the philosophy of art – quotes it inaccurately, or at least incompletely. I described Wagner's essays as astonishingly acute writings by an artist, though having the character of propaganda on his own behalf and being far removed from truly great essay-writing. Consideration kept me from commenting on the style of these 'essays' – a style which, regarded purely as prose and apart from all content, doubtless has a strong National Socialist element. This was, after all, a Memorial Address requested of me by foreign societies in Amsterdam and Paris, on the occasion of the fiftieth anniversary of Wagner's death.

What Mr Viereck does not know or has forgotten is that it was this very speech in 1933 which determined my emigration, or, more

* See note on p. 128.

correctly, my failure to return to Germany. Its enthusiasm was so faint that it put the Nazis into a transport of rage. This vermin is affected by shades of difference as is a bull by a red rag. Yet it is these very nuances of difference that are the most indispensable element in any discussion of Wagner.

May I say that I miss ever so slightly a sense of nuance in Mr Viereck's revealing characterization of Wagner? I mean the nuances of love, of passionate personal familiarity with this artistry, which is, after all, admirable and gifted beyond measure. Wagner was full of such naive wonder at his own works that he spoke of them as 'miracles' ('*Wunderwerke*'). And in the end – this is the proper word. No term better fits these unexampled manifestations; nothing in the history of creative art does it fit better – even though we, on our part, may not necessarily use that term as the absolute superlative. We were never similarly tempted to describe as 'miracles' other precious and indispensable cultural properties, such as *Hamlet* or *Iphigenia* or even the Ninth Symphony. But the score of *Tristan* is a miracle – especially in its irksome affinity with the *Meistersinger*, which almost defies mental grasp. It is still more of a miracle when both of these are taken for what they really are, mere relief from the minute, gigantic thought structure of the *Ring*. Wagner's work is a veritable eruption of talent and genius, the profoundly serious yet enchanting work of a sensuous sorcerer, drunk with his own wisdom.

It is a unique case, one subject to severe intellectual criticism (this must be admitted over and over) – this combination of poet and musician in which both qualities necessarily lose their pure character, becoming something different from what they usually are, on a big scale or small. As a poet Wagner was a musician; as a musician he was a poet. His relationship to dramatic poetry was that of the composer; his music forced his language back into a primitive state so that without their music his dramas are only half poetry; nor was his relationship to music purely musical; it was literary or poetic to the extent that the spiritual and symbolic content of his music, its significant charm and interpretative magic, decisively influenced this relationship.

It was from this dubious mixture of talents, developed to absolute greatness, that the *Ring des Nibelungen* grew. It is a work that stands by itself. It seems utterly beyond modernity, yet in the refinement, awareness and deliberate recency of its technique it is extremely modern. Again, in its pathos and its romantic, revolutionary urge, it is primitive – a world-poem interlaced with music and prophetic Nature. In it the original substance of life interacts; day and night hold colloquy; the mythical prototypes of man – the fair, blithe, golden-haired and those that brood in hate, grief and rebellion – engage each other in profound fairy-tale plot.

The tremendous thing about all this is a certain epic radicalism for which I shall never lose my enthusiasm. It is the radicalism of *beginning*, of going back to the first and original source of all things, the primeval cell, the first E-flat of the prelude to the overture. It is the obsession to rear a musical cosmogony, indeed, a musical cosmos, to be endowed with a meaningful life of its own – the ringing pageant of the world's beginning and end.

This blend of drama and music is often called impure, the work of a charlatan. I admit the charge. There are cases in which admissions of all kinds may be made – and still, something overwhelming remains. The parallelism between music and the creative world of things places the epic birth of the world in coincidence with the birth of music. The mythology of music is interwoven with that of the world. A mythical philosophy, a musical poem of Creation, grow up before our senses and proceed to unfold into a richly joined world of symbols rising from the E-flat major triad of the deep-flowing Rhine.

We are dealing with a work that is intensely German, to an exemplary degree. This conclusion is disquieting when we remember the relationships uncovered by Mr Viereck. It leads to identifications which we are today profoundly interested in repudiating. But the truth is that such a work could only spring from the German spirit. Perhaps – though this is not certain – Jewish blood did its share. Certain qualities of this art – its sensuousness and intellectualism – speak in favor of the assumption. But first and foremost it is German. It is the German contribution to nineteenth-century creative art in the monumental tradition – the type of contribution which in other nations pre-eminently took the form of the great social novel. Dickens, Thackeray, Tolstoy, Dostoevsky, Balzac, Zola – their works, heaped up with the same urge for moralizing grandeur, constitute Europe's nineteenth century, constitute the world of literary and social criticism. The German contribution, the form which this great-ness took in Germany, has no social element nor desires to have anything to do with it. Society is not musical; indeed, not even capable of creative art. The roots of creativeness go down into the pure humanity of the mythical age, into the timeless, non-historical proto-poetry of Nature and of the heart. That is what the German spirit desires. That was its instinct, long in advance of any conscious decision. So far as time and mind are concerned, the *Ring des Nibelungen* has a great deal in common with the Rougon-Macquart series. The essential and characteristic national distinction is that between the social instinct of the French work and the mythical, primitive, poetic spirit of the German. With the appreciation of this difference, the intricate old question: 'What is German?' perhaps finds its tersest answer. Essentially the German spirit lacks social and political interest. Deep down, that sphere is foreign to it. But its accomplishments do not permit a purely negative evaluation of such a fact. Still, one is fully entitled to speak here of a vacuum, a failure, a deficiency. And in so decidedly social and political a time as ours, this often so productive deficiency may truly take on a fateful, indeed, a disastrous character. In the face of the problems of the times it may lead to efforts at solution which are poor evasions and which are by way of being mythical substitutes for truly social solutions. But that brings us to National Socialism.

National Socialism means: 'I do not care for the social issue at all. What I want is the folk tale.' This formulation, to be sure, is the mildest, the most intellectual. The fact that in reality National Social-ism is also filthy barbarism springs from that other fact, that in the realm of politics fairy tales become *lies*.

National Socialism, in all its ineffable empirical vileness, is the tragic consequence of the mythical political innocence of the German spirit. You see, I go a little farther than Mr Viereck. I find an element of Nazism not only in Wagner's questionable literature; I find it also in his 'music', in his work, similarly questionable, though in a loftier sense – albeit I have so loved that work that even today I am deeply stirred whenever a few bars of music from this world impinge on my ear. The enthusiasm it engenders, the sense of grandeur that so often seizes us in its presence, can be compared only to the feelings excited in us by Nature at her noblest, by evening sunshine on mountain peaks, by the turmoil of the sea. Yet this must not make us forget that this work, created and directed 'against civilization', against the entire culture and society dominant since the Renaissance, emerges from the bourgeois-humanist epoch in the same manner as does Hitlerism. With its *Wagalaweia* and its alliteration, its mixture of roots-in-the-soil and eyes-toward-the-future, its appeal for a classless society, its mythical-reactionary revolutionism – with all these, it is the exact spiritual forerunner of the 'metapolitical' movement today terrorizing the world. This is the movement that must be beaten if a really new order is to arise in Europe.

Let us not deceive ourselves. National Socialism must be beaten. In practice this means, unfortunately: Germany must be beaten. It is meant, however, in a very definite sense – a spiritual sense too. For there is but *one* Germany, not two, not a good and an evil. And Hitler, in all his wretchedness, is no accident. He could never have become possible but for certain psychological prerequisites that must be sought deeper down than in inflation, unemployment, capitalist speculation and political intrigue. Yet it is true that nations do not always show the same face, that it depends on time and circumstances how their constant qualities appear. Germany today makes a frightful appearance. It torments the world – not because it is 'evil', but because it is at the same time 'good' – a fact with which Anglo-Saxon humor is fully familiar, as evidenced by the words of the estimable Harold Nicolson: 'The German character is one of the finest but most inconvenient developments of human nature.'

Germany must be beaten. That means it must be compelled to reactivate all the constructive social elements in its fund of tradition from earlier centuries. It must do so in order to fit into the European Confederation, the comity of nations for which Europe is ripe. Such federalism will require sacrifices in national sovereignty and selfishness from *every* nation. This war is waged in Germany's interest. It would be asking too much, of course, for Germany to see this at the moment. But the war is waged to bring about a state of affairs which will free Germany from the curse of power politics, more depraving for her than for any nation. It is waged for a pacified, depoliticalized Europe which alone can provide an atmosphere conducive to Germany's greatness and happiness. Such an atmosphere will restore political innocence to the works of Germany, and a clear conscience to those who admire them. They will no longer have to sigh: It is great, it is splendid, but it is 'against civilization'.

Yours very sincerely,

THOMAS MANN

To Agnes E. Meyer*

1550 San Remo Drive, Pacific Palisades, California
18 February 1942

[...] The essay on the *Ring* is a good deal older than the letter in *Common Sense*. It was a lecture that I gave in 1937 at the University of Zurich. As you can see, the way I talk about Wagner has no chronology or logical progression. It is and will always remain ambivalent, and I am capable of writing one thing about him today, and quite a different thing tomorrow. [...]

* Agnes E. Meyer (1887–1970), German-born American author and journalist, to whom TM addressed a great many letters. Her husband was sometime Editor of the *Washington Post*.

To Agnes E. Meyer

Pacific Palisades, California
5 May 1942

[...] Bermann and Landshoff have brought out a marvellous book: Verdi's letters, with a sensitively written introduction by Werfel.* All in all a magnificent character, infinitely more noble than his formidable counterpart, R. Wagner. I was deeply moved by the letter he

* *Giuseppe Verdi, 1813–1901: Briefe*, ed. Franz Werfel, trans. Paul Stefan (Berlin, 1926).

wrote to Ricordi under the immediate impact of Wagner's death: 'Triste triste triste!' And then he goes on to speak of the powerful (potente) influence of this *oeuvre* on the history of art, whereupon he crosses out the word 'potente' and substitutes 'potentissima'. Wonderful stuff! Yet he had had to endure so much because of this foreign genius, and he knew that Wagner had despised him. [...]

To Agnes E. Meyer

1550 San Remo Drive, Pacific Palisades, California
27 August 1943

[...] We were invited to the Schoenbergs',* and I talked music with him at some length during the evening. It is remarkable how much understanding and affection, even love, these composers of the modern school retain for the old, for the whole world of harmony – even for romanticism. On the subject of Wagner the conversation became very lively, and I liked the way he condemned Wagner's *longueurs*, but regarded the sort of cuts made by Weingartner as entirely unacceptable. But then again, how very typical that he *can't abide* Venice! [...]

* Arnold Schoenberg and his second wife Gertrud lived nearby at Brentwood Park, Los Angeles.

My Favorite Records*

Thomas Mann was an early and ardent partisan of the phonograph even when records sounded 'remote and diminutive, as though one were to look at a painting through the wrong end of an opera-glass' – to quote him in The Magic Mountain. *It is a privilege, then, to*

* *Saturday Review of Literature* (New York), 30 October 1948.

present his choices as the first in a series of phonographic preferences by laymen of note in public affairs. We note, in passing, Mr Mann's righteous complaint that a dozen choices could scarcely cover his indispensable records, and absolve him from any grievance that may incidentally arise.

FRANCK   Symphony in D minor. Pierre Monteux conducting the San Francisco Symphony Orchestra.

MENDELSSOHN   Concerto in E minor. Nathan Milstein, violin, and the Philharmonic-Symphony Orchestra of New York. Bruno Walter conducting.

MOZART and others   A Song Recital by Lotte Lehmann.

BERLIOZ   *Harold in Italy.* William Primrose, violinist, with the Boston Symphony, Serge Koussevitzky conducting.

BEETHOVEN   Symphony No. 3 in E flat ('Eroica'). Bruno Walter conducting the Philharmonic-Symphony Orchestra of New York.

WAGNER   *Parsifal*, Act III. Berlin State Opera soloists, chorus, and orchestra, Karl Muck conducting.

WAGNER   *Die Walküre*, Act I. Lotte Lehmann, soprano, Lauritz Melchior, tenor, Emanuel List, bass, and the Vienna Philharmonic Orchestra, Bruno Walter conducting.

BERG   Excerpts from *Wozzeck*. Charlotte Boerner, soprano, and the Janssen Symphony Orchestra, Werner Janssen conducting.

STRAUSS, JOHANN   Two Overtures and Two Waltzes. Various European orchestras. Bruno Walter and George Szell conducting.

SCHUBERT   'Der Musensohn' (Goethe) and 'Der Wanderer' (Schmidt von Lübeck). Gerhard Hüsch, baritone, and Hanns Udo Müller, piano.

SCHUMANN   'Romanze' (Geibel) and Schubert's 'Der Erlkönig' (Goethe). Heinrich Schlusnus, baritone, and Franz Rupp, piano.

ROOSEVELT   'A Prayer for the Nation on D-Day, 6 June 1944.' Franklin D. Roosevelt, recorded off the air.

From *The Genesis of 'Doctor Faustus'**

Adorno† gave me his very perceptive essay on Wagner to read, a work that is not without affinity to my own piece – 'The Sorrows and Grandeur of Richard Wagner' – in its critical ambivalence and lively scepticism (which yet never becomes wholly negative). It was probably my reading of this essay that prompted me to listen again one evening to the recordings of 'Elsa's Dream', with the magical entry of the *pianissimo* trumpet on the words 'In lichter Waffen Scheine – ein Ritter nahte da' [In shining armour bright/a knight to me drew nigh], and the closing scene of *Das Rheingold* with its many beauties and subtleties: the first appearance of the sword idea, the wonderful handling of the Valhalla motif, Loge's brilliantly telling interpolations, the lines 'Glänzt nicht mehr euch Mädchen das Gold' [If you maidens miss the gold's bright glow], and above all the indescribably affecting and sentimental words of the Rhinemaidens' final trio – 'Traulich und treu ist's nur in der Tiefe' [Truth and tranquillity/dwell only here below]. 'The triadic world of the *Ring*', the [*TM's*] diary confesses, 'is my true musical home.' Though it then goes on to add: 'And yet at the piano I never tire of the *Tristan* chord.' [...]

On the other hand one used to meet Hanns Eisler‡ at the Schoenbergs' house, a man whose sparkling conversation I always found immensely entertaining. I was often convulsed with laughter, especially when the talk turned to Wagner and the comic ambivalence of his attitude towards that master demagogue, when he 'twigged' him, shook his finger in the air and cried: 'You old rascal!' I remember how he and Schoenberg sat down at the piano one evening, at my

* *Die Entstehung des Doktor Faustus* (Amsterdam, 1949), English translation by Richard and Clara Winston under the titles *The Story of a Novel* (New York, 1961) and *The Genesis of a Novel* (London, 1961).

† T. W. Adorno (1903–1969), formidable writer on music, philosophy and sociology, a one-time pupil of Alban Berg. Much of Adorno's Hegelian philosophy of music found its way into TM's *Doctor Faustus*. The essay referred to is *Versuch über Wagner* (Berlin and Frankfurt, 1952), English translation by Rodney Livingstone under the title *In Search of Wagner* (London/New York, 1981).

‡ Hanns Eisler (1898–1962), the composer.

instigation, and went through the harmonies of *Parsifal* looking for unresolved discords. Properly speaking there was only one, in the part of Amfortas in the last act. This was followed by a discussion on archaic forms of variation, which I had enquired about for good reasons of my own; and Schoenberg presented me with a pencilled autograph, made up of musical notes and numerals, which illustrated some examples. [. . .]

We spent the evening with the Chaplins, the Dieterles, the Feuchtwangers and Hanns Eisler at the home of the philosopher Dr Weil and his American wife, and once again I had one of those conversations with Eisler on the subject of Wagner – a blend of honest enthusiasm and mischievousness – which used to amuse me so highly. Just around that time, however, I had received a letter, together with various enclosures, from a certain Dr Franz Beidler* in Bayreuth, the grandson of Wagner, and uncannily like him to look at. This letter exercised my mind for many days. I had known Beidler, who left Germany in 1933, from my time in Berlin and Munich, and later on in Zurich he and his wife were fairly frequent visitors to our house. On a few occasions he had read to us from the early parts of a book he was writing (still not finished, I suspect) about his grandmother Cosima – a highly critical book, needless to say.† Now the Mayor of Bayreuth, ambitious for his town, had turned to him with a view to reorganizing the Wagner Theatre and resuming the Festival performances 'in a spirit of democracy', and had offered him – who had always been firmly opposed to the Bayreuth of Hitler and the regime of his aunt – the directorship of the new enterprise. After a lengthy exchange of letters the Mayor had invited him to come to Bayreuth to discuss the matter in person. I fancy the main attraction of this trip for Beidler lay in the fact that it gave him an opportunity to study the Wahnfried archives, which had hitherto been closed to him – to the detriment of his book. But at the same time detailed discussions were held on the Mayor's plan, on the list of persons to be consulted

* Son of Wagner's daughter Isolde and her husband, also named (Wilhelm) Franz Beidler. See also p. 214.
† Beidler died in 1981 without completing his biography of Cosima Wagner. The manuscript is in the possession of the author's daughter, Frau Dagny Beidler, and Friedelind Wagner, who has read part of it, reports that 'It seemed very fair ... he was a brilliant writer.'

and on the establishment of a board of trustees: and Beidler had insisted, more or less as a precondition of his own collaboration, that I should become honorary president, a position that he now offered me in his very sincere and well-intentioned letter. It was a strange, weird, and in a sense shattering sensation. For a hundred different reasons, intellectual, political and material, the whole idea could only strike me as utopian, unreal and dangerous – part premature, part obsolete, overtaken by time and historical events. I was incapable of taking it seriously. All I could take seriously were the thoughts, feelings and memories that it stirred within me – memories of my lifelong allegiance to Wagner's world, which was only encouraged and reinforced all the more in my early years by Nietzsche's spellbound critique, memories of the tremendous and highly formative influence that the equivocal magic of this art had on my youth. Hideously compromised by the role it had played in the National Socialist state, it was now to be restored to its original purity (but had it ever been 'pure'?); and in belated reality I had been singled out to occupy an official position within the mythology of my youth. It was not a serious temptation, but it was a dream: and in truth I would have finished the last fifty pages of *Faustus* sooner than I did if this will-o'-the-wisp had not hovered before me for days on end – and if I had not been distracted by the evasively procrastinating letter that had to be written to Beidler.

To Emil Preetorius*

Pacific Palisades, California
6 December 1949

Dear Pree,

The interval between your letter and the arrival of the Wagner essay† has been longer than I would have wished. I realized how much the subject still means to me from the excitement with which I seized on

*Emil Preetorius (1883–1973), German artist and scenic designer who did important work at Bayreuth in the 1930s.
† *Wagner: Bild und Vision*, Godesberg, 1949.

the little book as soon as it arrived – despite all the other demands on my reading time – and which was sustained to the very last word as I read it through at one sitting. It is not often now that I get through something in one go; I tire easily, but on this subject, and with such a shrewdly and affectionately penetrating analysis, born of much profound study, there was no question of that. And of course one is carried along by the style, which becomes more elevated as the book proceeds. At first you appear to approach the problem strictly from the viewpoint of the modern stage designer; and the observation that from this particular point of view 'the timeless validity of the Wagnerian *oeuvre*, the possibility of its survival as a continuing artistic influence becomes a very curious, *highly proble-matic* and difficult-to-answer question' probably remains, when all is said and done, the central proposition of the whole work. But then the book grows and expands in scope until it transcends all specialized concerns and becomes a comprehensive account and explication of the whole vast phenomenon, written with the boldness of one who knows the subject inside out. And if at times the manner is a trifle *too* grandi-loquent, too inflated and 'German' – though never to the point where one forgets that one is in the company of a writer of highly refined aesthetic and philosophical sensibility – well, that is hardly your fault: the fault lies with the subject matter itself, which demands such a style.

And what a subject it is! I wish we could sit down together over tea and cigarettes for a good three-hour chinwag. We would find ourselves very much at one in our shared enthusiasm – and in its various sceptical nuances. In your essay you take Wagner too much at his word; you unconsciously – and perforce – omit too much of his ghastly side, and then you glorify his international success in a way that verges on the inadmissible. Do you seriously believe – surely you can't possibly believe! – that this triumphant conquest of the bourgeois world springs from a yearning to 'plunge back into the reuniting abyss and the sacred night' – and not, rather, from that characteristically German blend of barbarism and cunning with which Bismarck, too, subdued Europe – plus an eroticism such as had never before been exhibited in society? Can you still bear to listen to the Paris Venusberg music? There are times when it is really unsavoury. Or again, in a different vein: can you honestly stand Hans Sachs's theatrical cleverness, that ninny, 'dear little Eva', and the

'Jew in the thornbush', Beckmesser? Yet the latter's pantomime leading up to his discovery of the song is simply brilliant, the prelude to the act is quite magnificent, and the quintet is an exquisite piece. The man had so much ability, talent and interpretative skill – more than words can say. Yet so much affectation with it, such lordly pretension, self-aggrandizement and mystagogical self-dramatization – again, more than words can say or patience can bear. Why this *oeuvre* in particular, which, for all that it is a highly personal synthesis, draws its material from all over the place, should be the stuff that unites a nation and redeems the world – God alone knows. There is, in Wagner's bragging, his endless holding-forth, his passion for monologue, his insistence on having a say in everything, an unspeakable arrogance that prefigures Hitler – oh yes, there's a good deal of 'Hitler' in Wagner, and you've left that part out, as of course you had to: how could you be expected to associate the name of Hitler with the work that you wish to serve! It has been associated with his name for long enough.

The second act of *Tristan*, I find now, with its metaphysical ambience of ecstasy, is more suited to young people who don't know what to do with their own sexuality. But when I recently listened to the first act again, in all its realistic dramatic force, I was completely overwhelmed. Isolde's lines about the 'Kahn, der klein und schwach ...' [little boat, so small and mean ...], the tense scene between the two of them beginning 'Begehrt, Herrin, was Ihr wünscht' [Desire, O mistress, what thou wouldst], which is dominated by the opening theme, 'Wüsstest – du nicht, was ich – begehre' [Dost thou not know what I desire] – for sheer expressive power it beats everything. And yet the language here is kept within pure stylistic bounds by the epic model on which it is based. All the same, I couldn't take the whole of *Tristan* any more. It would be a different matter with *Lohengrin*, whose Prelude is perhaps the most marvellous thing he ever wrote, and whose silvery-blue beauty I probably love more dearly than anything else – it is a genuine case of youthful love that has endured, to be revived again with every fresh contact. I still have an old recording with the 'golden Delia'* (who unfortunately had to cut

* The soprano Delia Reinhardt (1892–1974) sang at the Munich Opera between 1916 and 1923. She emigrated to the United States after the Second World War and was often accompanied by Bruno Walter.

short her recent lieder recital here with Walter because she was feeling indisposed) in the part of Elsa, singing 'Einsam in trüben Tagen' [In lonely, gloomy times]; and with the entry of the *pianissimo* trumpet, on the words 'In lichter Waffen Scheine – ein Ritter nahte da' [In shining armour bright/a knight to me drew nigh], I am filled every time with sheer ecstasy, like a boy of 18. It is the very summit of Romanticism.

I should really like to see a *Lohengrin* that you'd designed! But have you never done *Parsifal*? His last work, much underrated, is actually the most interesting of all. It still contains the most marvellous music (the transformation in Act III), and the figure of Kundry is beyond a doubt his supreme poetic achievement. And he knew it.

My dear sir, I *never* write such long letters as this any more. It just goes to show how the subject of Wagner rejuvenates me! Many thanks for the stimulus and renewed excitement which your book has brought me. (...)

Yours,

THOMAS MANN

Richard Wagner's Letters*

This well-organized collection of letters, most of them hitherto unknown, written by the creator of *Tristan* at various stages of his life, is not only a real godsend for Wagner scholarship, but will also be read – or certainly should be – by everyone who has ever come under the spell of Wagner's work, and who has thereby been persuaded to study further one of the most fascinating, psychologically complex and artistically triumphant phenomena in the history of the human personality.

* 'Briefe Richard Wagners', a review in the January 1951 number of the *Neue Schweizer Rundschau* (Zurich). The celebrated Burrell Collection of Wagner letters and documents, formerly in the Curtis Institute of Music in Philadelphia, was first published in an English edition edited by John N. Burk under the title *Letters of Richard Wagner* (New York, 1950; London, 1951), and TM's review must be of this edition. The letters were not published in their original language until later: *Richard Wagner, Briefe: Die Sammlung Burrell*, Frankfurt, 1953.

Let me begin by recounting briefly how this volume of more than 650 pages came to be compiled. A few years after Wagner's death, an Englishwoman by the name of Mary Burrell, wife of the Hon. Willoughby Burrell and a passionate admirer of the German maestro's art, finding herself profoundly dissatisfied with all the accounts of his earthly life that had appeared so far, resolved to write the definitive Wagner biography, accurate, truthful in every detail and firmly based on documentary evidence, to the acquisition of which she was prepared to devote unlimited time and money, all her energies and all her detective skills. She began to travel throughout Europe, tracking down and contacting those individuals – or the descendants of those individuals – who had had anything at all to do with the deceased, buying up and hoarding every document relating to his life that she could possibly find: letters mainly, then musical and literary sketches, complete manuscripts, printed scores, pictures, concert programmes, birth and marriage certificates, contracts, passports, et cetera. Her principal concern was to uncover material that had hitherto been presented in any way untruthfully, that had remained in the dark or been deliberately kept in the dark; and it must be said that underlying her endeavours was a profound mistrust of the official version of her hero's life, of 'Bayreuth' and 'Wahnfried' and Cosima – a mistrust that was shared by many another who chose not to yield up his secret treasures to the Castle of the Holy Grail on the Roter Main,* and a mistrust for which I have a good deal more sympathy, I must confess, than the editor of this volume, who will not entertain the notion that 'Cosima had manipulated the Wagner documents to suit her ends.'

In my own view the estimable Mrs Burrell's instincts were entirely correct. Although she was a woman herself – or perhaps precisely because she was a woman – she had an intuitive understanding of the dangers involved when the literary estate of a man of genius is administered by a woman – dangers, not to say scandalous abuses, of which we have come to know more than she since the activities of Elisabeth Förster-Nietzsche. What happened in the Nietzsche archive is clearly what happened in essence and in principle – and in the same matriarchal spirit – at Bayreuth too. I am unable to judge whether the differences between the published edition of Wagner's autobiog-

* The little river running through Bayreuth.

raphy and the original version, of which Mrs Burrell unearthed a copy that had been kept back by an Italian printer, are indeed 'negligible'. I have no reason to doubt it.* But the detailed picture that this thoroughly candid book gives of the treatment that Wagner's letters to his old friend Uhlig underwent at the hands of Cosima and her blue pencil, all for the greater national glory of Bayreuth, is shocking enough in all conscience. Uhlig's daughter – Uhlig was a violinist with the Dresden Opera Orchestra – had sent the originals of these letters to Bayreuth, but had had the good sense to keep copies of her own, which Cosima tried her utmost to have destroyed. But they survived, passing eventually into the hands of our lady collector. As a result, we can now read things that Wahnfried would have censored for all time – things such as the incredibly telling letter to Uhlig in which Wagner gives free expression to that wild revolutionary ardour which survived the events of 1848, and his belief that the 'Augean stables' of our plutocratic civilization could not be cleansed through the political process, but must quite literally go up in flames in order to clear the air and give true art (i.e. his art) a chance to flourish in a climate of commercial innocence. All this may be just the foolish ravings of an artistic mind: but to suppress a biographical document of this kind is nothing more nor less than an unscrupulous act of self-serving corruption.

And yet such flagrant instances of suppression and falsification are not actually the main reason for concluding that Mrs Burrell's dislike of Cosima was only too well founded. One needs only to read the words, recorded in this book, that the daughter of Ferdinand Heine, another of Wagner's old friends from the Dresden Opera days, wrote to Mrs Burrell's daughter fifty years later, in 1895: 'After becoming acquainted with your dear mother and her noble aspirations, I would never make common cause with Wagner's widow. *How different* have the *once so noble festivals* of Bayreuth become through her, so different from what Richard would ever have guessed ...' – one needs only to read these words, I say, in order to be vividly reminded once more of the baleful influence that Woman, in the shape of

* TM should have. The differences between the first published edition of *Mein Leben* and the original privately printed version turned out to be considerable when the definitive text was eventually published (Munich, 1963: English translation by Andrew Gray, edited by Mary Whittall, *My Life*, Cambridge and New York, 1983).

Liszt's daughter, exercised on Man in his most corruptible manifestation – Wagner the man and artist – and on the administration of his *oeuvre*: an influence that has a good deal to do with that 'morass', which was Nietzsche's description of the *Bayreuther Blätter*, and which eventually degraded the Festival Theatre to the level of Hitler's private court theatre. I imagine we shall learn about these matters in great detail from the forthcoming biography of Cosima, now being prepared in Zurich by Wagner's grandson and son of Isolde, Franz Beidler.*

Having therefore amassed an enormous amount of documentary material, Mrs Burrell set about writing her great biography. But life had better equipped her to be a collector than a writer. Her book, as far as she got with it – which was not very far – was apparently an extremely clumsy piece of work; moreover, she insisted on quoting all the letters she had acquired only in the original, together with other eccentricities of a similar nature. The task proved too much for her. By 1898, when she died, she had managed to get as far as Wagner's twenty-first year and his first acquaintance with Minna Planer as a young provincial conductor – without having had an opportunity, as yet, to use any of her new material in her narrative. Her heirs published the biographical fragment as it stood. But the collection of documents remained untouched and inaccessible for many years. They were not catalogued until 1929, when at last some general notion of their contents began to emerge. In 1931 they were put up for sale, and an American lady, Mrs Mary Louise Curtis, now Mrs Efrem Zimbalist, donated them to the Curtis Institute of Music – 840 items, mostly letters, to which Mrs Zimbalist added a further 25 she had acquired separately. This vast mass of documentary material is now presented for the first time in the book in the clear, chronological chapter arrangement skilfully devised by its editor, Mr Burk, who has contributed passages of commentary and brief interlinking paragraphs between the texts which, in their intelligence and breadth of knowledge, their sensitivity and stylistic felicity, do indeed transform the book as a whole into the biography of Wagner that the late Mrs Burrell dreamed of writing, but failed to accomplish.

The principal achievement of this determined lady was to win the confidence of Natalie Bilz-Planer, the natural daughter of Wagner's

* See also pp. 207–8.

first wife, Minna Planer, who had passed her off as her younger sister. Their mutual trust was founded largely on a common dislike of Cosima: and as a result, by a combination of hard cash and gentle persuasion, Mrs Burrell was able to induce Natalie, who had inherited her mother's extensive collection of papers on the latter's death in 1866, to part with them twenty-four years later, until one by one she had acquired no less than 128 letters written by Wagner to Minna, which now form the *pièce de résistance*, so to speak, of the volume under review. Here we have, in Richard's letters to Minna and in hers to him, the whole bitter story of this marriage, from the first declaration of love to the final parting. And we learn a great deal from it – first and foremost, that Wagner's attachment to this woman was much stronger, much more deeply rooted and much more enduring than is generally supposed. He quite clearly loved her more passionately than all the others who later stole his heart from her: Jessie Laussot, Mathilde Wesendonck, Cosima von Bülow, in each of whom she was bound to see only a fiendish seductress, whereas in fact they simply understood Wagner's art better than she did. He never forgot the difficult times when she stood loyally by him, especially the years in Paris from 1839 to 1842; and even after he had signed the divorce papers he always treated her very decently as far as the financial arrangements were concerned – as she herself affirmed publicly shortly before her death. We learn also that the beautiful and successful young actress, who had already had her fair share of bad experiences (she had been seduced at the age of 15), did not lightly join her life to that of a man whose future destiny, wild, tempestuous and eccentric, at odds with all the ways of the world, was no doubt plain for all to see from a very early age. She had the shrewdness of her sex, was reticent and circumspect. But the magnetic force of his courtship was stronger – and therein lay his 'guilt'. Hers was a fate not unlike that of the poor Countess Tolstoy, who would have so liked her dear Leo to go on writing beautiful novels, instead of preaching primitive Christianity and condemning money, the military, the Church and civilization in general. As for Minna, she wanted to see her Richard pursue the career of a successful operatic composer, a career on which he had embarked so auspiciously with *Rienzi* and *Tannhäuser*. Even *Lohengrin* was not yet beyond the pale. But then, when he forfeited the desirable position of Kapellmeister at Dresden because of his accursed involvement in politics, and gave himself up to totally impractical chimeras whose demands were not of this world, vast, fantastic dramatic enterprises that were plainly unrealizable and unacceptable to the operatic stage as it then was – then she could no longer go along with him. The rock on which their marriage foundered, the thing that estranged her wayward husband from her, was her lack of faith – the very last thing that Wagner could forgive: he, a man filled with utterly unprecedented and unshakable faith in himself and his mission, who demanded the same measure of faith from everyone else, and saw decisive proof of the world's depravity in the fact that it denied him that faith – along with the necessary means of subsistence for the completion of his work, which ought to have been forthcoming first and foremost as the token of that faith.

Mr Burk finds suitably eloquent words to characterize Wagner's 'Wehwalt-der-Wölfing' [Sorrowful-the-Wolfling] relationship with the world, which caused poor Minna so much unhappiness. As for example when he writes:

> Wagner's basic problem through most of his career, but more than ever at this time [*around 1850*], was to find a living in a 'philistine' world only half inclined to bother with him, in order to fulfill his creative destiny and so conquer that world. It was a self-assignment that would have appalled anyone else, because it meant getting money without burying himself in routine to do it, writing scores prodigious in concept and complexity, following them through endless practical detail in production by performers whom he had to train, in a theater which he had to build, before audiences which had a totally different idea of what an opera should be. How protracted, how intense this struggle was can never be properly realized except by viewing his daily life at close range. The close view does not always present a likable person. It unfailingly presents an artist of incredible conviction and courage.

It could not have been better put or said with more understanding and fairness. 'A likable person' he most certainly was not. In fact he was an intolerable burden and a constant trial to those around him. Wagner the master borrower, the revolutionary who needed to wallow in luxury, the actor who played and promoted only himself, unspeakably immodest, totally self-absorbed, holding forth endlessly, boasting and bragging, setting the world straight on every subject under the sun; a man obsessed with theatre and fancy dress, that 'coiffeur and charlatan', as he was dubbed by Gottfried Keller, who of course had no time at all for that confused Wagnerian blend of worldly renunciation and worldly lust, for the archetypally Romantic exploitation of the unhealthy antithesis between sensuality and chastity in his work – such is the Wagner whom we now see before us again: and there is too much in him that repels, too much 'Hitler', indeed too much latent – or for that matter, manifest – Nazism for any real trust to seem possible, any reverence untrammelled by bad conscience, any love that need not feel ashamed of its name. And yet: who could fail to be moved or to feel suddenly at one with him on reading the lines that he wrote to Minna from Biebrich in February 1862:

> The time will come when men will look upon a life such as mine and realize with belated shame how carelessly I have been abandoned by others to worry and uncertainty, and what a *miracle* it is that I have created such works under circumstances such as these – including the one I am presently engaged upon.

It *was* a miracle, and the world stands shamefully condemned for its treatment of this insufferable egotist. But the world has no memory: and though it feasts on his works today, it forgets that it once found them absurd and impossible.

'The one I am presently engaged upon' was *Die Meistersinger*. One is overcome with admiration to think that the plan for that work was formed during those agonizing weeks in Vienna, when Wagner was fighting hard – and in vain – to get a production of *Tristan* off the ground. Was a major work ever before conceived in such a frame of mind? On the one hand lay the vast fragment of the *Ring*, probably unperformable for all time. On the other lay *Tristan und Isolde*, inspired by his liaison with Mathilde Wesendonck, unperformable even in the relatively accommodating atmosphere of the Austrian capital, where Wagner had been able to hear his *Lohengrin* for the very first time thirteen years after its creation. He had heard one of his youthful works – but everything he had written since seemed condemned to a twilight existence. Did this depress him deeply? Indeed it did. But *en route* from Karlsruhe to Vienna he had spent all of four days in Nuremberg; and there, evidently inspired just by the visual impact of the city, a nebula had been resolved into a star, a vague dream had become a concrete work project. Something aggressively German, filled with the revolutionary spirit of Protestantism, some bold and worthy work in a deeply popular vein, had long since lived in the half-light of his imagination, and his original ideas for a work on the theme of 'Luther's Wedding' were now channelled into the conception of *Die Meistersinger von Nürnberg*. All the torments, worries and tribulations he was going through on account of *Tristan*, profoundly though they affected his life at that time, formed merely the surface of his existence; in actual fact, in the stillness beneath that surface, all his thoughts and efforts and hopes were focused on the new work, on the work that was to be a glorious outpouring of the German spirit, a splendid celebration of German liberty and masterliness in C major.

Depression, adversity, hardship, despair are no barriers to great inspiration. In certain instances they may even be the best breeding ground for it. Dogged stamina is not an inborn attribute: it comes at the bidding of genius, and he who has a mission to fulfil is indestructible. As a child this man was puny and sickly, and in later life he was constantly afflicted by skin irritations, dyspepsia, insomnia and general neurasthenia. At the age of 30 he was in such a state that he would 'frequently sit down and cry for a quarter of an hour at a time'; he is afraid of dying before he can complete *Tannhäuser*, believes he is too old, at the age of 35, to undertake the execution of the Nibelung project, feels permanently exhausted, constantly 'done for', thinks 'daily about death' at the age of 40 – yet on the threshold of his seventies he will crown a life's work of veritably cosmic proportions, a vast, minutely wrought structure of magical intellectuality, with *Parsifal*. Say what you will: his was a marvellous, astonishing, endlessly fascinating life of creative achievement.

The present collection contains nothing like the great letter that Wagner wrote to Liszt in 1851, in which his plans for the *Ring* are solemnly unfolded and set forth. And yet there *is* a letter here that is almost as instructive, almost as revelatory of Wagner's personal creative technique, as that one to Liszt. It was written even earlier, on 30 January 1844, and is addressed from Dresden to Karl Gaillard in Berlin. At the age of 31 he writes as follows:

> I really do not pride myself on my abilities as a poet, and I confess that it is only out of necessity, and because no good texts have been offered to me, that I have set out to invent them myself. But I couldn't possibly compose a text alien to me for the following reason: My way is not to select any plot I like, put it into verse, and then ponder about how to add suitable music; if I should proceed in this way I would subject myself to the inconvenience of having to inspire myself twice, which is impossible. The way I produce is different: the only subject which can appeal to me is one which presents practical as well as musical possibilities. Before starting to write a verse, or even to outline a scene, I must first feel intoxicated by the musical aroma [Duft] of my subject, all the tones, all the characteristic motives are in my head, so that when the verses are finished and the scenes ordered, the opera proper is also finished for me and the musical treatment in detail is rather a calm and considered afterwork which the moment of real creation has preceded.

He goes on to say that he can make use only of subjects that lend themselves exclusively to musical treatment:

> Here we arrive at the point where opera and drama part completely ... While nowadays it is the task of the dramatist to purify and to spiritualize the material interests of our time, it falls to the poet and composer of opera to conjure up the holy spirit of poetry which has come down to us from the legends and sagas of past ages ... I have chosen for my next opera the beautiful and characteristic saga of the knight Tannhäuser ...

So young still – and yet such a clear-sighted and definitive assessment of his own unique brand of artistry! He also adds that in this way – his way – the opera can be raised to a higher level from a debasement that has come about through the treatment of unmusical (he means 'unromantic') subjects.

But enough. Let me just end with a few words about the history of the whole Festival idea, as it emerges, bizarrely enough, in this correspondence. It sprang from fundamentally revolutionary origins, and is already present *in embryo* in that impassioned letter to Uhlig referred to above, where he proclaims the necessity of putting a torch to the whole of bourgeois civilization along with its commercialized theatre industry. In the wake of this fiery cleansing, an isolated enthusiast here and there (like himself) might summon together the survivors of this despicable world and ask them: 'Which of you would like to help me put on a drama?' Then only men of truly disinterested motives would come forward, since it would no longer be possible to make money out of the enterprise. They would then gather together in a rapidly erected wooden building to show the people what art really is. The idea of a festival theatre dedicated to the people (in contrast to the despised 'court theatre') lived on tenaciously in his thoughts, and crops up repeatedly over the years. In Dresden, at the time of *Lohengrin*, when he was embittered by his failure to get the work performed, he outlined his wildly utopian notions of the ideal people's theatre of the future in conversation with friends. The building was to be placed on a hill, a temple of art visible for miles around. Then people would come together from the four corners of the land to be edified by a beauty pure and sublime. Only the most sublime works were to be given, in productions of the very highest standard. The nation itself was to be the sponsor and organizer of this festival, to which the public would be admitted free of charge. All those involved in the production would work for nothing, donating their time and talent freely in the service of the great cause – and so on. The sceptical objections of Wagner's friends were brushed aside in a torrent of Saxon dialect. At this point the festival theatre of the people already had the character of a permanent institution. Later on, when the *Ring* was in progress, he began to think again in terms of something more improvised. From Zurich he writes that he is determined, despite everything, to set his *Siegfried* to music (he is referring still to the original *Siegfrieds Tod*) – but he is equally determined that no conventional theatre shall be allowed to produce the work. Instead he has conceived the boldest of plans, the realization of which (however) will require not less than 10,000 thalers. He proposes to build his own theatre – on the banks of the Rhine, in Switzerland, or wherever – and send for the best singers and musicians; everything else he needs to mount the production must be specially made for the occasion, so that he can be sure of a perfect performance. Then he will issue invitations to all the devotees of his art, filling his theatre in this way with a receptive audience, and in the space of one week he will give three performances – with no charge for admission, of course. *Thereafter the theatre will be torn down*, and that will be the end of the matter.

Fantasies? Dreams? Time would make them come true – or if not exactly true, then at least in some sense 'real'. 'Bayreuth' would come into being, with tickets at twenty marks a time and an audience made up of kings and emperors and the vulgar international *nouveaux riches* and ghastly writers of Wagneriana, with profiteering and inflated house prices throughout the little town, and glittering receptions and garden parties (with fireworks) at the Villa Wahnfried – which, despite its name, was by no means free from Illusion [Wahn] or pretensions to papal infallibility in matters of art. Utopia had 'arrived'. And Nietzsche ran for his life ...

To Friedrich Schramm*

Bad Gastein
25 August 1951

Dear Sir,

How many professions and confessions I have already made on the subject of Wagner, for Wagner and against Wagner – it seems as if it will never end. 'Wagner without end' was the title used by the *Schweizerische Musikzeitung* recently when it published a letter† I addressed two years ago to a Munich friend of mine on the subject of a Wagner essay he had written. One of the things I talked about then was *Die Meistersinger*, that incredibly optimistic companion piece to *Tristan*, the larger-than-life comedy composed by a genius who was able to switch instantly and effortlessly from utter intoxication with death to the C major that signals radiant *joie de vivre*, German worthiness and roguishness in the grand manner – the work with which the Basle Opera is opening its Festival this year.

* Friedrich Schramm (1900-1981), director of the Basle Municipal Theatre.
† To Emil Preetorius, see pp. 208-11.

One should not be misled by a number of critical remarks concerning *Die Meistersinger* which found their way into that letter. They are the expression of an enthusiastic ambivalence which is the abiding characteristic of my relationship to Wagner, and which, for want of a better word, one might call 'passion'. All forms of expression are acceptable to this eternally youthful passion – the most sceptically critical as well as the most exaltedly laudatory. The disapproval – or apparent disapproval – conveyed in my words to Preetorius does not deter me in the least from introducing your new Festival production of *Die Meistersinger von Nürnberg*. I only wish I could do a better and more thorough job; but the baths are very tiring and I have been forbidden to do any work at all while I am here. So let me just send you these few words of greeting behind my doctor's back: you have chosen splendidly and well, for *Die Meistersinger* is a splendid work, a festival drama if ever there was one, a poetic work in which wisdom and daring, the worthy and the revolutionary, tradition and the future are wedded together in a gloriously serene manner that arouses a deep-seated enthusiasm for life and for art. In dark days of personal trial and tribulation, days of despair even, it was born of an inward exultation in strength and faith: and exultation it shall always invoke, now, even now, especially now – and in you too.

Please accept my warmest congratulations.

THOMAS MANN

Index

223